Recent Puerto Rican Theater: Five Plays from New York

John V. Antush

D1600033

Arte Publico Press
Houston
Texas
1991

This volume is made possible through a grant from the National Endowment for the Arts, a federal agency.

Arte Publico Press
University of Houston
Houston, Texas 77204-2090

Cover Design by Mark Piñón

Recent Puerto Rican theater: five plays from New York / edited by John V. Antush.
     p.   cm.
   ISBN 1-55885-019-8 (alk. paper)
   1. American drama–Puerto Rican authors. 2. Puerto Ricans–New York (N.Y.)–Drama. 3. American drama–New York (N.Y.) 4. American drama–20th century. 5. New York (N.Y.)–Drama.   I. Antush, John. V.
PS628.P84C66 1990
812'.5408097295–dc20   90-32908
                                                          CIP

The paper used in this publication meets the minimum requirements of the American National Standard for Permanence of Paper for Printed Library Materials Z39.48-1984. ∞

For my mother, Margaret Mary.

Contents

Introduction

Background

Hispanic theater's *gran florecimiento* in New York City during the sixties and the seventies continued unabated through the eighties. Now, though the bloom has faded somewhat, Hispanic theater moves into the nineties stronger than ever with a firm sense of purpose to forge a new understanding of what it means to be a Latino in the United States. In the summer of 1990, New York hosted two Hispanic theater festivals. Teatrofestival, co-sponsored by Pregones Repertory Theater and TENAZ (the national organization of Chicano theaters), brought ten theater companies from California, Colorado, Minnesota, New York, Texas, Mexico, and Puerto Rico to the South Bronx. The New York Shakespeare Festival celebrated its fourteenth annual Festival Latino, including an Hispanic film series along with live theater by companies from all over the Western hemisphere. All over New York City hundreds of young Hispanics are pursuing their theatrical ambitions with companies like the African Caribbean Poetry Theater, Duo Theater (Spanish English Ensemble Theater), The Family, Festival Latino, Hispanic Drama Studio, Latin American Theater Ensemble, Pregones, the Puerto Rican Traveling Theater, *El Repertorio Español*, ROSA (Ricans Organization for Self Advancement), Tango Productions Co., Shaman Theatre Repertory Co., *Teatro Moderno Puertorriqueño*, to mention a few. Other organizations such as HOLA (Hispanic Organization of Latin Actors) and INTAR (International Arts Relations) offer a wide range of theatrical services to anyone interested in the arts. With more than twenty legitimate theater companies operating successfully throughout the city and dozens of other performances, Hispanic theater has become a force in New York theater.

The quite considerable contributions of Puerto Ricans, however, have been subsumed under the not very precise categories of Hispanic, Latino, Caribbean, and Latin American. One purpose of this anthology is to bring more clearly into focus the achievements of a talented rising generation of new Puerto Rican playwrights. As Americans, Puerto Ricans stand in a unique relationship to other Hispanic cultures; as Hispanics, they enjoy a distinctive place in the ethnic diversity of American culture. A result has been that their literary achievements have been represented in anthologies and histories as marginal to several literary heritages at once. As Puerto Ricans and Americans, for example, they have been perceived as standing apart on both sides of the conjunction, as outsiders to both mainland and island cultures. Their marginality, working for and against them at the same time, has enabled them to see what more accustomed eyes have missed in the Brooklyn Navy Yard area, the South Bronx, and East Harlem (also known as "El Barrio" and "Spanish Harlem") and the Lower East Side (known as "Loisaida"). Their marginality sometimes involves the overlap of two cultures when the post-immigrant writer has grown up in New York, bilingual, with an easy mobility between communities, and considers himself or herself an expert on a variety of issues ranging from the quality of folk art to statehood. Early marginality in writers like René Marqués, Luis Rafael Sánchez, Pedro Pietri, Jaime Carrero, and Toni Mulett conveys a sense of alienation bred of culture shock at the disparity between island and mainland cultures. In some writers marginality also conveys a sense of adjustment to the more extreme condition of alienation bred by poverty and prejudice, as in the dramas of Miguel Piñero. Younger writers, like those in this anthology, Federico Fraguada, Cándido Tirado, Juan Shamsul Alam, Richard Irizarry and Ivette Ramírez, are onto something new and very important: the great promise of America as a challenging arena for some Puerto Rican values and assumptions that retard the quality of life even as they make that life possible and, to a degree, more comfortable. For example, in these plays, the relatively benign forms of racial prejudice, color consciousness, sexism, economic privilege, and class discrimination practiced in Puerto Rico manifest their full ugliness in the rough-and-tumble of the American social cauldron. These playwrights, while not discounting the impact of environment, are looking less toward external factors for solutions and more toward inner attitudes. This other, American, side of the margin finds a diminished nostalgia for primitive rural domesticity and an increased appetite for cosmopolitan integrity.

The five plays in this anthology, all written in the eighties, reflect the enormous changes in the Puerto Rican drama of New York City since the watershed production of Edward Gallardo's *Simpson Street* in 1979. As I wrote in the Introduction of *Simpson Street and Other Plays*,

> *Simpson Street* ... marks the end of the Puerto Rican diaspora. The general mood and feeling of plays written by Puerto Ricans in New York before 1979 was

one of exile and of a longing to return "home." The early playwrights tended to see the New York experience as too impersonal, materialistic, and secular to encourage the kind of human relationships that characterize the island culture. *Simpson Street* is the start of a whole series of plays that speak to that second generation who have no root memories of the island and who regard New York City as "home." Whereas the earlier plays generally looked back to a happier time and golden land, *Simpson Street* and its successors look forward to sharing in the unfolding history of a larger and more complex world. At the end of the play, Michael's attempt to create his identity as a Puerto Rican in this troublesome environment is the challenge out of which a whole generation of any ethnic origin must make of themselves, in one sense, a new people.

These plays stand where the past meets the future because these plays represent not only the changes in New York as well as the changes in San Juan, but also the unavoidable merger of Hispanic and American cultures on a larger scale. Even as American television broadcasts "L.A. Law" and major league baseball into Hispanic homes beyond our shores, American children idolize Jimmy Smits and Hispanic ballplayers, while adults admire Rita Moreno and Raul Julia. Other cultural totems in music, dancing, food, and literature are inexorably breaking down the resistance to assimilation and reaching toward a more universal fulfillment. As Richard Rodriguez has pointed out, the individualism of the Protestant Anglo North, proud of its separateness, is necessarily giving way to the larger view of an interconnected world. At the same time, the genius for synthesis of the Catholic Latino South, with its multiethnic Indian-African-European-Asian strains, beckons the United States into the Easter promise of being born again into a greater identity. The common condition of these five plays is the sense of belonging to the United States without betraying the nurturing culture of Puerto Rico. In this sense these plays are about the ways people create one another when they work together at those points where their different cultures touch their mutual identity.

The grammar of these plays is noticeably different from the plays of an earlier generation of Puerto Ricans. Like their contemporaries—Sam Shepard, Arthur Kopit, David Rabe, David Mamet, August Wilson, and others—these playwrights have been profoundly influenced by the movies and television. They use more cine-

matic devices and organize their material in a new kind of frag-
mented way to grab short attention spans. There is also a more
overt kind of political abstraction behind the structure of these
plays that derives from the avant-garde street theater, guerrilla theater, and open theater of the sixties and early seventies. Moreover,
they share with their fellow contemporaries a candid treatment of
sexuality, frank even brutal language at times, some bizarre comedy routines, and a political commitment to write openly, even
painfully, about previously taboo subjects such as homosexuality,
AIDS, drug addiction, the more deeply ingrained forms of racial
prejudice, and the plight of the homeless. Such candor has been
controversial within the Puerto Rican community and would have
been unacceptable only a short time ago. Even as these plays are
changing, they are changing the United States.

The Puerto Rican literary heritage has focused historically on
the *jíbaro* as a national folk hero. Although the origin of the word is
unknown, *jíbaro* has been translated as "peasant," "farmer," "yeoman," even "hillbilly." Like the British yeoman, the *jíbaro* is a
freeholder who farms his own land primarily to support his family, and sometimes he has a part-time home industry to get a little
ahead. Freighted with moral and spiritual qualities that transcend
physical traits, the *jíbaro* traditionally has personified the inner life
of the national identity. The *jíbaro*'s attachment to the land, family, and community constitutes his strength derived from a secular
ethnic heritage of Indian, African, Spanish ancestry. Though poor
and formally uneducated, he has been a man without a master.
He first came to literary prominence in the novel, *El Jíbaro* (1846)
by Manuel A. Alonso, and in the latter half of the nineteenth century writers used his persona to stress with passionate intensity the
Puerto Rican quest for liberty and redemption.

After Puerto Rico became a United States possession in 1898,
the encounter with an alien culture at first produced a certain
amount of bewilderment, confusion, and emptiness. Then the
threat to the survival of the Spanish language and its traditions
revived the native literature, and the *jíbaro* continued to symbol-
ize the strength of the people against the forces jeopardizing hege-
mony. Whether Puerto Rican writers were carving out their own
destiny within the Spanish domain or consolidating in the American sphere of influence the socio-economic structure forged by
Indian origins, African strength, and four hundred years of Spanish rule, a consistent strain of all the island's literature has been
to preserve the distinctive identity of Puerto Rican culture. This
theme has proved to be their most exportable literary commod-

ity to the mainland. Not in any of the literary arts, not even in the novel, has Puerto Rican individuality emigrated to the United States more effectually than in the drama.

For all practical purposes the modern theater began in Puerto Rico with the founding of the Areyto Group in 1938. The founder, Emilio S. Belaval, set the direction of the Group (named after an indigenous dance-drama) by writing several of the early plays himself, exploring Puerto Rico's cultural past and examining its present day problems. His most famous play, *La hacienda de los cuatro vientos* (1940 "The Hacienda of the Four Winds") concerns the island's struggle to end slavery. Manuel Méndez Ballester, sensitive to the emerging society—urban, mobile, mass—that was dislodging the traditional, communal, ethnic, religious bonds of the political structure, wrote plays for Areyto about the *jíbaro*. Two of his plays, *Tiempo muerto* (1940 "Dead Time") and *Encrucijado* (1956 "Crossroads") trace the human costs of inexorable social progress. In *Tiempo muerto* a poor *jíbaro* family forced off the land to work in the sugar mills becomes disoriented as it loses its emotional and communal props to its dignity and integrity. *Encrucijado* depicts a similar *jíbaro* family that is destroyed by its move to New York City, where it experiences extreme forms of tragic alienation with which it cannot cope. Francisco Arriví, who in 1944 founded the experimental theater, *Tinglado Puertorriqueño*, wrote highly psychological plays as well as realistic plays firmly rooted in social problems. *María Soledad* (1947) concerns a highly sensitive woman's obesession with chastity and the code of honor that demands that her husband kill her poet-lover. His *Club de solteros* (1953 "Bachelor's Club") is an absurdist sex farce depicting the sexual superiority of women. *Un cuento de hadas* (1967 "A Fairy Tale") is a Pirandellean comedy about repression and the loss of identity. However his trilogy, *Máscara puertorriqueña* (1956–58 "Puerto Rican Masquerade") established his reputation as the second most important modern Puerto Rican dramatist after René Marqués.[1]

The great transitional figure between the drama in Puerto Rico and Puerto Rican drama in New York is René Marqués (1917–1979). Already a renowned dramatist in Puerto Rico, Marqués was awarded a Rockefeller Foundation grant to study playwriting in New York in 1949. However much the training at Columbia University and at Piscator's Dramatic Workshop might have enhanced his dramatic skills, it also opened up his imagination to the Puerto Rican experience in New York City. Soon after returning to San Juan he wrote his most influential play, *La carreta* (1951

"*The Oxcart*"). The simple three-act structure of this play belies its political, emotional, and symbolic complexity. The first act dramatizes the economic and psychological plight of the *jíbaro* who moves his family from its mountain farm to San Juan to better its condition. In the second act the family is unable to adapt to the San Juan slum "La Perla." Out of desperation they migrate to New York City where, in the third act, they suffer even greater degradation and the *jíbaro* is killed by the machinery he admires so much. Much chastened by the terrible price they have had to pay for leaving the land of their communal ties, the source of their emotional and spiritual sustenance, the rest of the family moves back to Puerto Rico. No bare outline can begin to do justice to all the complex issues raised by this play. René Marqués is the "father of Puerto Rican drama." Not that Puerto Ricans were not writing plays in New York before Marqués nor Americans before O'Neill.[2] But the extraordinary quality of Marqués's and O'Neill's plays, the impact on their successors, and the direction they charted for the future of the drama separate these two playwrights from all their predecessors and make them emblematic of an important beginning.

The birth of Puerto Rican drama in New York might be dated December 19, 1966, the English-language opening at the Greenwich Mews Theater of René Marqués's *The Oxcart* for an Off-Broadway run of eighty-nine performances. This auspicious beginning had been gestating since its 1953 Spanish-language production in New York had caught the imagination of the widely-acclaimed Puerto Rican actress, Miriam Colón, who played the part of Juanita in both productions. Miriam Colón and others founded the Puerto Rican Traveling Theater (PRTT) primarily to bring this play, free of charge, to the people of New York. In 1967, funded largely by mayor John Lindsay's Summer Taskforce, Miss Colón's troupe toured New York City's parks and playgrounds performing *The Oxcart* in English and Spanish. The enthusiastic reception the Puerto Rican Traveling Theater received in all five boroughs from appreciative, theater-hungry audiences provided the impetus for one of the most remarkable theatrical ventures in the history of New York City.

The PRTT also grew out of that impulse to more creative experimentation in the playwriting and production of the sixties that became known in New York as "Off-Off-Broadway." By the sixties, even the Off-Broadway theaters, like Circle-in-the-Square and the Phoenix Theater, enjoyed such success that they became safer and more convention-bound. The swift reaction was a new breed of writers, directors, and producers influenced by Artaud, Pirandello, Brecht, and others who were committed to extreme political attitudes and radical changes in the mode of presentation. 1961 saw the birth of the Judson Poets Theater, Ellen Stewart's La Mama Experimental Theater Club, and Joe Cino's Caffe Cino in which hundreds of experimental plays found a venue where anything could be (and was) attempted. By 1963 Joseph Chaikin and Peter Feldman were exploring open-ended scripts with the whole company of the Open Theater. They and others were improvising, performing on the streets and in the parks where actors and audience mingled with each other. Two years before Roberto Rodríguez produced the English version of René Marqués's *The Oxcart* in New York City, The American Place Theater established itself as a playwrights' theater dedicated to the exploration of indigenous material. When Miriam Colón and the others took *The Oxcart* into the neighborhoods to bring Puerto Rican culture to the people, these rather humble beginnings were part of a movement that had a profound influence on the whole course of writing and production in the American theater. In the seventies, the PRTT graduated from Off-Off-Broadway to the more respectable Off-Broadway. The PRTT, along with Circle Rep, The Ensemble Theater Studio, the Manhattan Theater Club, Playwrights Horizons, and others, is one of the more prestigious survivors of the sixties, when experimental theater companies seemed to spring up like weeds and die as easily.

From the desire to extend this one production and present it to even more people, the PRTT has grown into a full-blown organization with a touring unit, a training unit, a playwright's unit, and a permanent theater. The touring unit has mounted 20–30 performances each summer for the last twenty-four years before more than 300,000 New Yorkers. The training unit has given free instruction in acting, dancing, singing, diction, and so on to more than 5,000 youngsters over the age of 14. The playwrights' unit, started in 1977, has provided free beginning and advanced classes to writers of all ethnic backgrounds who have developed in their workshops over 125 new American plays. In that same year, 1977, the PRTT inaugurated its permanent theater at 304 West 47th Street in the heart of the theater district. There is no question that a breakthrough in sensibility has occurred, that it is changing the cultural climate, that Puerto Rican writers feel they have a place in New York and a position in American drama. The dual objective of the PRTT is being realized: to establish, in the words of Miriam Colón "a bilingual theatrical organization which would emphasize the dramatic literature of Puerto Rico and Latin

America, highlighting the contributions of Hispanic dramatists in the United States, and to make these theatrical presentations accessible to the people." Two of the plays in this edition, *Bodega* and *Family Scenes*, were developed in the playwrights' unit and *Bodega* was produced in the permanent theater. Two other plays, *First Class* and *Midnight Blues*, were written for and produced by the African Caribbean Poetry Theater. *Ariano* was developed in a playwrighting class of the M.F.A. program at New York University and produced at the PRTT.

In synoptic form, the history of the African Caribbean Poetry Theater recapitulates the history of Puerto Rican drama in New York City. Just as Puerto Rican theater in New York before the sixties consisted mainly of *zarzuelas*, musical recitals, and poetry readings, so did the original Afro-Hispanic Poetry Theater founded by C.D. Grant in 1980. For the first three years the theater sponsored almost exclusively dramatic poetry readings, sometimes accompanied by music. One night, after seeing a performance of *Hakim*, a one-act play by Juan Shamsul Alam, at the Museo del Barrio, Grant invited the young playwright and his wife, Sandra María Esteves, to take over the theater so that he himself could devote more time to publishing. On September 30, 1983, Juan and Sandra accepted the offer, and Sandra became the Executive Director. Her first official act was to change the name to the African Caribbean Poetry Theater (ACPT).

Mr. Alam and Ms. Esteves brought with them several members of The Family, a theatrical group founded by Marvin Felix Camillo for prisoners in the Bedford Correctional Facility in upstate New York. On the outside, The Family provides further theatrical experience for ex-prisoners as well as for people who have never been in prison. Some members had grown restless with the same three or four plays a year Marvin had them do in repertory and were looking for new outlets. Marvin let them go with his blessing, often referring to the ACPT as "The Family #2." This influx of new blood tilted the balance heavily toward drama, but the group never lost sight of its original mission to celebrate the combined heritage of Black and Puerto Rican history and to address the present-day problems of the community. From 1983 to the present the ACPT has staged dozens of plays at the Duo Theatre, the New Rican Cultural Center, the State University of New York at Rochester, the Aaron Davis Center for the Performing Arts, the Invisible Performance Workshop, the Kiss Lounge, Bronx Community College, Hostos Community College, and elsewhere. Several of their plays, characterized by personal dramatic tension infused with humor, have been developed in their own playwriting workshop.

A major significance of the PRTT and the ACPT has been their role in uniting the disparate elements of the Hispanic community and in breaking the codes of American society. For years now the two repertory theaters have dramatized the problems of the Hispanic community, clarifying the misunderstandings and pitfalls of the American experience, pointing toward solutions, and creatively bridging the gap between cultures. Although these plays still fulfill that community role in some respects, they have also moved well beyond it into the mainstream of American drama. These plays are closer to the high art of their island ancestors—Marqués, Belaval, Arriví—and their New York contemporaries— Shepard, Mamet, Kopit—than the folk art of the *zarzuelas*, comedy sketches, and poetry readings out of which they evolved. These two companies in particular and the more than twenty other Hispanic theatrical companies in New York are not supported by Hispanics alone. The quality of their art, the human complexity of subject, and their bilingual productions have captured a highly appreciative cosmopolitan audience. This broad appeal, along with the reviews in the major newspapers and other media (*Show Business* recently gave front-page coverage with a seven-page pull-out section on Hispanic theater in New York), the cross-fertilization of all aspects of theater between Hispanic and non-Hispanic companies, and more—all attest to the very substantial place Puerto Rican drama now holds in the whole tradition of American drama.

BODEGA

Bodega by Federico Fraguada first opened at the PRTT on January 20, 1986, for a limited run. The timeliness of the subject matter—the robbery of a South Bronx bodega and the murder of its owner by two drug addicts—and its reputation in the community made this play "a smash hit." Night after night overflow crowds had to be turned away. At the last performance, sensing the importance and the popularity of this play, Miriam Colón announced that for the first time in the twenty-year history of the PRTT she would bring *Bodega* back the following year. The May–June, 1988, revival was not as successful. The ill-fated second run fell victim to a host of circumstances ranging from the failure of the air-conditioning system to the near-fatal heart attack of the publicity director. Perhaps the single most telling blow against the play was the sponsorship of the series by the Coors Brewing Company. That year Coors expanded its sales market to New York. Coors's troubles on the West Coast with the unions and Hispanics

created a spontaneous boycott, and at the very least an unenthu-
siastic response among many people to anything associated with
Coors.

In 1988, however, Puli Toro, the actress who starred in *Bodega*,
was instrumental in arranging to have the Institute of Puerto Rican
Culture bring the play to Puerto Rico. On January 28–31, 1988,
the play ran for five nearly sold-out performances at the Centro de
Bellas Artes in Santurce. On Feburary 2, the play was a rousing
success for more than 1100 theatergoers at the Teatro La Perla in
Ponce, the oldest theater on the island. Finally, on Feburary 4, the
play moved to the University of Puerto Rico, where a crowd of
students, intellectuals, dignitaries, and working people (conserva-
tively estimated at 1800) jammed into the school auditorium to
see this play whose popularity had steadily gained momentum.

The people of New York loved *Bodega* because it addressed
some of the basic dreams and fears of all New Yorkers; the people
of Puerto Rico loved it for the same reasons and also because they
were fascinated by the conditions and fate of their countrymen in
New York. *Bodega* crosses the American Dream of financial success with the Puerto Rican Dream of spiritual harmony and produces a hybrid dream of artistic fulfillment. The father, Máximo
Toro, dreams of expanding his small bodega in the South Bronx
into a super bodega, perhaps even a chain of super bodegas. His
wife, Elena, wants to return to the Puerto Rico she left twenty-six
years earlier and a better quality life. Their high-school daughter,
Norma, ambitions a career in dance that will release the creative
energy of her mind and body.

Although this play may be categorized as "realistic" (as all the
critics did) with its mundane details and straight narrative plot
line, its real power lies in its appeal to a radical vision that does
not necessarily reaffirm the social order but holds it up for critical
examination. *Bodega* is a ritual reenactment of a mythic immi-
grant experience of a "mom and pop" grocery store, made famous
by waves of Italian, Jewish, Hispanic and more recently, Korean
and Vietnamese immigrants. At the same time this play is heavily
influenced by the archetype of the Western gunfight, particularly
the one depicted in the movie, *High Noon*. Likewise, these characters, although drawn from real life, are all stock characters: the
individualistic *macho* father as the successful Puerto Rican who
is in the process of "making it" in New York, the supportive but
peace-loving wife who just wants to go home to Puerto Rico, the
rebellious teenage daughter distancing herself, she thinks, from her
parents by her radical "Americanness," the junky who had great

promise. *Bodega* is not simply "about" a single slice-of-life, realistic incident; it is about the culture as a whole, consisting in all the systems of meaning by which a society thinks and acts. This play, no matter how much it may seem to reflect life directly (Fraguado actually worked in such a bodega), nevertheless reflects it through the cultural system in which it functions. *Bodega* operates within a dramatic tradition as a whole, and concentrically within many other systems of mythology, ritual, natural ordering, social structure, and so on. Among other things, this play is about a family in transition; it is about the code of *machismo* and how that code is handled by women; perhaps finally it is about a gun—the social, economic, political, tradition of violence in America.

FIRST CLASS

Cándido Tirado's *First Class*, first produced at the African Caribbean Poetry Theater in June, 1987, cast a new director, Michael Carmine, in the role of Speedy. Michael later became very successful appearing with Robert de Niro in the critically acclaimed Off-Broadway production of *Cuba and His Teddy Bear* as well as in the Stephen Spielberg movie, *Batteries Not Included*. Michael believed in the honesty and dramatic power of this play and invested his own money in it. Unfortunately he died of AIDS two years later. In May–June, 1988, the PRTT mounted its production of the play, which became highly controversial, especially within the Puerto Rican community. The English-speaking newspapers reviewed the play more favorably than the Spanish-speaking newspapers. The problem for the playwright was that the audience found it difficult to perceive his literary shaping out of the parameters of the experience described. The largely working class audiences were struggling with characters like Speedy and Apache on the streets and did not want to be associated with them. Nevertheless, this play opened their hearts to these characters and forced audiences to face issues they would rather leave behind. The harsh naturalism of the play, which Tirado believed must be rendered honestly if it is to offer any element of transcendence, moves toward compassionate utterance. It was not uncommon to see audiences, especially the men in the audience, weep during the performance. The author himself felt conflicted because suddenly people were arguing over his ideas on television and radio talk shows, in newspaper columns, in restaurants, and in their homes. *The New York Times* review ended by summing up the conflict this way, " ... Paul-Félix Montez creates an Apache whose tenderness is the source of his toughness and whose cunning self-questioning in a very limited vocabulary makes him a most attractive character."

First Class made a major contribution to New York theater in ways that have not yet been fully acknowledged. By wrapping urban realism, Aesopian fabulism, abstract political symbolism, and the history of U.S.-Puerto Rican relations in a highly sophisticated classical dramaturgy, Tirado engages the imagination in several different ways at once. As rewarding as *First Class* is on the personal level with its rich motivation and complex nuance of value, the play also works anagogically. For example, the traffic island in the middle of Broadway where the two brothers, Apache and Speedy, work out their salvation is literally a "home" where the family braces for an assault from outside social forces, symbolically the island of Puerto Rico within the American sphere of influence, allegorically the American theater amid the crass commercialism of Times Square, and anagogically Prospero's magical isle where the apparently discordant clashes of man and nature are transmuted into an harmonious moral significance. Politically, Maurice represents the corporate power structure of the United States, raping and imprisoning its own children in a mad pursuit of control over other people's lives; Grizzly stands for the outlaw arm of the bureaucracy. However, at its heart, *First Class* is about male bonding, friendship. Apache's prostitute mother took in the very young child, Speedy, from off the streets. The two men raised as brothers are, as we all are, brothers under the skin. The influence of Guillermo Gentile's "fantastic realism" is apparent in their character development, and action rather than dialogue reveals their inner selves. The fundamental story here is confined and intimate. Two men of opposite sensibilities, trapped in a world they never made, teach each other the meaning of work, of self-respect, and of self-sacrifice. The audacious ambition of this play is nothing less than an investigation into what it means to be a man, in the highest moral sense, regardless of background, past offenses, or social position.

MIDNIGHT BLUES

The original version of *Midnight Blues* received a staged reading in April, 1984, at the Invisible Performance Workshop. In May, 1987, Sandra María Esteves, Executive Director of the African Caribbean Poetry Theater, co-produced the play as part of a series of shows in the South Bronx at Malka Percal's Invisible Performance Theater. The critics praised the play, calling Juan Shamsul Alam "one of our most gifted playwrights." The opening night audience itself contributed to the show's critical success. When the audience gave some unexpected laughs to the stage prop of an E.T. doll that resembled the bald-headed actor, Ralph Marrero, who played Jackson Vera, the cast used the humor effectively to satirize the macho father's attempt to clone his sons into exact replicas of himself.

Midnight Blues is a play about a man who, like Willy Loman, has all "the wrong dreams," and who also like Willy Loman has a long-suffering wife named Linda. Jackson Vega, the patriarch of the play, is a moderately successful businessman. However, Jackson's dream of success is embedded in a larger, more destructive dream of the macho husband and father. His desire to pass on the business to his sons goes beyond the business itself to his desire to make his sons conform to his own image. Jackson's tyranny over his family takes the form of a machismo that is not peculiarly Latino nor exclusively American; it has no national nor cultural boundaries. But it is an echo of the darkness that lurks inside our lives and our whole society. While he indulges his wife's shopping sprees, he abuses her verbally and emotionally. As he prods his children to fight each other, he tries to restrict their individual development to one that closely resembles his own. Jackson's machismo tries to mask a misogyny and a homophobia that destroys his favorite son, breaks up his family, and leaves him split against himself. On a larger, political scale, Jackson is part of that grinding system of coercion that parades itself as manly or superior or "smart."

What makes *Midnight Blues* an outstanding American play are the poetic devices of the plastic theater and the imagery used to explicate the often subconscious levels of the play. These subtle techniques keep the disintegration of Jackson's psyche at the center of the action. The play covers only a few hours of Jackson's life and moves from his physical incapacity to go to work in the morning, to painful memories, to hallucination, and finally to complete isolation later that same day. The setting is a womb-like basement apartment that connects to an upstairs duplex. Jackson, however, never leaves the basement during the course of the play. His physical life, imaging his emotional development, is severly constricted. At the play's opening, Jackson takes a fetal position on the sofa and cradles a tin box. At the end he is groveling on the floor in a similar fetal position while his family emerges to a new life leaving him behind stillborn. The occasion of Bobby's birthday brings the whole family together, including Bobby. The appearance of Bobby merges the present action with the root-action in the past and conjures up scenes that make up the life of the mind that is dissolving before us. Past and present exist without any clear distinction of what is happening when. Thus, we come to witness, not just by report, the reenactment of the methodical estrangement by which Jackson has cut himself off from the vitality of love and mutuality with his family. This treatment of time heightens the impact of his complete isolation at the end of the play.

ARIANO

The first small production of Richard Vincent Irizarry's *Ariano* at an Off-Off-Broadway theater in 1984 featured the little-known but rising young actor, Jimmy Smits, in the title role. From the very beginning and in every reincarnation, this play has enjoyed great popular and critical success. Its word-of-mouth fame spread quickly and crowds overflowed the small theater. After further development in the PRTT workshop, the Puerto Rican Traveling Theater mounted the first major production of *Ariano* to an even larger critical and popular sucess in January, 1988. On some nights audience participation in the performance itself was high: women would give motherly advice to the characters; sometimes they scolded Ariano for his faithlessness. But one and all—intellectuals, other theater people, and ordinary citizens—got their money's worth of entertainment. When Miriam Colón revived the play at the PRTT in January, 1990, the *New York Times* reviewer, after praising the play for the "tidal sweeps from shoes off down home comedy to supercharged melodrama," mused wonderingly at "the audience of whites, blacks, Spanish-speakers and English-speakers" who responded so enthusiastically to this play. In the spring of 1990, *Ariano* was invited to take part in the Festival of Latin American Theater at the University of Puerto Rico and also the Ninth Anniversary Celebration of *El Centro de Bellas Artes*.

Richard Irizarry's play, *Ariano*, deals with the most difficult cultural adjustment Puerto Ricans must make when moving to the mainland: racial bigotry. Puerto Ricans are the first large group ever to immigrate to the United States with a tradition of widespread racial integration. When they arrive, Puerto Ricans encounter a type of racial discrimination and segregation they do not experience on the island. Moreover, Puerto Ricans find that they themselves are simplistically placed into one of two categories: white or non-white. Finding their acceptance into the larger, more affluent white community much more difficult if they are regarded as non-white, Puerto Ricans soon realize the social and economic advantages of being white in America. This newly-confronted color awareness often triggers identity confusion and extreme distortions of Puerto Rican cultural values. One distortion involves an unnatural tension between Puerto Ricans themselves. Those who can pass for white may assimilate with the white community and separate themselves from those who cannot pass for white. The incredible force of American racial bigotry can sometimes overcome even blood ties. The color barrier may split husbands and wives, brothers and sisters, even children and parents.

In Puerto Rico, where segregation of the type seen in North America is almost unknown, a person's identity never depends solely on color; the racially sophisticated culture factors in too many other characteristics for identification. Social class, education, occupation, wealth, and other facets of one's personality all contribute to how someone is accepted. However, color discrimination does exist in Puerto Rico in a very complicated way. Opposed to the crude either/or discrimination of black or white on the mainland, Puerto Rico boasts over a dozen words to disciminate among color and racial characteristics. For example, *blanco*, or *hincho* is white; *mulatto* carries both white and black features; *trigueño* (color of wheat) is deep tanned skin but perhaps straight hair and white features; *jabao* means very light skin and hair but black features; *grifo* is a white person with kinky hair; and *negro* is black. However, *negrito* or *negrita* is a term of endearment applied to anyone. Richard Irizarry claims that underlying all these language discriminations is the common prejudice that "you better the race the lighter you marry." Most Puerto Ricans, he says, consider themselves white, and they are shocked in New York to find themselves perceived as black. On the island they can live the lie; they do not have to get an apartment in a lily-white neighborhood. In New York they "grow-up very fast." As relatively benign as Puerto Rican racial prejudice may be in comparison to mainland bigotry, Richard Irizarry's play shows how this prejudice paves the way for Puerto Ricans to adopt this cross-cultural value system when they come under pressure in a racist society. *Ariano*, however, is more than a play about color prejudice; it also has to do with *machismo*, self-esteem, and the Latin soul.

FAMILY SCENES

The last play in this anthology, *Family Scenes*, continues the thematic concern for the dynamic of the family. Although this is the only play here that has not yet been produced, it won the 1989 New York Drama League Award and it was a finalist in the 1989 McDonald's Latino Dramatists Competition in New York. This contest was "created to identify the best writing on the contemporary Hispanic experience in America." The play also received a staged reading at the PRTT in June, 1990.

The ironically named *Family Scenes* by Ivette M. Ramírez is a sonata in a minor key which explores the fragile, tentative nature of human relationships. They are a real family, of course, the mother and her two daughters, but they are not the "family" they pretend to be. These characters so live within the crease between their perceptions and misperceptions of each other that we can never feel confident about assigning final blame to one or the other. Margarita, to protect and console her children (and herself), fictionalizes herself as a conventional wife abandoned by her husband. She fabricates a whole identity in which estrangement and loneliness are evoked only to be dispelled by the "white lie" of her marriage. The audience sees the actress performing the role of mother who performs yet another role for her children who in their turn perform roles for their mother. This metadramatic dimension of the play offers an ironic image of the power of the theater to console.

Simplicity is the keynote to this rather spare play which has no violence and little overt physical tension. *Family Scenes* is not "scenic" in the theatrical sense, a second irony of the title. However, behind the simple plot outline a more complex play emerges from the ambiguity of the ostensibly shared experience offered by the theater when it depicts alienation. For the most part, this play seems to end reassuringly; derailed relationships are back on the right track, some fears have been allayed. However, the future falls far short of the characters' dreams and everyone is the less for it. The sense of loss is not dominant but very strong. It is impossible to rebuild the family relationships that were never forged in the first place, to replace what has been lost. The simple gesture of self-revelation is a step in the right direction, but it is not powerful enough to neutralize the lies and disrelations of a lifetime. So the reassuring aspect of the ending is partially subverted, and the incompletions and isolations exposed by the dramatic action of the play create an awareness that the dissonances are more important than the deceptive harmonies. As Sophia says toward the end, "Oh, Mom, you can't hide that kind of truth forever. The lies hurt more than the truth." The lies told to children are merely the first of many lies to help control their fears. But when these lies present only pleasant or wish-fulfilling images, they offer only escapism or defeatism to the real problems of life. This play stands as a critique of the kind of theater that is implicated in such deceptions.

These five plays suggest the broad range of Puerto Rican playwriting in New York in the eighties. They are presented only technically in the chronological order of their production. They are so close together in time and in their human concerns that their chronology is only of incidental interest. Their most compelling interest lies with the common thread that binds these plays together, the classical Greek question "What is man?" What is it to be a man or a woman in the fullest sense under the conditions of modern life? What does it mean to be Puerto Rican on the American mainland? The most telling rubric under which they fall is their diversity of theme and technique. The use of television's underlying, unstated grammar and a fiercer, more difficult moral vision distinguish *Bodega* (1986). The powerful Brechtian reversal in *First Class* (1987) magically reveals that under the rags and rough manners the foul-mouthed Apache is really a decent, caring, wise person. Juan Shamsul Alam's imaginative staging in *Midnight Blues* (1987) probes the deep psychological recesses of male homophobia complicated by AIDS. *Ariano*'s (1988) pungent humor and moving melodrama crack the American color code and pave the way for the new breed, *el nuevo puertorriqueño*, proud of his or her rainbow heritage. The irony under the surface simplicity of *Family Scenes* deconstructs theatrical performances, on and off stage, for their value in helping us discover who we really are. Finally, a word of appreciation should be said about Mr. Allen Davis III, Director of the Playwrights Workshop at the PRTT, who had a hand in the development of these five playwrights. His work has helped sharpen the talents of numerous aspiring playwrights and has opened up for them the possibilities of production and publication. Except for the plays of Miguel Piñero and Edward Gallardo, few plays by Puerto Rican playwrights have been published in English. This anthology is intended to help fill that void. There are in the New York area dozens of unpublished plays by Puerto Ricans—well over a hundred—many of them (like the plays in this anthology) having enjoyed great popular and critical success. Hopefully, many more of these plays will be published in the near future. Their theattical success has already been recognized; now their literary merit needs to be assessed and preserved in our libraries and classrooms.

John V. Antush
Fordham University

[1]For a fuller sketch of the development of the drama in Puerto Rico, see the following books to which I am greatly indebted:

George R. McMurray, *Spanish American Writing Since 1941: A Critical Survey* (New York: Ungar Press, 1987) and Manesba Hill and Harold Schliefer, *Puerto Rican Authors: A Biobibliographic Handbook* (Metuchen, NJ: Scarecrow Press, 1974).

[2]For an excellent description of Puerto Rican drama in New York before René Marqués, see Nicolás Kanellos, *A History of Hispanic Theater in the United States: Origins to 1940* (Austin, TX: University of Texas Press, 1990).

Bodega

by

Federico Fraguada

Characters:

ELENA TORO, late forties, wife.
MAX TORO, late forties, husband.
NORMA TORO, sixteen years old, daughter.
RAFY LOPEZ, mid-twenties, friend, local drug-addict.
DOÑA LUZ, late sixties, customer, friend of family.
DON LEOPOLDO, late sixties, customer, friend of family.
MICHAEL PETERSEN, mid-twenties, customer.
HOOD 1
HOOD 2

Time: Present.

Place: South Bronx.

Stage is a typical Spanish-American bodega (grocery store) in the South Bronx. Stage left is the exit to street. Neon signs decorate the store windows. A subway entrance is partially visible from the bodega. It's the entrance to an elevated platform station. A large counter-top extends from the street exit to U.S.C. Upstage center there is an exit that leads to the interior living quarters. A curtain hanging on a string serves as a door. Behind the counter there are various shelves containing items, such as cigarettes, mouthwash, toiletries, aspirins, a radio, etc. There is also a wall phone next to the interior exit. Part of the counter flips up by the window end. On the counter-top there is a cash register, meat-slicer, candy jars, T.V. Guides, and dried beef sticks. Above the counter, hanging by a cord, are items, such as boxing magazines, aluminum pots, coffee strainers, potholders, etc. There are two freezers that support the counter-top. One is for ice-cream and sometimes beer. The other is for frozen foods and T.V. dinners. There is a large window sill down stage left where you will find tropical fruits displayed in open boxes. Stage right there is a large refrigerator. On all of the shelves throughout the bodega there are typical Hispanic products with familiar company names, such as Goya, Condal, Iberia, El Paso, etc. Above each of the exits you will find some sort of religious memorabilia, such as a crucifix made of palm leaves, a large black rosary, or portraits of the Sacred Heart or Last Supper. The sounds of the street are constant throughout the play; they include police sirens, fire sirens, burglar alarms, a loud radio playing. Whenever the elevated train passes, its silhouette is seen throughout the bodega.

ACT ONE

.... SCENE ONE ....

    At rise ELENA *is standing behind the counter, returning change to a customer. The customer exits and a delivery boy enters carrying a box that he places next to some others already on the floor.* ELENA *comes from behind the counter and inspects the delivery, then signs the invoice. The delivery boy exits,* ELENA *shuts the door behind him. The store radio is audible.* ELENA *looks at the store clock above the interior exit, then she looks out the window towards the train. An expression of disappointment appears on her face. It's six p.m. late Fall.*

MAX: (*Offstage.*) Elena! Elena! (ELENA *does not respond.*) Elena! Are you out there? ¡Oye!

ELENA: (*Walking up to the counter.*) What do you want?

MAX: (*Offstage.*) Can you hear me?

ELENA: (*Annoyed.*) No, I can't!

MAX: (*Offstage.*) Stop the joking! Are you ready?

ELENA: (*Impatiently.*) I've been ready for two hours!

MAX: (*Offstage.*) Is the front door shut?

ELENA: Yes, it's shut.

MAX: (*Offstage.*) Good! When I yell, open it ... You open it, okay? You got that?!

ELENA: (*Impatiently.*) Just hurry up, will you?

MAX: (*Offstage.*) Open it! (ELENA *returns to the front door and opens it. Suddenly, the piercing siren of an alarm shatters the silence and the lights dim slightly from it.* ELENA, *startled momentarily, rushes over to the alarm box and tries turning it off. Frustrated, she bangs on the box and turns off the radio. She rushes back to the door and tries shutting the door to turn off the alarm. The alarm continues ringing. She runs back behind the counter and yells inside to* MAX.)

ELENA: Máximo! Máximo, come turn this thing off! Máximo I said turn this thing off! (*After a pause,* MAXIMO TORO *enters, he's wearing a triumphant smirk across his face. He*

deliberately walks slowly, admiring his alarm box.) ¡Por
favor, Max! Please hurry!

MAX: Let it ring. That's what I want! Let everybody hear it!

ELENA: Máximo!

MAX: All right, take it easy, nena. (MAX *turns off the 274 alarm
and taps it.*) There! ¿Te fijas? Nothing to it! Not bad, if
you ask me. (*Beat.*) What do you think, Elena? (*Elena
does not respond.*) Oye, didn't you hear me?

ELENA: Ay, I heard you! And, you already know what I think!
(MAX *begins to pick up the wires and pliers he was using
and pack them into a box.*)

MAX: Oh, yeah? Well, I think I got us a good deal, if I say so
myself.

ELENA: You keep saying that.

MAX: That's right, I do and for good reason.

ELENA: Max, I don't understand what's wrong with you. Why did
you buy this new alarm? There wasn't anything wrong
with the old one.

MAX: What are you talking about, eh? What don't you understand? I've explained it a hundred times by now. When
it comes to alarms, they don't make any better than this
one. This is the state of the art, nena. And, when it comes
to the security of my family, only the best will do.

ELENA: Well, I think it's a waste of money. Especially since there
wasn't anything wrong with the old one.

MAX: Is that what you think? This is a waste of money! (*Beat.*)
Who asked you, anyway, eh?

ELENA: Ay, then leave me alone and put it up yourself. (ELENA
*goes over and begins to unpack the boxes and inspects the
contents.*)

MAX: Oh yeah, then, tell me something . . . what happens if there's
another blackout, eh? Did you think about that? I'm
not losing everything I worked hard for because my alarm
won't work in a blackout! No sir. ¡A mí, sí que no! This
one will! It'll ring eight solid hours on batteries. You can't
get a better buy anywhere, I'm telling you, Elena.

ELENA: Ay, who cares?

MAX: Who cares! Who cares! I'll tell you who cares! I care! That's
who cares! I'm not going to stay up all night like the last
time. When this system is put in, punks are going to find
out that breaking into Fort Knox is easier than breaking
into Toro's Bodega! I care! You should too!

ELENA: (*Begins pricing and shelving delivery.*) Well, I think you're silly.

MAX: We'll see who's silly. (MAX *resumes working on the alarm. A train rumbles into the station, its shadow is cast throughout the bodega.* ELENA *stops what she's doing, looking expectantly at the door.* MAX *is mumbling to himself.* ELENA *resumes working.*) There! That should do it. Elena, come over here and give me a hand.

ELENA: ¡Ay, esa porquería! Don't bother me with that stupid alarm. I've had it with it!

MAX: ¿Cómo que stupid alarm? There's nothing stupid about my alarm! Sometimes I don't understand you, nena!

ELENA: I'm the one who doesn't understand! Everybody else is moving out of the neighborhood and you're wasting money putting up new alarms.

MAX: It's an investment, not a waste! And, not everybody is moving out, we still have customers. Just wait until those abandoned buildings across the street get renovated, you'll be singing and dancing all over the place. (*He exits into interior with tools.*)

ELENA: (*Stopping work. Dreamily.*) I wish they would renovate them, all of them! And get rid of all the junkies and bums that live around here. Then you and me wouldn't have to worry all the time about Norma. It would be nice to see this neighborhood clean, finally. We could plant flowers and trees ... see decent people around and have children laughing and playing outside our bodega. (*Sighs.*) Ay, that would be so nice. (*Beat.*) But, don't kid yourself, they'll never pick up the garbage around this place. Those buildings will never be renovated, you're dreaming.

MAX: (MAX *enters, he picks up a staple gun from behind the counter and begins working near the tropical fruits. A customer enters during the following.*) The governor's visit wasn't a dream. He came to my bodega and shook my hand and told me, "Mr. Toro, it's small businessmen like yourself that are the backbone of the United States economy. Your struggle is the struggle of our nation. My administration will be dedicated to protecting the integrity of small businesses. I personally guarantee you that those buildings across from your bodega will be renovated and filled with tenants that will stimulate your business." That's what he said. You were here, you heard him! I am the backbone of the U.S. economy! That wasn't a dream.

(MAX *stops working and goes and rings up the customer's purchase and half-fills the bag, leaving the customer waiting while he continues the discussion with* ELENA. *The customer, frustrated, packs the bag and exits.*)

ELENA: That's right, it wasn't a dream, that was a nightmare in the Bronx. He was so full of hot air, he could fill a balloon large enough to carry the state capitol. I can't believe you fell for it.

MAX: He's on record. He said it on public television.

ELENA: That's where they always say it so the public can't feel the hot air.

MAX: It wasn't hot air. He'll keep his promise.

ELENA: Pero, Max, you didn't vote for him.

MAX: So what? What does that have to do with anything? He doesn't know that.

ELENA: It's been two years and nothing has happened yet.

MAX: Things take time. You know how much red tape people have to go through to get things done. Remember how long it took us to get all the paperwork done for this bodega?

ELENA: It wasn't two years, that much I know.

MAX: Anyway, it doesn't matter, I'll be here when they finish. I have it all figured out. If business gets good, I'll get a loan and expand next door. I'll call it Toro's Super Bodega. It'll be the first Super Bodega in the Bronx, maybe the whole city. How about that, nena?

ELENA: (*Laughing.*) A super bodega? I can't believe you sometimes.

MAX: Yeah, like a super market, except, Puerto Rican style. I'll keep all Latino products.

ELENA: They already have supermarkets Latino style.

MAX: So what? They don't call theirs Super Bodega. And, they won't be anything like my Super Bodega. I'll own a chain of them.

ELENA: I have a better idea. Why don't you open a disco-laundry. I can see it now, Toro's Dance and Clean. The only place you can dance your laundry clean. I'm sure you'll clean up.

MAX: Chuckle, chuckle, are you going to help me or not?

ELENA: I'm busy now.

MAX: (*Opening curtain.*) That's fine with me. (*Yelling.*) Norma! Norma, come down here, I need you to help me with something!

ELENA: (*Goes and looks out the window.*) Stop yelling, she can't hear you, she hasn't returned from school yet.

MAX: (*Goes in front of counter and glances at clock.*) What?! Where is she? Do you know what time it is? It's six. Look how dark it is outside. It doesn't take three hours to get to the Bronx from Manhattan. She's supposed to be here at three-thirty. What happened?

ELENA: She's on her way, she told me she would be a little late because of her rehearsals. (*She sits by the window.*)

MAX: A little late! I've told you I don't like the way you're spoiling that girl!

ELENA: ¿Ay, de qué hablas ahora?

MAX: You know exactly what I'm talking about, the way you carry on with her about that dancing nonsense of hers. I've told you a thousand times not to encourage her.

ELENA: It's not nonsense, I think she's a good dancer. With practice and dedication she can get far.

MAX: That's exactly what I'm talking about. Don't you know that being good isn't enough nowadays. There's thousands of dancers roaming the streets and begging and starving; you know why? They're starving because they're good dancers, that's why! It takes more than just being good.

ELENA: Ay, thinking that way, she doesn't stand a chance before she starts.

MAX: (*Pacing.*) That's right! She doesn't. I'm a realist, I don't want my daughter chasing after a wild dream. She needs to learn something concrete, something she can use for the rest of her life.

ELENA: And, what might that be?

MAX: (*Proudly.*) Business! That's what! She should be learning business. That's where her rice and beans are! Not in some flaky dancing career. And, what better place for her to get a solid foundation in business than right here in my bodega. This is where her future is!

ELENA: (*Laughing.*) ¿Aquí? Ay, no me hagas reír.

MAX: I don't see what's funny.

ELENA: Some realist you turned out to be. Do you think I slave sixteen hours a day so my daughter ends up doing the same?

MAX: I don't see anything wrong with it. Hard work is good for her. If she's busy working sixteen hours, then she won't have any time to get into trouble. Just wait until they finish renovating those buildings, you'll see.

ELENA: I don't care if they renovate the entire city. Norma is not going to spend the rest of her life behind a counter. No sir, as long as I have something to say about it, Norma's becoming a dancer. That's all there is to it! (*Enter* NORMA, *she kisses* ELENA, *then crosses D.S.R., sits on a stool and looks through her bag. She pulls out a phone book and begins copying a number written on her hand.*)

NORMA: Hi, guys, sorry I'm late. Brrr, it's cold out there, feels like winter. We ran behind schedule all day long. How's the new alarm coming along, Papi?

MAX: (*Walking over to* NORMA.) Don't try to Papi me! It feels like winter because it's blacker than a bat's ass out there! Do you know what time it is? Where have you been, it's past six!

ELENA: Máximo, watch how you speak!

MAX: All right, all right! (*To* NORMA.) So, where were you?

NORMA: I told you, we ran late.

ELENA: (*Stands and walks to the middle of the counter.*) How did you get home? You weren't on the last train.

MAX: (*Impatiently.*) Answer your mother, she asked you a question!

NORMA: I got a lift.

MAX: (*Looking at* ELENA, *then at* NORMA.) A lift from who?

NORMA: (*Putting address book back in bag.*) From one of the guys in the show, nobody you know.

MAX: (*Turns to face* ELENA.) One of the guys from the show, what guy? How come he didn't bring you to the door?

NORMA: Papi ... (*She gets up to get a soda.*)

MAX: (*Turns to face empty stool, then follows* NORMA.) Papi nothing! Ahora sé yo ... a lift from a guy. This is the last time. This is it! From now on no more rehearsals. You want work? I have work for you. I'm putting an end to this nonsense. Go change and come give me a hand. I'm going to show you what work really is, not that silly dancing of yours.

NORMA: But, Papi, I didn't do anything wrong. (*To* ELENA.) Mami ...

ELENA: (*Trying to mediate.*) Norma, you know how dangerous this city is. You know your father and me worry about you when you're out and it's dark.

NORMA: I know that. That's why I accepted the ride home, so you guys wouldn't worry.

MAX: Stop calling us you guys! I'm your father, not some guy from the streets!

NORMA: But, Papi ... I have the lead role in the school's Christmas show. You don't want me to quit now. What will everybody say? You're the one who's always telling me, "A Toro never quits." Mami, not now, not after all I went through to get the part.

MAX: (*Walking away from* NORMA.) First, let's get one thing straight: I'm not asking, I'm telling you! You should have thought about that before you came in this late. You're a young girl and I don't want my daughter out in the streets with strangers. I never wanted you to take up dancing in the first place! Second, I don't need you to quote what I tell you! And, third, you can forget about any phone calls tonight. I'm putting the lock on it right now!

NORMA: (*Protesting.*) Papi ...

MAX: Papi, nada! Now, get upstairs!

NORMA: (*Picking up her bags and going to* ELENA.) Mami, what am I going to do? (ELENA *hugs* NORMA, *trying to comfort her as they walk towards the curtain to the interior.*)

ELENA: Nothing. Just do as he says, you know how stubborn he gets. Nothing you tell him will change his mind. We'll talk about it tomorrow, okay? (*They both exit inside. MAX follows them and makes sure they've left. Satisfied, he laughs to himself and places a lock on the phone. He starts to hide the key in the usual spot, but, changes his mind and hides it in his pocket. He then opens the curtain.*)

MAX: (*Yelling.*) And, don't take forever! I need you now, not tomorrow! (*To himself.*) I'm not stupid, that's why I keep only one phone. (MAX *grabs a broom and begins sweeping the bodega. Enter* RAFY, *a young junkie wearing an extra large raincoat.* MAX *puts down broom to remove a box that is in the way of sweeping. He resumes sweeping.*)

RAFY: Yo, bro, ¿qué pasa, Mr. Toro? How's it going?

MAX: (*Stops sweeping.*) Oh no, not you. Mira, Rafy, it's not going. I haven't made any money yet, so whatever you're selling, forget it, I'm not buying. (MAX *resumes sweeping.*)

RAFY: Yo ... chill out, Mr. Toro, check out this deal I have for you. (RAFY *pulls out a box of government cheese from inside his jacket and slams it on the counter.*) I gots three dozen of these bad boys left. I saved them, you know, just for you. So, how's about it? I'll give you a good deal on them. (*Following* MAX *with the cheese in hand.*)

MAX: (*Stops sweeping.*) How did you get three dozen boxes of this cheese?

RAFY: Yo, bro, come on, Mr. Toro, like you don't, you know, expect me to give away my trade secrets now, do you?

MAX: (*Resumes sweeping.*) Mira, Rafy, I told you already, I'm not buying anything today. Especially not government cheese. That cheese is for the poor and I don't want any part of it.

RAFY: Yo, bro, I'm poor! Why the hell do you think I'm selling it?

MAX: Forget it! I wouldn't sell my customers that garbage. They would sue me for giving them a bad case of killer farts and diarrhea.

RAFY: Diarrhea! Yo, bro, you don't know what you're talking about!

MAX: Believe me, they would fart themselves to death. Have you ever tried it? You ought to some time ... just make sure you keep plenty of toilet paper with you.

RAFY: (*Following* MAX *as he sweeps.*) Bro, this is U.S.D.A. inspected. Shit, just the other day I offered, you know, thirty boxes of this same stuff to this, you know, very high-tone restaurant downtown.

MAX: (*Stops sweeping, faces* RAFY.) You sold this stuff to restaurants?

RAFY: You got that right, bro.

MAX: How about the ones around here?

RAFY: Are you kidding, bro? I'd sell it to Kentucky Fried, if they made a cheese chicken.

MAX: (*Holding his stomach and walking away.*) No wonder I've been toxic ... I knew there was something wrong with that grill cheese I had at Charlies.

RAFY: (*Following* MAX.) All right, bro, don't jump the gun. I mean the cheese is on the money, you know, Mr. Toro, but, if you don't want, I'm not gonna force you. Hey, Mr. Toro, you know I wouldn't give you anything if it wasn't righteous.

MAX: (*Resumes sweeping.*) Yeah, I bet you wouldn't. (RAFY *puts the cheese on the counter, then reaches into another inside pocket and pulls out a machete. He begins swinging like a Samurai warrior.*)

RAFY: Yo, bro, check this out! This blade is so sharp, you know, it cuts itself! Check it out, bro ... this bad boy is guaranteed for life! It's got the same blade the Japanese use for their Samurai swords. You'll have no problems, you know, cutting anything with this. Shit, you can use it to chop a motherfucker's head off. Swoosh!

MAX: (*Stops sweeping.*) Please, put it away, Rafy. You already sold me one two weeks ago.

RAFY: (*Putting machete back in coat.*) I did? Oh, then, maybe you're in the market for something else? (MAX *resumes sweeping.* RAFY *pulls out a portable radio/cassette player and follows* MAX, *almost mimicking his motion.*)

RAFY: Check this out, bro. What you're looking at here, you know, is the baddest damn "Walkman" ever made. Listen bro, I don't have to tell, you know, a smart man like you, how bad the Japanese are when it comes to electronics, you know, they is tops. Hey, with this bad boy you can play or record, nothing to it. Let me give you a quick, you know, demonstration and then tell me what you think. Check it out, look it's a "SONY," bro, you got nothing, you know, to lose and mucho to gain. (*Places tape recorder in* MAX's *hand; he returns it.*)

MAX: Rafy, por favor, try somebody else. Can't you see I'm busy?

RAFY: Yo, Mr. Toro, I want you to have first crack at this deal, you know, at the price I'm selling it, it's a steal, you know, bro? You can't even find a better deal on Delancey St. (*Hands* MAX *the recorder.*)

MAX: (*Returning recorder.*) I can't help you, I'm not buying anything today.

RAFY: (*Putting arm around* MAX's *shoulder.*) Yo, bro, this is the latest thing, you know, on the market. I'm letting it go only because I wanna, you know, get myself a real box to go to the beach. Before you make up your mind, check it out, bro. Go ahead, I don't charge for looking.

MAX: (*Reluctantly grabbing recorder and walking away.*) Oh, what the hell, let me see what you got.

RAFY: (*Going over to* MAX.) Believe me, bro, it's what you always wanted. You won't regret this.

MAX: I regret it already. (*Beat.*) Rafy, you didn't steal this ... did you? (*Police sirens are heard in the background.*)

RAFY: (*Backs away, faking a bruised ego.*) Wow, Mr. Toro, do you think, you know, I would do you like that? I wouldn't do something like that to you ... my main man. Wow, bro, you know, you hurt my feelings saying that. I'll sell it to somebody else. I was just trying to do you a favor, that's all. Nothing more. (RAFY *grabs the recorder and pretends he's walking out.* MAX *crosses over behind the counter and gives in.*)

MAX: All right, hurry up, I have things to do around here. I can't spend the whole night talking to you. This is the last thing you show me ... nothing else ... you got that?

RAFY: (*Returning to the front of the counter.*) You got it, bro ... this'll make a good gift for your, you know, daughter's birthday.

MAX: (*Fidgeting with recordor.*) Her birthday was two months ago.

RAFY: You can give it to the Mrs. for her birthday.

MAX: I don't think so.

RAFY: Hey, bro, like you don't have to give gifts only on holidays, you know, you can give them any time.

MAX: So, what's the big deal with this? It's nothing but a tape-recorder. (*Puts it to his ear, then down.*) I can't hear a thing. Are you sure this thing works? (RAFY *throws his leg up on the counter and pulls out a set of earphones from his socks and plugs them into the recorder.*)

RAFY: Of course, it works. I personally guarantee it. What you need is this earphone here. With this bad boy you'll be able to hear everything in super galactic stereo. Complete privacy, just you and your tapes.

MAX: Rafy, why don't you give your motor mouth a break?

RAFY: (*Plugs earphone into* MAX*'s ear and raises volume.*) Sure thing, bro. Here let me help you.

MAX: (*Removing earphones quickly.*) Ahhh! What are you trying to do? Blow my ears off?

RAFY: (*Laughing.*) Bad, bro, I just wanted you to check it out, you know, the sound and all. And, those are dead batteries too, imagine if they were new and all.

MAX: (*Puts recorder on counter and picks up broom.*) Yeah, yeah, very nice, Rafy, pero, I don't think so. (RAFY *throws the other leg on the counter and pulls out some tapes and a strap for it and slams them on the counter.*)

RAFY: Yo, bro, chill out. Tell you what I'll do for you. I'll toss in these tapes and the strap for free. Look, you can keep your hands free to do whatever you have to in the bodega. It's like having a disco in the bodega.

MAX: (*Stepping in front of the counter.*) Mira, Rafy, I told you ... (*Beat.*) Did you say disco? (RAFY *reaches for the recorder, puts it on and begins to dance and sing.*)

RAFY: That's right, bro. Look, no hands.

MAX: Hmmm, disco, let me take a look at it, maybe I can use it, after all.

RAFY: (*Excitedly hands him the recorder.*) That's what I've been trying to, you know, tell you. I'm not, you know, trying to waste your time, Mr. Toro. Here.

MAX: (*Putting on the recorder carefully.*) How much?

RAFY: (*Pacing around.*) Well, seeing like I really don't want, you know, to get rid of it, you know, after all it has, you know, sentimental value to me, but, since I like you, say fifty bucks.

MAX: (*Listening to recorder.*) How much did you say?

RAFY: (*Removes one plug and whispers in* MAX*'s ear.*) Fifty beans.

MAX: ¿Estás loco? (MAX *takes off recorder and places it on the counter, he takes the broom and begins sweeping behind the counter.*)

RAFY: (*Following* MAX.) Come on, bro, it's a "SONY," they don't, you know, make anything better. Yo, Mr. Toro, that's rat cheap. Anybody would, you know, jump on this price.

MAX: (*Pushing* RAFY *from behind counter.*) Yeah, jump right out of your way, thinking you're nuts or something.

RAFY: (*Going up to* MAX*'s face, then, breaking away.*) Don't do me like that!

MAX: (MAX *crosses over in front of the counter.*) Sorry, I can't help you, Rafy. (*Reminiscing.*) Funny thing is I can still remember the first time you came in here. You were this tall. (*Indicating with hand.*) It sure doesn't seem that long ago, let me think, ah, sí, you came in, ha, trying to trade a broken top for some bubble gum. I remember. You remember? You were quite a kid back then. Good looking, smart, strong, everybody thought you were going to win a gold medal in boxing. Now look at yourself. What a disappointment.

RAFY: (*Pacing around uncomfortably.*) Okay, okay, Mr. Toro, like, you know, this is really gonna hurt me, but, I'll let you have it for thirty ... only don't get into memory lane, all right, bro?

MAX: I can't help it ... you even won a Golden Glove championship back then. You had the world in your hands.

RAFY: Okay, okay, make it twenty-five.

MAX: It was the other kid, what was his name? Nothing but trouble; from the first time I saw him I knew he was bad news. Right now you could be the champion of the world ...

instead, look at you. (*Beat.*) Lucky, that was his name! Some luck he turned out to be. Where is he now? You could be rich right now. Instead, you're the undisputed drug champion of the Bronx. You can still do something with your life. Why don't you try going to one of those . . .

RAFY: (*Interrupting.*) Okay, Mr. Toro, don't start with the rehabilitation bullshit again. How much are you willing to give me?

MAX: (*Studying recorder.*) Fifteen. (*A customer enters and purchases a pack of cigarettes during the following heated argument, then exits.*)

RAFY: Fifteen dollars! For a Sony?! Yo, Mr. Toro, you can do better than that! As long as you've been in this bodega, I know you got some serious bucks stashed around somewhere.

MAX: That's the best I can offer.

RAFY: Bro, you're putting a hurting on me, you know, you're lucky I need the bread. Give me the fifteen. (MAX *hands him the money and quickly hides the recorder from* RAFY.)

RAFY: (*Reaching in his back pocket.*) Hey, Mr. Toro, maybe you can use a pair of gold earrings for the old lady? I got here an eighteen carat Panamanian gold set . . .

MAX: (*Interrupting.*) No, no, forget it. This is it for me. Go try Don Alipio, he might be interested in buying something. This is my limit for the day.

RAFY: Yeah, I think I better. He knows a deal when he sees one. I don't have to, you know, argue with him over some chump change. See ya on the rebound, Mr. Toro. (*RAFY exits.* MAX *crosses over to the door just as* DON LEOPOLDO *enters.* MAX *chases some teenagers from the front of his bodega.*)

MAX: Hey, fellas no hanging out in front. (*To* LEOPOLDO.) Hola, Don Leopoldo, how are you feeling tonight?

LEOPOLDO: (*Coughing.*) Fine, Don Max.

MAX: You should see a doctor about that cough.

LEOPOLDO: At my age it don't matter much. I don't have many more years to live. If I die tonight, I would have lived a long life.

MAX: You'll never hear me say that. I want to live forever. By the way, what number came out today?

LEOPOLDO: Don Max, don't you think that if your number had come out, I would tell you?

MAX: I know I didn't win, Don Leopoldo, I just wanted to know how close I got.

LEOPOLDO: The number for Brooklyn was 819 and New York was 443.

MAX: One day I'm going to hit and when I do, watch out, 'cause it's going to be big. Real big! You'll see, Don Leopoldo.

LEOPOLDO: You should be playing what Don Alipio plays, he's always hitting. Just last week he hit it for two thousand two hundred. That's a lucky man, almost left my bank broke.

MAX: Then stop telling people about his luck, or they'll break your bank for sure.

LEOPOLDO: Guess you're right, I shouldn't volunteer information. (*Beat.*) I wonder what he does with all that money?

MAX: I'll tell you what he isn't doing, putting it to good use! You know how many times I've asked him to invest in my Super Bodega idea? And, every time it's the same answer, "I don't know, it sounds too risky." Can you believe that? Fifty percent I offer him and he thinks it's too risky! Sometimes ... ahhhh ... that's another ... (*Beat.*) So, how's the wife?

LEOPOLDO: Ahhh, Martha is doing fine. She's found herself a new Bingo spot, now she spends all her time there. (*Sighing.*) A marriage made in heaven. Of course, sometimes she ruins it by insisting I drive her to some Indian reservation where they have some sort of Super Bingo.

MAX: Why don't you take her sometime. It might be good for you.

LEOPOLDO: It's somewhere in Colorado or Nevada or someplace like that.

MAX: She must love her Bingo.

LEOPOLDO: Up to any new inventions lately?

MAX: Naw, just trying to improve this alarm I bought yesterday.

LEOPOLDO: What are you planning to do?

MAX: (*Demonstrating a light to him.*) I want to connect this light to it, but I have to buy another for the inside.

LEOPOLDO: Why do you want to connect the light to the alarm for?

MAX: To make it easier for the police to locate where the alarm is coming from, and, to scare the hell into whoever dares break in here.

LEOPOLDO: (*While fetching some beer.*) I hope it works better than that sand sprinkler you put up last year.

MAX: That could have happened to anybody. How was I to know the sensor was so sensitive?

LEOPOLDO: Sensitive? That was ridiculous, all you had to do was light a cigarette and it was spitting sand all over the place. You should have left it connected, *that* was a crime stopper if I ever saw one.

MAX: (*Annoyed.*) Will that be it, Don Leopoldo?

LEOPOLDO: (MAX *handing him the bag.*) That's it for now, write it in the book, I'll pay you what I owe tomorrow. Do you want me to put you down for the same numbers tomorrow? (MAX *nods.* DON LEOPOLDO *exits.* MAX *writes the amount in a composition book and resumes studying the light. He grabs a chair and goes over to the front door, he stands on a chair and tries determining where the light should go.* NORMA *enters, she has changed clothes.*)

NORMA: I'm ready, Papi.

MAX: Good, give me a hand over here.

NORMA: Papi, getting back to the rehearsals, I'm sorry I got home late. I promise it won't ever happen again. So, I was thinking, maybe, you might want to think about it some more before making a hasty decision. I mean, like we should talk about it ... (*Lights slowly fade to black.*)

.... SCENE TWO ....

The following morning, MAX *is behind the counter measuring and cutting wire.* NORMA *enters, she is wearing a leotard.*

NORMA: Good morning, Papi. Bendición. (*She kisses his cheek.*)

MAX: Dios te bendiga, nena.

NORMA: You still haven't finished with that alarm?

MAX: I'm having trouble finding the proper wires.

NORMA: Why can't you buy a system with everything done already, wouldn't that be easier?

MAX: It would be easier, nena, but it wouldn't be as enjoyable as doing it yourself. I'm going downstairs to see if I can find what I need. You cover here for me.

NORMA: Have you considered what we talked about yesterday?

MAX: I'm still considering it. (*He exits inside.* NORMA *goes about preparing herself something to eat.* RAFY *enters dressed as before.*)

RAFY: (*Rushing in.*) Hey, Mr. Toro, today is your lucky day, you know, look what I gots for you. (*Seeing it's* NORMA.) Oh, I'm sorry, I didn't think you were here. I'll come back later. (*Starts to exit.*)

NORMA: Wait, don't leave, Rafy.

RAFY: (*Straightening his appearance and speaking softly.*) You look great, Norma.

NORMA: Thank you. So, how's your mother doing?

RAFY: (*Sadly.*) She's still at the home.

NORMA: I feel terrible. I've been so busy I haven't gone to visit her.

RAFY: It doesn't matter, she wouldn't, you know, recognize you no how. She don't even recognize me, her own son.

NORMA: I'm sorry to hear that, she was very nice to me. (*Beat.*) It's been some time since I've seen you. What's been happening?

RAFY: Nuthin' much. Same old same old. I hear, you doing good in school.

NORMA: It's okay, I guess.

RAFY: I'm surprised you here. I thought you'd be rehearsing or something.

NORMA: Well, you gotta take some time off some time.

RAFY: When do you finish?

NORMA: This is my last year.

RUFY: That quick?

NORMA: Yeah, I was skipped from ninth to eleventh.

RAFY: You were always smart like that.

NORMA: So, are you still messing with that stuff?

RAFY: I've been cutting down, I was just telling your father yesterday, I'm, you know, entering a detox clinic tomorrow.

NORMA: (*Disbelieving.*) Is it for real this time?

RAFY: (*Crosses himself.*) I swear, I'm legit this time. Do you think, you know, I wanna be a dope fiend forever?

NORMA: I don't know, I never knew with you. But, I hope you're on the level this time, I don't want to hear you had an O.D. or caught AIDS.

RAFY: Aaaw, come on, Norma, why you wanna wish something like that on me?

NORMA: I'm not wishing anything on you. I just don't wish to see people I care about being hurt, that's all.

RAFY: I'm careful, you don't think, you know, I'm gonna share my needle, do you?

NORMA: There you go, missing the whole point again.

RAFY: (*Sadly.*) I know ...

NORMA: (*Interrupting.*) No! I don't think you do. A lot of people have cared about you, Rafy, myself included, the only problem is you have never cared about yourself.

RAFY: I promise, Norma, may I die if I'm lying, this is it! No more. The next time you see me, I'll be a different man. Word.

NORMA: All right, I'll take your word for it. So, what you want to see Dad for?

RAFY: It was nothing important, I can, you know, talk to him some other time. I have to be booking, see you on the rebound. Good luck with your dancing. I know you gonna, you know, make it some day. (RAFY *exits as* MAX *enters, he notices* RAFY *leaving.* MAX *walks up to the door and fidgets with it.*)

MAX: What was he trying to sell this time?

NORMA: (*Defensively.*) He wasn't trying to sell anything, he just wanted to talk to you.

MAX: Thank God he left, I didn't feel like talking to him. Look, nena, I'm going to the hardware store to get some things I need to finish this. Lock the door behind me and don't let anybody in. I don't want this mechanism getting messed up. (MAX *exits, carefully shutting the door behind him.* NORMA *locks the door.* ELENA *enters from inside.*)

ELENA: Where's your father? I thought he was working on the alarm?

NORMA: He needed some things from the hardware store. All he said was keep the door locked until he got back.

ELENA: He hasn't had his coffee yet. (DOÑA LUZ *appears at the door, finding it shut, she knocks and waves at* ELENA.) Ay muchacha, look what you've done, you locked Doña Luz out. Open that door.

NORMA: Oh no, Mami, Papi told me not to let anybody in.

ELENA: Don't be silly, Norma, he didn't mean Doña Luz. Open that door.

NORMA: (*Reluctantly goes and opens the door.*) Well, I hope she doesn't start bothering me about that stupid church of hers again. (DOÑA LUZ *enters stopping at the door.*)

LUZ: (*In exaggerated Evangelican fashion.*) In the name of the Father, the Son and the Holy Spirit, may our Lord Jesus Christ protect this bodega and all inside it from the evil malevolent forces that would seek to bring harm to us. Amen. (NORMA *shuts the door and sits by the win-*

dow. DOÑA LUZ *crosses herself, then the bodega, as she approaches* ELENA.)

ELENA: Why, thank you, Doña Luz. (*To* NORMA.) Honey, you better go eat your breakfast before it gets cold. And, put your father's breakfast in the oven so it won't get cold. (NORMA *exits inside.*)

LUZ: You wouldn't believe who I just saw ... Milagros Fonseca. (*Pause.*) Don't you remember? Doña Belén's daughter, she ran off with her mother's boyfriend.

ELENA: Ohhh, that Milagros.

LUZ: You won't believe what I heard.

ELENA: (*Dryly.*) What did you hear?

LUZ: She's pregnant. And, that's not the worse of it! He died, and, it was AIDS! (*Pause for effect.*) Now, she's seven months and finds out the baby has AIDS!

ELENA: Oh God, that's terrible. Then she must have it also.

LUZ: If she had been going to church like she was supposed to, she wouldn't be in this mess now.

ELENA: This is terrible, she's so young and pretty.

LUZ: (*Sitting on a nearby crate.*) It turns out he had an operation some years back and that's how he got it. (*Pause.*) I thought you knew already, you know how fast news travels in this neighborhood, especially bad news. You know how I hate being the bearer of bad news. (*Beat.*) Anyway, guess who I was speaking to last night.

ELENA: Doña Luz, I'm not good at guessing games.

LUZ: Reverend Cruz.

ELENA: (*Sarcastically.*) How nice.

LUZ: You'll never guess what he told me.

ELENA: (*Impatiently.*) Doña Luz, why don't you just tell me.

LUZ: (*Rising proudly.*) He told me he's interested in buying this bodega. He asked me to find out if you're interested in selling.

ELENA: (*Interestedly.*) Reverend Cruz is interested in buying this bodega?

LUZ: Yes. He feels the best time to grab sinners is when they're on their way to work or returning home at night. And, this bodega is in the right spot with this EL next to it. He believes a location like this makes the word of the Lord more accessible to sinners who find it difficult getting to church.

ELENA: You'll have to talk with Max about it.

LUZ: Do you think he'll go for it? (*Looking over bodega.*)

ELENA: I don't know. But, it doesn't sound like a bad thing to
me.

LUZ: I know Reverend Cruz is willing to make him an attractive
offer. Maybe God might help persuade him.

ELENA: Just don't tell him you mentioned it to me or he'll think
it was my idea and say no. (MICHAEL PETERSEN, *a
young white male in his late twenties, enters. He goes to
freezer and takes out a soda.*)

MICHAEL: Good morning ladies. I do hope you lovely ladies
are enjoying this beautiful weather we're having. (*Both
women study him.*)

LUZ: (*Leaning towards* ELENA.) What a polite young man. I wonder if he goes to church.

ELENA: (*To* MICHAEL *perusing magazines.*) Can I help you?

MICHAEL: I'm glad I found this place. I've been looking for
a store for the past couple of blocks now. Every place
seemed closed down. You seem to be the only grocer in
the neighborhood.

ELENA: Do you live around here?

MICHAEL: (*Placing items on counter.*) Yes, a few blocks from
here. My grandmother and I just moved into New York.

LUZ: (*Following* MICHAEL *while delivering this in her usual exaggerated evangelical style.*) In the name of the Father,
the Son and the Holy Spirit, I bless this fortunate meeting. This accidental meeting is not as accidental as it may
seem. Our Lord Jesus Christ works in very mysterious
ways, and this is one of them. Doña Elena, this young
man has come to your bodega because it was the Lord's
way of allowing this fortunate young man to become ac-
quainted with me. So that I can inform him about the
services we offer at the Church of Our Shepherd and, in
that manner, begin his path toward God.

ELENA: (*To* LUZ.) There's nothing mysterious about the Lord's
workings, it's his servants who are mysterious.

LUZ: (*Ignoring* ELENA *and approaching* MICHAEL.) I knew you
weren't from around here. This is an act of grace. What's
your name, young man?

MICHAEL: (*Taken aback by her aggressiveness.*) Michael Petersen,
madam. And, you must read minds. It just so happens I
am looking for a church my grandmother can attend.

LUZ: (*To* ELENA.) There! You see! (*To* MICHAEL.) I know a
church your grandmother and you can attend. You do
attend church, young man?

MICHAEL: Yeah, I do ... sometimes.

ELENA: What else can I get you?

MICHAEL: Er ... I'll have two packs of Marlboros, a small box of unsalted crackers and a jar of peanut butter.

ELENA: (*Gathering items.*) Do you want creamy or chunky?

MICHAEL: Creamy.

ELENA: What size?

MICHAEL: Small.

LUZ: (*Taking a calling card from her bible.*) Now let me give you this card, that way you won't forget it.

ELENA: Anything else?

MICHAEL: No, this'll be all for now. How much do I owe you?

ELENA: (*Packing everything except the soda and magazine, which* MICHAEL *carries.*) Let's see ... that's eight twenty-five. (MICHAEL *hands her a ten dollar bill and starts for the door.* DOÑA LUZ *awkwardly blocks his path.*)

LUZ: Here, give this to your grandmother. I hope I'll see you two at tomorrow's services.

MICHAEL: (*To* LUZ.) Thank you much. (*She moves out of his way and behind him.*)

ELENA: (*Handing* MICHAEL *his change.*) Here you are.

MICHAEL: (*Having to get around* DOÑA LUZ *to get his change.*) Thank you much. Do have a nice day. (*He exits.*)

LUZ: (*Almost clinging to the door.*) Ahhh, what a polite young man. I wonder why they moved here in the South Bronx. What do you think Doña Elena?

ELENA: Ay, no sé. I have other things on my mind.

LUZ: Hmmm, I wonder if they're planning to gentrify the South Bronx ...

ELENA: (*Interrupting.*) Gentri what?

LUZ: You know, whiten the neighborhood. They could be the first wave of Anglos.

ELENA: Mira, Doña Luz, before they gentrify the South Bronx, they'll gentrify the Amazon jungle.

MAX: (MAX *enters carrying his supplies. He stops momentarily and stares at* DOÑA LUZ *before continuing inside.* DOÑA LUZ *sits down by the window.*) Where's Norma?

ELENA: She's inside eating breakfast. (*Beat.*) What do you have there this time?

MAX: The wires I need to finish this job.

ELENA: Are you hungry, honey? Let me warm up your breakfast. By the way, Max, Doña Luz has something she wants to talk to you about. (ELENA *exits inside.* MAX *goes behind*

counter *looking for his tools and* DOÑA LUZ *comes up
    behind him. He turns suddenly, causing the both of them
    to shriek.*)
MAX: (*Annoyed with what just happened.*) So, what can I do for
    you, Doña Luz?
LUZ: Now that you mention it, Don Max, there is something you
    can do for me ... well ... it's really not for me. I have this
    friend who has some money and he's looking to invest it.
MAX: Bien, what is he looking to invest it in?
LUZ: Well, he's interested in investing in real estate, so I told him
    I would speak to you.
MAX: (*Packing some cakes on the counter.*) I'm sorry, Doña Luz,
    pero, you've come to the wrong man. I don't know any-
    thing about real estate.
LUZ: But, you own this bodega, Don Max.
MAX: (*Replacing magazines strewn on counter.*) Ahhh, that's true.
    And, it was the first and only good investment I ever
    made.
LUZ: That's exactly what I'm talking about, your bodega.
MAX: (*Turning to face her.*) Wait, I must have missed something
    here. What are you talking about?
LUZ: (*Taking his arm and walking with him.*) Well, you see, it's like
    this ... personally, I think it's an honor, and you should
    be proud that Reverend Cruz is interested in buying your
    bodega.
MAX: (*Shocked, he pulls away.*) WHAT?! Did I hear you right?
LUZ: Yes, he's very excited about the possibility of converting this
    into his new church.
MAX: (*Excitedly.*) Un momento, before you bring in the altar,
    I think you should know I'm not selling my bodega. I
    don't know where you or Reverend Cruz got that idea,
    but wherever it came from, send it back. The answer is
    no. Did Elena put you up to this?
LUZ: No, no, it's not that at all, Don Max. This has nothing
    to do with Elena. It's just that Reverend Cruz likes this
    location. He likes it so much he's willing to pay you fifty
    thousand dollars for it.
MAX: I don't care if it's a hundred thousand dollars! I'm not
    selling! This isn't just any bodega. (*Caressing the counter-
    top.*) This is me! I can't sell this place, not after all the
    work I've put into it. Look, look at this wood. Look at
    this job. (*Sniffing wood.*) Smell it, go ahead, smell it!
    (*Bangs the counter.*)

LUZ: (*Shocked, she walks away and sits down on the crate.*) Don Max, please, I'm not going to smell it.

MAX: Está bien, it doesn't matter. I'll tell you what you would smell. Me! That's what you would smell. My sweat mixed with the best wood money can buy. My hands did everything you see here. Ask Elena, she'll tell you. This work will outlast both of you.

LUZ: I understand, but Reverend Cruz and I thought that since there's so much drugs and crime in this neighborhood, you might be thinking about taking your family away from here.

MAX: I'm not afraid! If you or Reverend Cruz think some punks are going to chase me from my bodega, you're dead wrong. (*Pacing.*) ¡A mí, sí que no! Don't you worry about my family, I can take care of them. Don't you think you and the Reverend have enough to worry about with your church than to interfere with us?!

LUZ: (*Standing and heading for door.*) I can see you're in no mood for conversation. I'll let you think about it and I'll come back later when you're in a better mood. Tell Doña Elena goodbye for me. (*She exits.*)

MAX: (*Following her to the door and yelling out.*) My mood has nothing to do with it. The answer will be the same! (MAX *slams door behind her and sits by the windows.* ELENA *enters with coffee and breakfast for* MAX. *A customer enters,* MAX *jumps thinking it's* DOÑA LUZ. *The customer crosses over to the shelves.*)

ELENA: Where's Doña Luz? Did you speak to her?

MAX: She's gone, thank goodness.

ELENA: Why do you say that?

MAX: Hmmm, this coffee is delicious.

ELENA: What did Doña Luz tell you? (ELENA *crosses over to the refrigerator and begins unpacking juice from the box in front of it. The customer places his items on the counter and selects some cakes.*)

MAX: I can't believe her! She's really got a lot of nerve. Imagine, she told me it was a great honor to have Reverend Cruz interested in buying my bodega. She wants to convert *my* bodega into a church! Hey, it doesn't bother me when she tries converting me, but not my bodega. Of all things she wants to convert it into a church. Está loca.

ELENA: How much was he offering?

MAX: Whatever the price, it's not enough.

ELENA: I don't understand, why won't you sell?

MAX: If I sold this bodega, where would all my customers go?

ELENA: They can always go to the supermarket.

MAX: (*Gets up and rings up the customer's purchase.*) Supermarket? Ha, sure, as long as they have money. But, what
happens if they lose their job? Remember when Fernando
Sánchez lost his job? Or what about Doña Yeya who had
her disability check stolen? Do you think the supermarket
would give any one of them food on credit? (*He begins
bagging the purchase, but, stops.*)

ELENA: Maybe that's true, but they're not our problem.

MAX: (*Walking towards* ELENA, *forgetting customer.*) You're
wrong! They are my problem. They're my people. (*The
customer becoming impatient, bags his groceries and exits
while* ELENA *and* MAX *continue arguing.*)

ELENA: Pero, Max, we have Norma to think about. I don't think
anybody else will give us a better deal.

MAX: (*Picking up cup and plate from the window.*) This bodega
is not for sale! If the Reverend wants a bodega, he can
buy Don Alipio's! This one will remain a bodega. I don't
want to discuss it anymore, punto!

ELENA: Pero, Max ...

MAX: Pero nada! (MAX *exits inside. A train passes overhead.*
ELENA *disposes of the empty juice box.* MAX *enters
cleaning his teeth with a toothpick.*) Anyway, it doesn't
matter, I've got some new ideas on improving security
around here.

ELENA: What are you talking about, security? Security de qué?
All the security in the world didn't help that old man they
killed last month.

MAX: Aha, that's true, but he didn't have what I'm going to in-
stall ... surveillance cameras. (*Pause.*) What do you think
about that, eh, nena? I'll put up two! One here (*Demonstrating.*) and the other above the door. That way no matter where they are, the camera will catch them. There'll
be no place to hide. I'm telling you, Elena, it's perfect.
That's what that old man needed. If he had a camera,
he'd be alive today. I'm telling you, I know what I'm talking about. As soon as I put them in we won't have a thing
to worry about, tú verás.

ELENA: Do you really think that? (*A fire truck siren in background.*)

MAX: I don't think, I know! Why do all the banks have them?

ELENA: I don't know why, they still rob banks. Why should it stop them from robbing here?

MAX: What's the matter with you? Are you trying to jinx us? Nena, can't you see I'm doing this to protect you and Norma?

ELENA: No, I can't.

MAX: Don't worry, nena, if they try to rob us, I'll be ready for them. Just you watch.

ELENA: Oh, sí, you're ready for them ... ready to get killed. Is that what you're ready for? Do you really believe all these fancy gadgets will protect you?

MAX: Ay bendito, Elena, what do you want from me?

ELENA: Ay, qué hombre más cerrao tú eres.

MAX: You'll see! As soon as they renovate those buildings across the street, you'll be thanking me for not listening to you. You'll see, we'll be rich to top it off. What else can you ask for?

ELENA: Peace, that's all I'm asking for.

MAX: (*Walking away from her, he puts one foot on stool.*) Peace? Peace is a dream, an illusion. There's no place on earth that can guarantee it. That's what they told us this neighborhood was, remember? A peaceful neighborhood.

ELENA: (*Crosses over to him and leans on him.*) That was fifteen years ago. It's not the same anymore.

MAX: I know that! Why do you think I go through all the trouble of putting up all these security devices? It may be hard to live with at first, but, after awhile we'll get used to it. I'll tell you something else, if it weren't for you I'd get me a gun.

ELENA: (*Taking arm off* MAX.) What?

MAX: A gun, yes.

ELENA: (*Walks away behind counter.*) Forget it and don't mention it again.

MAX: Why not?

ELENA: Do you think I would allow a gun here, and kill somebody?

MAX: (*Walking up to* ELENA.) Who said anything about killing? You don't have to kill them. You can just maim them for life. That's all. Nothing serious, just make sure they never walk or see again.

ELENA: Forget it! The answer is no! (*Walks away.*)

MAX: But, what if they were trying to kill us, nena? (*Following her.*)

ELENA: That's what I mean, I don't want to be put in that position. I don't know what I would do, but, why be exposed to all this when we can live a better life in our own country?

MAX: Puerto Rico! Now I know you're nuts. If there's one place you don't go to get away from violence it's Puerto Rico.

ELENA: Ay, you don't know what you're talking about! (MAX *goes to the magazine rack and grabs a newspaper. He waves it defiantly, then, looks through it.*)

MAX: Oh yeah, how about this, "Jockey and his horse killed at Comandante Racetrack." (*Pause.*) Or, how about this, "Nine decapitated in Guayanilla." Don't you ever read *El Vocero*?!

ELENA: *EL Vocero* is like the *Enquirer*, they exaggerate everything. (*Suddenly, the bodega is filled with blaring disco music annoying* MAX.)

MAX: What the hell! Why is she playing that now?

ELENA: I told her she could rehearse after breakfast. She has to rehearse sometime.

MAX: I've told her a thousand times not to play it that loud! (*He goes to the curtain and yells.*) Turn that damn music off!

ELENA: Máximo Toro! Don't speak to your daughter that way! What's the matter with you?!

MAX: This is not a disco! This is a bodega! I've had it with this nonsense. I'm going to settle this once and for all! (MAX *is about to exit inside, but* ELENA *prevents him. She pulls him aside.*)

ELENA: No, déjame a mí, I'll talk to her.

MAX: Don't talk. Just turn that damn music off before I get really angry. (ELENA *exits inside.* DON LEOPOLDO *enters.*) Good morning, Don Leopoldo, the usual? (LEOPOLDO *nods.* MAX *goes to the refrigerator and takes out a six-pack of beer. He begins to bag it.*)

LEOPOLDO: Here, this should cover what I owe you, and this. (*Beat.*) How are you feeling this morning?

MAX: (*While summing up the tab from his book.*) Entre Guatemala y Guatepeor.

LEOPOLDO: How's Doña Elena?

MAX: That's Guatemala.

LEOPOLDO: ¿Y Norma?

MAX: That's Guatepeor. (*Hands* LEOPOLDO *his change.*)

LEOPOLDO: Don't worry, things will get better.

MAX: (*Escorting* LEOPOLDO *to door.*)   Here, put ten dollars
     on each, I feel lucky today. (LEOPOLDO *takes money.*)
     Adiós, Don Leopoldo. (NORMA *enters from inside.*)

NORMA: Papi ...

MAX: (*Interrupting.*) Haven't I told you not to come here dressed
     like that? When you come into my bodega, I want you to
     dress proper, not half-naked like you are now.

NORMA: Papi, I'm not half-naked, these are leotards.

MAX: I don't care what you call them, you shouldn't be wearing
     them down here. Somebody can walk in and see you.

NORMA: So what? They're not going to see anything. They'd
     have better luck seeing something at the beach than down
     here.

MAX: Just once I would like to say something without an answer
     from you.

NORMA: Papi, how am I supposed to rehearse if I can't hear my
     music?

MAX: Don't tell me you can't hear it, a deaf man can hear it.

NORMA: We made an agreement. You said I could rehearse, since
     you didn't allow me to go to rehearsals, remember?

MAX: Well, I've changed my mind.

NORMA: Papi, if it's any lower, I won't be able to get into it. It
     has to vibrate me.

MAX: Vibrate?! You've vibrated the whole building! How much
     vibration do you need?

NORMA: But, Papi, it's louder than that at school.

MAX: This is a bodega, not a dance school, so forget it!

NORMA: What else am I supposed to do if I can't hear my music?

MAX: (*Going behind the counter, he gets the recorder and hides it
     behind his back.*) I never said you couldn't listen to music.
     All I said was I don't want that stereo blasting, now, come
     over here a minute.

NORMA: What for?

MAX: Did I ever tell you, you ask too many questions?

NORMA: Why should I?

MAX: (*Coming from behind the counter, hiding recorder.*) Because
     I have a gift for you. If you don't want it, then I'll give it
     to somebody else.

NORMA: (*Turning to face him.*) What is it?

MAX: (*Mimicking her.*) Why don't you come and find out? (NOR-
     MA *begins walking slowly towards* MAX. *He shows her the
     "Walkman" and she runs to him taking it and spinning
     with delight.*)

NORMA: Oh, Papi, it's a "Walkman," I can't believe you got me a "Walkman!" Oh, it's fresh!

MAX: Yeah, fresh like you. (*Slight pause and beat.*) Nothing but the best for my little girl. (*Embracing and stroking her hair.*) Mira, honey, I want you to understand something, when I get angry at you it's not because I want to make it hard for you or because I don't love you, but you're young, you're my daughter and I want to make sure you don't have to put up with what your mother and I did. Do you understand? (*She nods.*) Well, do you like it? (*She kisses him and gives him a gigantic hug.*)

NORMA: Are you for real? I love it. I've wanted one of these for the longest. Thank you, thank you. You're the greatest father in the whole world.

MAX: Funny, it didn't sound that way a little while ago.

NORMA: (*Trying on the "Walkman."*) A little while ago I didn't have a "Walkman."

MAX: The way I see it ... now you can do all the rehearsing you want without having to blast that stupid stereo. You can hear it as loud as you want. You can hear it in super galactic stereo. I even got you a couple of tapes to go with it. They have all the latest hits on it. El Gallito de Manatí, Pat Boone, El Trío los Panchos, Frank Sinatra ... now you can vibrate all you want.

NORMA: (*Dancing with "Walkman" on.*) Oh, Papi, it's perfect.

MAX: Good, I'm glad you're happy. Now, if you don't mind, please go upstairs and get into something decent. Better yet, go upstairs and rehearse.

NORMA: (*Saluting.*) Yes, sir, right away, sir. (*Starts to leave. MAX goes to the window and begins hanging bananas on twine.*)

MAX: Cut the funny stuff.

NORMA: Oh, no.

MAX: What is it now?

NORMA: This is not going to work.

MAX: What are you talking about, eh? It works perfect, I checked it out myself.

NORMA: I don't mean that. I mean, how am I supposed to dance, if I need one hand to hold the "Walkman?"

MAX: ¡Qué pregunta! Use the strap that comes with it, that's how.

NORMA: What strap?

MAX: ¿Cómo que what strap? It must be in the box.

NORMA: What box?

MAX: The box behind the counter.

NORMA: (*Rushing behind counter.*) I'll get it.

MAX: (*Stops what he's doing and chases behind her.*) No! I'll find the strap! Don't open that box!

NORMA: Papi, there's a gun in ... (MAX *grabs the box from her and puts his finger to his lips and looks behind the curtain.*)

MAX: Ssssh! Keep quiet. I don't want your mother to find out.

NORMA: But, who's is it? What's it doing here? (MAX *goes back to the curtain and looks inside, then he goes and locks the front door and lowers the blinds. He returns behind the counter.*)

MAX: First, you have to promise you won't tell your mother.

NORMA: I won't have to. She'll find it just like I did.

MAX: No, she won't. She never looks in there. It's been there over a month and she hasn't found it. Do you promise?

NORMA: Yes, yes, I promise. Whose is it?

MAX: Mine, of course.

NORMA: Yours? Really? Is it loaded?

MAX: (*Unloading gun.*) Of course it's loaded. What good is it if it isn't?

NORMA: Why do you keep it in that box? Won't it take too long to get it out in an emergency?

MAX: Naw, the box is perfect, mira. (MAX *pushes* NORMA *aside. He replaces the unloaded gun in the box and hides it. Then, pretending there's a holdup, he draws the gun quickly.*) Fua! Fua! (*Comes out in front of the counter and points at victim.*) You're dead, sucker!

NORMA: You mean you'd kill him?

MAX: ¿Qué, qué? If I thought he was going to hurt you or your mother, I wouldn't think twice.

NORMA: Wouldn't you be scared?

MAX: I'd be scared not to. Norma, I don't want your mother finding out about this. You know how hysterical she gets about guns. That's why I haven't told her about this. I don't want her worrying, you understand?

NORMA: You don't have to worry about me, my lips are sealed tight. Can I hold it?

MAX: (*Checking gun again.*) Sure, here. (*He hands her the gun.* ELENA *enters unobserved. Shocked at what she sees, she remains silent.*)

MAX: Would you like to learn how to use it?

NORMA: Are you serious?

MAX: Of course I'm serious, you never know when you might need it.

NORMA: Yes, of course, I'd love to learn. (NORMA *squats as if
in target practice.*) Fua! Fua! Fua! (*Blackout.*)

ACT TWO

.... SCENE ONE ....

Later that evening NORMA *is behind counter talking with a
female customer. There are several young people just hanging out,
one reading something from the magazine rack, two others talking
by the window.*

NORMA: (*To customer.*) So, when she found out Mr. Barnes gave
me the lead part, she went straight to the head of the
drama department and complained that I shouldn't be
permitted to do it because I was Puerto Rican and the
role was obviously meant for an American white. Can you
believe that girl? (*Customer shakes her head in disbelief.*)
ELENA: (*Offstage.*) Norma, come here, I need to talk to you!
NORMA: (*Yelling inside.*) I have customers out here! Papi hasn't
returned.
ELENA: When he gets in, I want you up here!
NORMA: All right! (*To customer.*) So, then she started telling
everybody in school I was trying to steal her boyfriend,
just like I stole her part. Can you believe her? Now,
who in their right mind would want to steal that turtle
face boyfriend of hers? Even a pet shop would give that
boy away. (DOÑA LUZ *enters in her usual exaggerated
evangelical fashion. An overhead train drowns out some
of her speech. The customers quickly flee upon seeing her.
They all exit.*)
LUZ: In the name of the Father, the Son and the Holy Spirit, may
our Lord Jesus Christ protect this bodega and all inside
it from the evil malevolent forces outside that would seek
to bring harm to us. Amen. (*Yelling behind customers.*)
Our Lord awaits all of you in his home! (*To* NORMA.)
What about you, my child? We haven't seen you at God's
house for some time. When you were younger we saw you
all the time.

NORMA: I've been busy with the show. Sometimes I even have rehearsals on Sunday. (*Yelling inside.*) Mami, Doña Luz is here! (NORMA *goes and sits by the window, shaking her head in disbelief.*)

LUZ: I understand your show is very important to you, my child, but you have to make time for your saviour. (ELENA *enters.*)

ELENA: Hola, Doña Luz. What a surprise seeing you this evening.

LUZ: Ay, Doña Elena, you don't know what I've just witnessed. It was horrible, horrible. There was a fire in Don Alipio's building. Everything was ruined. The firemen had to destroy everything in order to save him and Silvia. They were both trapped in the rear of their bodega. It was a miracle nobody got hurt. I was praying to our Lord that nobody would get hurt.

ELENA: (*Crossing herself.*) Oh, dear God. How did it happen?

LUZ: They don't know yet, but they're lucky to be alive. I was just coming out of church and then I heard all the fire trucks. They just left to Brooklyn, it's so sad, they're going to spend the night at Silvia's sister's house. It's horrible, they may not be able to open for at least a couple of months.

ELENA: What they should do is retire. They're too old for this kind of work. Which reminds me of something I want to tell you, Doña Luz. You tell Reverend Cruz that Max and I want to talk to him about his offer.

LUZ: (*Excitedly.*) I knew the Lord would not fail the church. Meeting that young man earlier was a clear sign that this will make a wonderful church. I'm so glad he changed his mind, Doña Elena.

ELENA: He doesn't know he's changed his mind yet. (*Beat.*) Doña Luz, it's always a pleasure talking to you, but right now I have to get back to something very important. As always, if there's anything I can do for you, please don't hesitate to ask.

LUZ: Well, now that you mention it, there is a little something, Doña Elena.

ELENA: And what's that?

LUZ: Errr, I was hoping I could get a few things until tomorrow. I don't have any money on me and, you know (*Sitting on crate.*) how difficult it is for me to climb up those five flights. With my arthritis every time I get to my floor, I feel I'm going to die.

ELENA: Well, we don't want that to happen.

NORMA: (*Gets up and goes behind the counter.*) But if it did happen, at least you'd be closer to heaven.

ELENA: Norma!

NORMA: I'm sorry, it was just a joke. I was practicing for the Christmas show. It's all in the timing.

ELENA: Well, your timing is terrible.

LUZ: Don't worry, Doña Elena, I understand. I used to be young myself. I'm sure she meant no harm. I can bring you the money first thing in the morning.

ELENA: Of course, Doña Luz. Norma, you see that Doña Luz gets whatever she needs, and don't forget to write it in the book. When your father gets in I want to talk to you. Adiós, Doña Luz. (ELENA *exits.* DOÑA LUZ *walks up to the counter.*)

LUZ: Thank you, Doña Elena, and may God bless you. (*To* NORMA.) I need a dozen eggs, a quart of milk, a loaf of bread, a bottle of achiote, a can of tomato sauce, a bottle of rubbing alcohol number seventy, twelve white candles, a bottle of Florida water, half a pound of cod fish with bones, but not too much salt ... (NORMA *rushes to get each item, but slows down after the bread and returns slowly to the counter, slamming bread on the counter. Blackout.*)

.... SCENE TWO ....

A sidewalk near an alley. RAFY *is standing, rubbing his hand. Obviously, he is in need of a fix.* MICHAEL *enters stage left. Still that evening.*

RAFY: (*Approaching* MICHAEL.) Mira, bro, can you spare any change?

MICHAEL: No.

RAFY: All I need is a few bucks.

MICHAEL: (*Annoyed.*) Man, do I look like welfare to you?

RAFY: No bro, you don't. It's just ...

MICHAEL: (*Interrupting.*) Then don't bother me!

RAFY: Take it easy, bro, I just, you know, wanted to see if you're interested, you know, in this Cuban gold chain I got here.

MICHAEL: Man, who do you think you're talking to, some fool?

RAFY: Yo bro, this is eighteen carat, real gold.

MICHAEL: Yeah, gold plated.

RAFY: (*Demonstrating.*) No bro, check it out, take a look at this.

MICHAEL: (*Pushing it away.*) Man, you think 'cause I'm white I
    don't know what's going on? I'm going to tell you some-
    thing, I've been around ... you understand? I'm not in-
    terested in that Mickey Mouse gold chain you have there!
RAFY: Look, bro, I'm sick, all I need is five bucks to get myself
    straight ... how about it?
MICHAEL: I don't believe in hand-outs, buddy.
RAFY: (*Walking away.*) All right, bro, thanks anyway.
MICHAEL: Hey mirror, where's the action in this town. I thought
    New York was supposed to be fun.
RAFY: Help me get straight and I'll show you where all the fun
    and action is.
MICHAEL: Sorry, I can't do that, it creates a bad habit. Besides,
    you don't know where the action is. I have this friend
    back in Omaha with the same problem you have. The
    difference is he doesn't beg for his habit like a wimp.
RAFY: Bro, are you calling me a wimp?
MICHAEL: What do you think, man?
RAFY: I ain't no wimp, bro. I can take care of myself ... and I
    can take care of you.
MICHAEL: In your condition I don't think you can handle a cock-
    roach.
RAFY: Bro, you're a long way from home, you know, to be talking
    about me like that in *my* neighborhood.
MICHAEL: You're planning to do something ... junkie?
RAFY: What's your problem, bro?
MICHAEL: Seems to me you're the one with the problem, man.
RAFY: I'm warning you, bro ... you don't know who you're mess-
    ing with.
MICHAEL: I know exactly who I'm messing with ... a loser ...
    nobody.
RAFY: I've had it with you, bro. (*As* RAFY *finishes these words
    he throws a combination that misses, while* MICHAEL
    *ducks and counters with two blows he delivers to the mid-
    section of* RAFY. RAFY *buckles, collapsing to the ground.*
    MICHAEL *stands over him threateningly.*)
MICHAEL: Is there anything else you want to say, man?
RAFY: No, bro, I'm sorry ... I didn't know what I was doing, I
    swear, bro.
MICHAEL: I should just finish you off. I've already fulfilled my
    "be a nice guy" quota for the day.
RAFY: Come on, bro, give me a break, bro. You know how it is
    when you're sick.

MICHAEL: (*Sharply.*) No! I don't know what it's like! I get my
    thrills differently. Don't ever compare me to you, again
    ... you hear me, man?

RAFY: Yeah, bro, I hear you.

MICHAEL: I think I have an idea how to take care of your prob-
    lem. You interested, man?

RAFY: Sure, bro, I'm interested ... just as long as I get straight,
    I'm down ... I'm your man. (MICHAEL *helps* RAFY *to
    his feet, they begin to walk. MICHAEL takes out the card
    DOÑA LUZ gave him and shows it to RAFY as they both
    exit stage right. Light fade slowly.*)

.... SCENE THREE ....

NORMA *is behind the counter returning change to a customer.
The customer exits, bumping into* DON LEOPOLDO *and* MAX-
IMO *as they enter the bodega.*

NORMA: (*To* MAX.) Well, it's about time, Mom's been calling
    me every ten minutes for the past hour. She's driving me
    crazy! (NORMA *exits inside.*)

LEOPOLDO: I understand she gets on your nerves, but she does
    a lot of good.

MAX: Why can't she learn to leave people alone?

LEPOLDO: Because if *she* had been left alone, she wouldn't be
    who she is today.

MAX: I thought she was always this way. Ever since I've known
    her she's been preaching the word of God.

LEOPOLDO: She wasn't always like this. I've never told you,
    well, maybe, because I thought you knew, anyway, I don't
    like talking much, but in her younger days she was called
    (*Whispering.*) "Lucy the Firebird."

MAX: Naw, not our Doña Luz.

LEOPOLDO: She was one of the hottest numbers down on the
    Avenue.

MAX: I can't believe this!

LEOPOLDO: You never met the people who remembered her back
    then. If not for Reverend Cruz, she would still be out
    there. He's helped her a lot. That's one thing I can say
    about the Reverend, he's a good man. Even the hoodlums
    respect him. Not one of them would dare do anything to
    that man, or his church.

MAX: How did they ever meet?

LEOPOLDO: It turns out she picked him up! He was dressed like you or me. So she took him to her room, he paid her, took out his Bible and began praying for her soul. She's been with his church ever since.

MAX: You know, Don Leopoldo, now that you mention it ... I don't think I ever remember Doña Luz talking about her or the church being robbed or anything ...

LEOPOLDO: That's what I'm trying to tell you ... nobody bothers them ... that's how good they are, people love them. (NORMA *enters from inside. She pulls* MAX *aside.*)

MAX: (*To* NORMA.) This better be good ... what is it now?

NORMA: Mami's packing.

MAX: What do you mean, packing?

NORMA: Mami is packing her clothes.

MAX: (*Turns to face* LEOPOLDO.) Excuse me, Don Leopoldo, I have ...

LEOPOLDO: (*Turning to leave.*) No problem, Don Max, I have to pick up my wife from the Bingo. I'm late already. (*He exits.* MAX *escorts him to the door.*)

MAX: Good night, Don Leopoldo. (*Turning to* NORMA.) You didn't tell her anything, did you?

NORMA: Of course not! I promised I wouldn't.

MAX: I better go upstairs and see what's going on. You stay here and lock the door. (NORMA *prepares herself a sandwich.*) ¡Oye, aguántate! Save some of that for the customers!

NORMA: All right! All right! (MAX *exits inside.* NORMA *goes, gets a soda, then goes and shuts the door. She stands in front of the counter and pretends the bottle is a microphone. She goes into her act, imitating an M.C.*) Ladies and gentlemen, tonight it gives me the greatest pleasure to introduce to you, not only a funny comedienne, but also an excellent dancer, the singularly exciting and vibrant MISS NORMA!! (NORMA *runs behind counter and spins with delight, transforming herself into MISS NORMA. She steps in front of the counter feigning modesty as she bows to her imaginary audience.*) Thank you, thank you. It's really a great honor to be here tonight. This is one of those situations you always dreamed would happen, but never honestly believed would happen, but has happened. (*Beat.*) I want to take a moment to thank my mother for being so supportive throughout the years, and especially my father, whose constant opposition to my dancing was the strongest motivation I had. But, enough talk, I want to perform for you the Puerto Rican version of Swan Lake. El Cuchifrito Lagoon. (NORMA *begins to dance her interpretation of El Cuchifrito Lagoon. Suddenly* ELENA *enters, storming past her, almost knocking her down.* ELENA *is followed by* MAX, *who enters pleading with her.*) Hey, you two ... watch it!

MAX: Pero, nena, what is it? Was it something I did? Elena, will you talk to me? Háblame, m'ija. (MAX *and* NORMA *exchange looks.*)

NORMA: Listen, you guys, I'm going upstairs, you two look like you want to be left alone.

ELENA: (*Fuming, she paces circling the bodega.*) Stay right where you are! (*To* MAX.) I bet you two really thought you could get away with it! (*Pause.*) Well, didn't you?!

MAX: Get away with what? For Christ's sake, Elena, what are you talking about?

ELENA: ¡Tú sabes! Don't play dumb with me, Máximo Toro! I can't stand it when you try to play dumb. You know exactly what I'm talking about! (*To* NORMA.) And, I haven't forgotten about you!

NORMA: Me? Wait a minute, what did I do? All I did was come down for a sandwich.

MAX: Elena, please tell me what you're talking about, nena.

ELENA: What I'm talking about?! ¿Quieres saber? Is that it, huh? I'll show you what I'm talking about! (ELENA *storms past* MAX *and goes behind the counter to get the gun.* MAX *follows her to attempt to stop her.*)

MAX: Oh, oh, wait, wait a minute, nena. What do you want back there? Stay away from there. Oye, what are you doing? (ELENA *pulls out the gun.* MAX *and* NORMA *try to stay out of the aim of the gun, which* ELENA *waves recklessly.*)

ELENA: Qué carajo is this doing in here?

MAX: Just calm down, okay? Just be careful with it, eh? Be very careful. Elena, listen to me, it's loaded. Can you hear me? The gun is loaded. Cálmate, nena. Just put the gun down, all right? Can you do me that favor?

NORMA: Mami! Please, put it down before somebody gets hurt.

ELENA: (*To* NORMA.) Don't you speak to me! You, you traitor! You and your father, you were going to keep this a secret from me, ah? (*To* MAX.) That's right! I know about your plans to teach her.

MAX: Aha, so that's it! Mira, nena, if you give me a minute I can explain it to you.

ELENA: Forget the "nena" bit. I want it out of here, now! This second! No explanations. Just get it out of here! Ahora!

MAX: For Christ's sake, Elena, please put the gun down before somebody gets hurt!

ELENA: That's exactly what I don't want!

MAX: (*Approaching her.*) Good! Then we're in agreement! Give it to me before something you don't want to happens. Dámelo, nena.

ELENA: (*Backing away.*) Stay away.

MAX: Take it easy, nena. I just want to put it away, that's all.

NORMA: Mami, please put it down.

ELENA: All the time you were talking about surveillance cameras, you were taking me for a fool!

MAX: That's not true, nena. I'm getting the cameras ... it's just that this makes me feel safer.

ELENA: How long have you been hiding it there?

MAX: Since yesterday.

ELENA: ¡No soy pendeja, Máximo!

MAX: All right, I've had it for a month, since they shot that guy last month.

ELENA: Why didn't you tell me?

MAX: I couldn't tell you I had a gun.

ELENA: You lied to me!

MAX: I didn't lie, I just didn't mention it, that's all. What did you expect me to do?

ELENA: Not this.

MAX: Awww, what's the use. Mira, give me my gun. ¡Damelo! (MAX *lunges towards* ELENA, *grabs her hand with both of his and aims the gun away from them as a struggle ensues.*)

NORMA: Stop it! Mami! Papi! Stop it! Stop it! Stop it! (NORMA *rushes up to them and grabs the gun from them. She runs behind the counter with it and hides it back in the box. Both* ELENA *and* MAX *react terrified at* NORMA *having the gun.*) There! Now, let's talk like adults. (*Pause.*) Well, which one of you two wants to start. (MAX *starts for the box, followed by* ELENA. NORMA *prevents them from getting it, by hiding it behind her back.*) What's wrong with you two? Why don't you start, Papi?

MAX: Start what? There's nothing to start. It's my gun and that's all there is to it!

ELENA: That's not all there is to it!

MAX: This is my bodega, and I'm the one who decides here, punto!

ELENA: ¡Ahora sé yo! This is *our* bodega, not yours! I have my money invested here too! This is a family business!

NORMA: Stop shouting! I mean, nothing is going to get done if you keep shouting at each other.

ELENA: Something is going to get done, all right. (*To* NORMA.) You get upstairs and start packing right now, we're leaving tonight. ¡Vete! (NORMA *reacts to each command as if she were a puppet on a string.*)

MAX: You stay right where you are!

ELENA: I said, go pack!

MAX: You stay right there!

ELENA: I'm your mother and I told you to go pack! (ELENA *starts to leave.*)

MAX: (*To* NORMA.) You stay right there and don't move!

NORMA: (*Pleadingly.*) Hey, you guys!

MAX: (*Grabbing* ELENA *and spinning her around.*) And, where the hell do you think you're going?

ELENA: That's none of your business.

MAX: What are you, crazy? You're *my* wife! Everything you do is my business! (*Stomping.*) I'm the MACHO here! ¡Yo!

ELENA: (*Folding her arms in amusement.*) No me digas. Is that so? (NORMA *quietly grabs some popcorn and sits on a crate out of the way while she observes.*)

MAX: That's right!

ELENA: Since when did I become your property?

MAX: They day you married me!

ELENA: I don't remember that.

MAX: Sure, you do. When the priest said, "to love, to honor and *obey* till death do us part."

ELENA: Well, you can forget about that, Mr. Macho!

MAX: Where will you spend the night?

ELENA: We'll sleep in the streets if we have to, but we're not staying here, that's for sure. If you think I am, you got another thought coming, Mr. Macho!

MAX: Nena, be reasonable. We need some sort of protection.

ELENA: (*Pointing to the alarm.*) I thought we had protection? Then what's all this shit for?!

MAX: (*Pause.*) Deterrent!

ELENA: Deterrent?! Who are you now, General Patton? Are you expecting Gadafy to invade this bodega?

MAX: Worse! Much worse than that, your local junkie. That's why I need the gun. Just in case my deterrent doesn't work.

ELENA: I can't believe how that mind of yours works. I think you should see a doctor, you need help. You're ... you're, what do they call it?

NORMA: The word is paranoid.

ELENA: Paranoid! Yes, that's it! You're paranoid!

MAX: (*Furiously.*) Paranoid! I'm not paranoid! Just because I want to make sure my family and business is safe doesn't make me paranoid.

ELENA: If you're really thinking about our safety, you'd take Reverend Cruz's offer to buy this bodega!

MAX: I knew it! You put her up to it, didn't you?

ELENA: So what if I did? I'm getting sick of all this. I can't take it anymore. All these gates and alarms make me feel like I'm living in Riker's Island, not a home. ¡Hombre, estoy harta ya!

MAX: Riker's Island! You're comparing my bodega to a prison? Are you crazy or something?

ELENA: What else can I compare it to? All you have to do is look around. Go ahead, be honest with yourself. Míralo, what do you see? And now this, you're the macho of a prison, and we are your prisoners.

MAX: This is not a prison. You can come and go as you please.

ELENA: Ah bueno, I'm glad you said that. (*To* NORMA.) How come you're still here? I thought I told you to go and pack! ¡Echa!

NORMA: But, Papi said ...

ELENA: Forget about what he said. I'm the woman here!

MAX: Nena, you just can't pack and leave. This is everything we've struggled for ... you can't leave.

ELENA: Just watch. Either the gun goes or we're gone! What's it going to be?

NORMA: But, Mami, where are we going to stay?

ELENA: With Doña Luz!

NORMA: Doña Luz! Oh no! Come on, you guys, you're not serious? Not Doña Luz.

ELENA: It's Doña Luz or the church! Either one is fine with me!

NORMA: Hey, you guys, there's got to be a better way ... Papi?

MAX: (*Defensively.*) Aren't you supposed to be upstairs?

NORMA: Papi, is it worth keeping that gun?

MAX: (*Hesitantly.*) Hmmmmph!

ELENA: Then get rid of it! Take it back and get your money back!

MAX: I can't.

ELENA: Why?

MAX: It's a little complicated. I can't explain it now.

ELENA: I don't care how complicated it is, get rid of it! ¡Bótala!

MAX: Throw it away, just like that? Just because you say so?

ELENA: I want it out, Max.

MAX: Do you have any idea how hard it was for me to get this,
    eh? I couldn't go get it from a regular gun shop, not with
    all the red tape involved, that would take forever. I had
    to make special connections.

ELENA: Are you trying to tell me you got this gun in the streets?

MAX: How else was I supposed to get it?

ELENA: Dios mio, how can you be so stupid to buy something
    like that in the streets? You don't even know where it's
    been. For all you know, somebody could have been killed
    with that gun and you'll get the blame for it.

MAX: I don't care where it's been, or what it's done. It's mine
    now and I'm keeping it to protect what's mine.

ELENA: Max, can't you see this isn't worth it? (*Silence.*) Ay, forget
    it. It's no use talking to you, we're leaving, vámonos! You
    know what to do if you want us to stay! (*To* NORMA.)
    ¡Muévete! (NORMA *doesn't budge.* ELENA *grabs her
    and shoves her inside.* NORMA *exits.*)

MAX: Elena, why are you being so difficult?

ELENA: Are you going to get rid of it or what?

MAX: Let's talk about it.

ELENA: There's nothing to talk about.

MAX: There's everything to talk about ... there's the bodega ...

ELENA: (*Interrupting.*) As far as I'm concerned, the alarm is
    stupid, and this bodega is stupid!

MAX: (*Shocked.*) My bodega stupid? I suppose you have some-
    thing smart?

ELENA: Yes, sell this bodega and let's get out of here a family!

MAX: Ah, that's brilliant!

ELENA: I don't know why I bother talking to you. ¡Si la pendeja
    soy yo! (ELENA *exits inside.* MAX, *frustrated, leans on
    the counter as a train passes by. After a pause,* NORMA
    and ELENA *enter.* ELENA *is dragging* NORMA *by her
    ear.*)

NORMA: But, Mami, I haven't packed anything!

ELENA: I don't care. We'll send Doña Luz to pick up our things.

NORMA: Mami, she'll have me dressing like I'm a nun.

ELENA: (*Unlocking the door.*) Don't argue with me, let's go!

MAX: (*Blocking their path.*) Está bien, you win. All right?! I'll get rid of it.

ELENA: When?

MAX: Jesus! (*Sighs.*) Give me a couple of days.

ELENA: I want it out of here now! Tonight, not a couple of days.

MAX: Ay bendito, Elena, give me a couple of days ... let me try and get my money back.

ELENA: I want it out tonight!

MAX: Nena, be reasonable.

ELENA: ¡Carajo! I don't want it here! (*She attempts to leave.*)

MAX: Jesus! All right, all right! Tomorrow morning it's gone, how's that?

ELENA: I don't want it in the bodega overnight.

NORMA: Mami, come on, he said he'll get rid of it!

ELENA: Don't you side with him. Don't you defend him, traicionera!

NORMA: I'm not defending him. And I'm not a traitor. You could at least let him get his money back.

MAX: I promise it'll be out of here first thing in the morning. What do you say, eh? Mira, nena, if it bothers you having it down here in the bodega, then I'll hide it in our bedroom, how's that?

ELENA: Don't you dare take that thing into my room!

MAX: (*Hiding the gun behind counter.*) All right, I'll leave it down here tonight, eh? It'll be gone before I brush my teeth.

NORMA: Good! Then it's settled. Listen, you guys, I'm getting back to my rehearsals if you don't mind? (NORMA *exits.*)

MAX: (*Approaching* ELENA *and putting his arms around her shoulder.*) Don't worry, nena, everything will be okay.

ELENA: (*Walking away.*) ¡Dejame! Don't touch me!

MAX: Nena, I'm sorry, really. I didn't want to upset you. I don't understand why we're fighting. Okay, maybe the gun was a bad idea, but a man who isn't prepared to defend his family isn't a man. You know that. Mira, sometimes, I make bad decisions, but you must admit I'm always thinking of our best interest. We just can't get up and run the first time there's trouble, we've put too many years into this place. Things will get better, just wait. (*Pause.*) Nena, I know things look bad to you, but if we're not willing to fight for what's ours, who will?

ELENA: Why does everything have to be a fight or violence with you? (*Beat.*) It would be nice to go back home.

MAX: It's not like it used to be in Puerto Rico, nena. Over there you can't leave your doors open anymore. Now every house has rejas. It's the funniest thing you ever saw: the good people are behind bars and the criminals are out in the streets. The island has become a giant prison. It's no longer the island of enchantment; now it's the island of incarceration. There's nothing there for us anymore, we've been here too many years now.

ELENA: I know what you're saying, but over there we'd be with our own people.

MAX: Our people! You know what they would call Norma over there? A Nuyorican! I hate that word. What happens if you live in Chicago? What do they call you then? A Cagaorican? (*Pause.*) I'm only thinking about our future. We don't have to move there to escape violence. Violence is everywhere, in the Middle East, in Latin America, in Africa, in the middle of the street and even in the middle of the ocean. Violence is all around us.

ELENA: So, because, as you say, there's violence all around us, you feel it's all right to bring it into our lives?

MAX: No, wait one minute! I didn't say I wanted to bring it into our lives, nena, I ... I just don't want to get caught off guard, that's all.

ELENA: You want to invite violence, that's what you want!

MAX: I don't want anything, except to be prepared.

ELENA: Be prepared for what?!

MAX: All right, look ... I promised to get rid of it in the morning, right? Right! Now, how about if we come to some sort of compromise or deal?

ELENA: (*Suspiciously.*) What kind of deal?

MAX: A deal where we fight less and hug and cuddle a little more?

ELENA: Why should I agree to that?

MAX: Because I love you. (*Reaching into his pocket.*) Oh, I almost forgot, I bet you can't guess what I have here? Take a look at this. (*She does not respond.*) These are the pictures we took when we first bought this bodega.

ELENA: (*Excitedly.*) What?! I can't believe it! I've been searching for those pictures for years! Let me see them. (ELENA *reaches for the photos, but* MAX *hides them behind his back and steps away.*)

MAX: No, no, no ... do we have a deal or not?

ELENA: Max, stop playing, let me see them.

MAX: Oh, I don't know. I'll have to think about it.

ELENA: Okay, we have a deal. Satisfied? (*He hands her the pictures.*) Where did you find them? (ELENA *sorts through the pictures.*)

MAX: I found them beneath some old milk crates I have downstairs. I was making some space down there when I moved this crate and, fua, there they were on the floor.

ELENA: I thought they were lost forever. Look at this one! Do you remember when we took it? Can you believe she was that small when we got this place?

MAX: Sure seems like a long time ago.

ELENA: That was sweet of you to get her that recorder she wanted. You can be such a nice guy when you want to ... you should try it more often. (MAX *nods in agreement.* ELENA *kisses him on the cheek.*)

MAX: I really got it for myself. This way I won't have to listen to that lousy stereo all the time.

ELENA: I know you better than that, Máximo Toro. I haven't been married to you for eighteen years for nothing. You may jump, scream and carry on about her dancing, but deep down inside it makes you proud, very proud.

MAX: (*Proudly.*) She does dance good, doesn't she? Remember the first show she was in?

ELENA: Who could forget that?

MAX: She was so cute dressed as an apple, tap-dancing in that forest.

ELENA: I guess we both found out that night she was special ... different. (*He nods.*)

MAX: I guess we're pretty lucky with Norma. She could have turned out like some of her friends she grew up with.

ELENA: What a shame seeing teenage girls with two or three kids already. All just to prove their womanhood.

MAX: Our Norma is too smart to fall for that nonsense.

ELENA: It's terrible, I have to place the blame on the mothers. It's their fault. What will those poor girls do with their lives?

MAX: What else, live on welfare.

ELENA: Well, let's be glad Norma broke away from that crowd and got interested in dancing, even if it is hard to make a living at it.

MAX: That's why I still think it's not a bad idea if she trains in something else, just to be on the safe side, in case it doesn't turn out for her.

ELENA: It will turn out for her. (ELENA *is going through the pictures when* MAX *stops her to reach for a special shot.*)

MAX: Wait a second, let me see that one again, ahh, yes ... you always knocked them dead when you wore that dress.

ELENA: (*Embarrassed.*) Ay, stop that, Max. (*An auto alarm is heard in background.*)

MAX: (*Embracing her from behind.*) You still knock them dead today.

ELENA: (*Walking away from him.*) Max, I haven't forgotten about the gun.

MAX: Elena, nena, we've settled that.

ELENA: Hmmm ...

MAX: (*Approaches and embraces her again.*) Remember our agreement ... anyway, that's the same dress you were wearing the night we met. I'll never forget that night. We danced all night.

ELENA: That's because nobody else would ask me.

MAX: It's not my fault they were afraid to dance with you.

ELENA: You know very well you threatened to beat up anybody who asked me to dance.

MAX: You must admit that impressed you, eh? Or why else would you dance with me all night?

ELENA: I wasn't going to let you ruin my evening.

MAX: Ruin your evening! I was the best dancer in town. What are you talking about, eh? And, if I remember correctly, you weren't too bad yourself. (MAX *takes* ELENA *in his arms and begins to dance slowly, holding her very close while he sings in front of the counter. Singing.*) "Mujer, si puedes tú con Dios hablar ... pregúntale si yo alguna vez te he dejado de adorar ... "

ELENA: (*Singing.*) "... te he buscado por doquiera que yo voy y no te puedo hallar ... para qué quiero tus besos si tus labios no me quieren ya besar ... " (MAX *picks up the pace and they both sing in unison while displaying some fancy footwork. They slow down, dancing in place with* MAX *behind* ELENA.) (*Sigh.*) Wouldn't it be nice to go back in time and live it all over again? To be young again, to swim in clean waters ... to fall asleep to the coqui's singing in the night ... to wake up to the smells of fresh fruit and roosters singing.

MAX: (*His expression reflects that he is not keen on the idea.*) Not me! I don't want to go through all that struggling again. Besides, roosters don't sing, they crow.

ELENA: (*Sighing.*) You sure were something back then. You were so crazy, you had me scared for a while.

MAX: Come on, you always say that, I didn't really scare you.

ELENA: You have no idea how frightened I was seeing you following me from school every day.

MAX: Nena, I've told you a million times I wasn't following you, I was trying to protect you. (ELENA *starts laughing.*) What's so funny?

ELENA: I don't remember you trying to protect me after Dad chased you with that sugar cane.

MAX: I didn't think that was funny.

ELENA: That's because you didn't see yourself climbing that avocado tree.

MAX: If I didn't climb that tree, you would have damaged goods today.

ELENA: If you weren't so persistent, my father wouldn't have chased you.

MAX: When I think about it, I can't believe I spent the whole night up in that tree.

ELENA: You were lucky he was too old to climb that tree and I didn't have any brothers.

MAX: I guess I should be thankful for that.

ELENA: Max, if you could go back in time, would you do anything different?

MAX: Let me see ... yeah; there are some things I would do different.

ELENA: What about me? Do you have any regrets?

MAX: ... Yeah.

ELENA: (*Pushing away from* MAX.) What?!

MAX: I regret I didn't marry you sooner. (*Pulling her into a long kiss.*) Now, how about if we call it a night and continue this upstairs?

ELENA: (*Still holding each other.*) It's still early.

MAX: It's a slow night, we're not going to make any more money.

ELENA: I don't know ... you haven't been good today.

MAX: I have these new steps I've been dying to teach you.

ELENA: (*Suspiciously.*) Really?

MAX: (*Cuddling more romantically.*) We can even go back in time some more, if you want. (*Kissing her neck.*) It's been a long time, nena. What do you say?

ELENA: Máximo Toro, are you trying to seduce me?

MAX: (*Feigning innocence.*) Me? Do you think I'm capable of that? I just want to teach you some new moves I have, in case we want to go out dancing some night.

ELENA: How come I don't believe that?

MAX: I give you my word as a gentleman.

ELENA: That's what got me in trouble with you the first time.

MAX: Do you have any regrets?

ELENA: None. Let's go upstairs. (*Suddenly the front door swings open. A hood wearing a ski mask enters. He's brandishing a gun and is followed by a second hood who enters.*)

HOOD 1: Don't anybody move! Stay right where you are! Hurry, lock the door! Lock the door, man! (HOOD 1 *turns off the lights, while* HOOD 2 *shuts and locks the door behind him.* ELENA *shrieks in horror.*)

HOOD 2: All right, bro! I already did! (HOOD 2 *crosses over to* MAX *and* ELENA *and pulls* ELENA *away from* MAX. MAX *attempts to prevent this, but* HOOD 1 *points the gun directly at* MAX.)

HOOD 1: You, step back! Nice and easy! Slow! (MAX *backs away.*) And, don't say a fucking word unless I ask you!

ELENA: Oh, dear God, protect us. (HOOD 1 *maneuvers* MAX *over by the window at gun point while a train passes overhead and casts its shadow.*)

HOOD 2: Sit down! Quick man! I said, sit down! Move it!

ELENA: Please don't hurt him! We don't want any trouble mister!

HOOD 1: (*Pointing the gun at* ELENA.) Man, shut the fuck up, lady, or I'll blow his brains out! (*To* HOOD 2.) Get some rope and tie this motherfucker down! Now! (ELENA *crosses herself and begins praying as* MAX *sits slowly.*)

HOOD 2: The rope! Where's the rope, lady? (ELENA, *terrified, is unable to answer.* HOOD 2 *sees rope overhead and pulls it down, causing everything to crash on floor. He goes over to* MAX *and ties his hands behind his back.* HOOD 1 *places the gun muzzle at* MAX*'s ear.*)

HOOD 1: Lady! I'll make this brief and to the point! Where's the bread or I'll blow his face apart!

ELENA: In the register! Everything we got is in the register! Take it all! But please don't hurt us! (ELENA *goes behind the counter and hits the register's keys opening it.* HOOD 1 *gestures to* HOOD 2 *to get the money.* HOOD 2 *takes his knife and points it at* ELENA, *moving her away from the register. He looks through the register and a disgusted look appears on his face.*)

HOOD 1: What's the matter? Take the fucking bread, man! Hurry!

HOOD 2: God dammit! Yo, bro, there's only, you know, thirty beans here! Shit!

HOOD 1: What?! Lady, I told you I don't have time for games! (HOOD 1 *returns to* MAX *and places muzzle right up his nostril.* HOOD 2 *is rummaging behind the counter.* ELENA *rushes to aid* MAX, *but stops when* HOOD 1 *points gun in her direction.*)

ELENA: (*Hysterically.*) Don't hurt him! Please don't hurt him! That's all we got!

HOOD 1: I said shut the fuck up, lady! (*To* HOOD 2.) This really burns me up, man!

ELENA: Please, for the love of God, don't hurt us!

HOOD 1: I said, shut the fuck up, lady! (*To* HOOD 2.) What the fuck is going on, man? You told me these people had some bread. I knew I should have hit the church instead of listening to you!

HOOD 2: (*Nervously.*) They do! I swear, bro, they do! They've, you know, been here for years. She's got to be lying, bro.

ELENA: I swear by everything that's sacred, it's all we got.

HOOD 2: She's lying, bro! I'm telling you she's lying. They been here for years, they've got it hidden somewhere here. I swear. This place is meant to be had, you know, bro.

HOOD 1: (*Picking up* MAX *by his vest.*) All right, mister, it's your life, where's the bread? (MAX *doesn't respond and* HOOD 1 *punches him in the stomach twice.*) Speak motherfucker! (*He punches his face.*)

ELENA: I'm telling you, we don't have any more money! Tell him, Max! Tell him we don't have any more money! Your friend there, he's lying, that's all the money we made!

HOOD 2: I ain't lying bro! They got cash stashed somewhere here! (*Both hoods stare at each other.* MAX *gestures to* ELENA *to go for gun, but she's too terrified.* HOOD 1 *drags* MAX *to center stage.*)

HOOD 1: Don't make me re-arrange your fucking face, mister! I guarantee you won't like it, man!

MAX: She told you the truth, there isn't any money. (HOOD 1 *knees* MAX *in the groin.* MAX *collapses to ground.* ELENA *screams and tries to aid him, but* HOOD 2 *grabs her, holding her at bay with knife.*) You must feel like a real big man, eh? Hitting a man who's tied down and can't fight back. Real tough.

ELENA: Máximo! Shut up!

HOOD 1: That's right, man. It makes me big and bad. And it makes you small, you fool ass sucker. So tell me where the bread is before I kill you, asshole.

HOOD 2: Yo, bro, we ain't, you know, got time for this ...

HOOD 1: (*To* HOOD 2.) Shut your face, man! It's your fault I'm here and not at the church!

HOOD 2: Yo, bro, maybe I'm wrong, you know, like maybe there ain't no money, after all. Let's take what we got and book, bro. (HOOD 2 *shoves* ELENA *to the ground and crosses over to* MAX *and* HOOD 1.)

HOOD 1: (*Rising.*) I said keep quiet, man! I do the thinking around here and don't you forget that! Just keep that bitch over there quiet while I think.

MAX: (*To* HOOD 2.) Hey, don't I know you?

ELENA: Shut up, Max!

HOOD 2: Yo, bro, let's get out of here.

HOOD 1: (*Kneeling next to* MAX.) The bitch has brains, you'll be lucky to get out of this alive, never mind who you know. Where's the bread?

MAX: We told you, there ain't any more.

HOOD 2: (HOOD 1 *is pointing gun at* MAX*'s head.*) Yo, bro, I told you, I ain't down for this, you know?

HOOD 1: (*Rising to face* HOOD 2.) Listen, my man, I'm not about to waste my time, if something's to be had, then it's to be had. Dig?

HOOD 2: Yo, bro, ain't nothing to be had 'cept us.

HOOD 1: (*Pointing gun down at* MAX.) The money.

MAX: We can't give you what we don't have.

HOOD 2: Yo bro, come on, let's split.

MAX: (*To* HOOD 1.) Hey, punk, why don't you untie me so I can settle this, man to punk.

HOOD 1: Shut the fuck up! (HOOD 1 *straddles* MAX *and knocks him unconscious with a blow to the head as a train passes overhead.* HOOD 1 *rises slowly and heads towards* ELE-NA.) What about this cunt, my man?

HOOD 2: Shit, bro, you're crazy! (HOOD 1 *stops, turns and heads to* HOOD 2. *He puts gun on the throat of* HOOD 2.)

HOOD 1: Let me tell you something, asshole, don't ever call me crazy again, do you understand?

HOOD 2: I'm sorry. I'm sorry, bro. I didn't mean it, you know. Whatta you say we get the hell out of here?

HOOD 1: (*Turning to face* ELENA.) That's out! Maybe you're satisfied with that chump change, but I'm not. Something has to be had. I say it's the cunt, otherwise ... (*Facing* MAX.) I'll blow this faggot away.

ELENA: No, please don't hurt us. We gave you what you wanted.

HOOD 2: Yo, bro, you promised you wouldn't kill anybody.

HOOD 1: Just be glad it isn't you. Here! (*They exchange weapons.*) Keep an eye on that motherfucker over there. If he comes to, let me know. (HOOD 2 *drags* MAX *over by the window.* HOOD 1 *slowly approaches* ELENA. *She begins to rise slowly.*)

ELENA: Stop! We don't have anymore money, your friend, he's right, you don't have time for this, have mercy, the police are on their way.

HOOD 1: (*Grabbing* ELENA *by the hair, he finishes pulling her up.*) There's nobody on their way, lady.

ELENA: Agggh, please, for the love of God.

HOOD 1: (*Dragging her to front of the counter.*) Don't worry, lady, if you don't struggle you won't get hurt.

ELENA: Please, I'm begging you, don't do this.

HOOD 1: (*Leaning her body back against counter.*) You sure have a nice body for an older woman ... real nice ... (*He rips open her blouse and begins to caress her with the knife.*) Man these are real pretty ... real pretty.

MAX: (*Coming to and trying to get loose.*) I'll kill you, bastard! I swear it! If you touch her I'll hunt you for the rest of my life! I swear it! (ELENA *re-buttons her blouse.*)

HOOD 1: Gag him! (HOOD 2 *gags* MAX *with a bandana* MAX *is wearing around his neck.*) Man, you're lucky I don't blow your brains out, you're just lucky I don't like violence when I'm having sex. It's your fault, man, all I wanted was the bread. You didn't give up the money, so now I'll take your honey. (*Putting arm around* ELENA.) Ha, ha, funny isn't it? I made a rhyme, shit, I'm a poet. (*He points knife at* ELENA.) Kneel bitch! You have something to take care of down there. Remember, my buddy has the gun on that brave faggot of yours, you understand what I mean? (ELENA *begins to kneel slowly while* HOOD 1 *begins to unzip his pants.* MAX *is frantic, trying to free himself.* HOOD 1 *reaches inside pants when* NORMA *enters listening to her "Walkman" and wearing her leotard. She is unaware of what is happening.* HOOD 1 *rushes to* NORMA *and grabs her by the neck, putting the knife to her throat.*)

ELENA: Don't shoot! Don't shoot! It's my daughter! (ELENA *gets up and rushes to* HOOD 2 *to prevent him fron shooting.* HOOD 2 *shoves* ELENA *to the ground and nervously points gun at* NORMA.)

HOOD 1: I'll cut her throat! I'll cut her throat! Don't nobody move! Who else is inside? (*To* HOOD 2.) Go check inside! Make sure you check everywhere! I don't want no more surprises, man! You hear me! No more surprises! (HOOD 2 *exits inside.*) Well, well, what have were here? This is a pleasant surprise ... hmmmmmmm ... calm down, honey. (HOOD 2 *enters.*)

HOOD 2: The place is empty, nobody else in here, bro. Let's get the fuck out of here!

HOOD 1: Good! Go check the front door and make sure nobody's out there.

HOOD 2: (*Checking outside.*) There's nothing happening out here, we can book, bro.

HOOD 1: Perfect!

NORMA: Let me go! Let me go!

ELENA: Please don't hurt my baby! Please let my baby go!

HOOD 2: Hey, bro, let the girl go, I'm not down for this.

HOOD 1: I don't give a fuck what you're down for! You hear me, junkie? You do as I say or your ass is mine. You dig? Can't you see things are beginning to look up here?

ELENA: Please don't hurt her ... I won't tell anybody!

HOOD 1: You must think I'm stupid or something? (*To* HOOD 2.) What are you standing there for? There's two now, you don't have to have sloppy seconds. You can do your own thing.

HOOD 2: This isn't right ... I don't want any part of this!

HOOD 1: You fucking asshole! Don't you get moral on me now! I'll cut her throat right now and slice your guts out, man! I'm sick of your whimpering!

ELENA: (*Hysterically.*) No! I'll do anything you want!

HOOD 1: It's too late for deals, lady. You can do whatever you want, 'cause I'm going to do whatever I want with this young thing here, yes, indeed, whatever I want. (HOOD 1 *caresses* NORMA*'s body with his hands, then rips her leotard from the top, exposing her breast.*)

NORMA: (*Kicking.*) Get your hands off me! Don't touch me! Stop! Papi! Somebody help me! Get off of me, you pig!

HOOD 1: Ain't nobody going to help you, girl. So, just relax and maybe you'll learn something.

ELENA: (*Crawling on her knees to* HOOD 1.) She's just a baby ... take me! Take me! (ELENA *opens her blouse, but,* HOOD 1 *presses his knife to* NORMA*'s neck, bringing* ELENA*'s crawling to a stop.*)

HOOD 1: Whoa, I'm doing you a favor, lady. I'm going to tell you if your baby is still a virgin. (*To* HOOD 2.) If you're smart, you'll get on some of this action yourself, otherwise keep an eye on these bozos. (*To* NORMA.) Baby, you're going to love this. Just relax and it'll be over before you know it. (HOOD 1 *picks up* NORMA *and carries her over by the refrigerator and lays her down on the floor.* HOOD 2 *nervously approaches them while also trying to keep an eye on* MAX, *who is still trying to free himself.*)

HOOD 2: Bro, please don't do this. We don't have time for this shit! (HOOD 1 *ignores* HOOD 2 *and continues attempting to rape* NORMA. MAX *has freed himself by now, he rushes to* HOOD 2 *who is unaware.* MAX *pulls* HOOD 2 *and punches him in the stomach, followed by a punch in the face.* HOOD 2 *falls to the ground.* MAX *is about to attack* HOOD 2 *when* HOOD 2 *points gun, stopping* MAX. HOOD 2 *stands up and exits bodega running.* MAX *quickly turns to* HOOD 1 *who is atop his daughter and pulls him off* NORMA. HOOD 1 *elbows* MAX *in the ribs then feigns a stab.* MAX *stops* HOOD 1 *by grabbing the knife with his hand.* MAX*'s other hand is on* HOOD 1*'s head.* MAX *pulls off the mask; it turns out to be Michael Petersen and they both separate.* MAX *quickly wraps the mask around his hand for protection.* MICHAEL *stabs at* MAX, *but misses. They both circle each other.* MAX *swings at* MICHAEL, *he ducks and comes up stabbing* MAX. MAX *falls.* MICHAEL *stands over* MAX *squeeling with delight.* ELENA *screams, stands up and runs behind the counter to where the gun is.* MICHAEL, *seeing her, follows her behind counter.* ELENA *pulls out the gun and shoots* MICHAEL *once. He falls behind the counter.* ELENA *runs over to* MAX*'s fallen body, she places the gun on the corner of the counter closest to* MAX *and joins* NORMA, *who is already there.*)

NORMA: Papi! Papi!

ELENA: Max! Max! Get the police! (NORMA *exits bodega running.* ELENA *takes off the sweater she's been wearing and places it on* MAX*'s fallen body. She crosses herself and folds her hands in prayer.*) No, God, please! Our Father who art in heaven, hallow be thy name, thy kingdom come, thy will be done, on earth as it is in heaven, and give us this day, our daily bread, and forgive us our trespasses, as we forgive those who trespass against us, and lead us not into temptation but deliver us from ... (MICHAEL *stands up from behind counter, coughing and holding the wound in his stomach. He has managed to crawl to the far side of the counter.* ELENA *leaps to her feet and quickly goes to where she placed the gun.* ELENA *grabs the gun and watches* MICHAEL *as he slowly approaches her.*)

MICHAEL: (*Coughing.*) I'm hurt, I'm hurt, I need a medic. I'm sorry, this was a mistake, honest, I didn't mean to hurt anybody. I just wanted to have a little fun. (*Cough.*) I wasn't planning to hurt anyone. You don't need that gun, lady ... he attacked me! What was I supposed to do?! Please, lady, put down the gun. It was the other guy's idea to hit this place ... not me ... it was Rafy's idea. I don't want to die, lady, please put down the gun ... have mercy. (MICHAEL, *still walking toward her, reaches out.* ELENA *aims the gun and fires once.* MICHAEL *collapses. Blackout.*)

.... SCENE FOUR ....

Next day, early morning. A beam of light illuminates the bodega. ELENA, *dressed in black, is sitting by the window. She's staring at a portrait.* NORMA, DOÑA LUZ *and* DON LEOPOLDO, *also dressed in black, enter from inside.* NORMA *and* DOÑA LUZ *are each carrying a suitcase. They stop, remaining at a distance.*

NORMA: (*Softly.*) Mami ... Mami.
LEOPOLDO: Doña Luz ...
LUZ: We've packed a few things for you.
NORMA: Doña Luz says we can stay with her. Don Leopoldo can keep an eye on the bodega.
LEOPOLDO: That's right, Doña Elena, you don't have to worry about a thing. I'll take care of everything. (ELENA *doesn't respond, she just stares blankly at the portrait.*)
NORMA: (*Whispering to* LUZ *and* LEOPOLDO.) She hasn't said a word since we got back. I don't know what to do.
LUZ: You're doing just fine, my child.
LEO: (*To* NORMA.) She's still in shock. The same thing happened to my sister, Gloria, when she lost her husband in an earthquake back in Colombia.
NORMA: But, she doesn't move from there.

LEOPOLDO: She'll be all right. Don't worry, it just may take her some time.

LUZ: (*Getting closer.*) Doña Elena, we're ready to leave.

ELENA: (*Without looking up.*) I want to thank you, Doña Luz, for taking care of Norma. In all my life I had never been to jail.

LEOPOLDO: Don't worry, Doña Elena, my lawyer friend says there isn't a jury on earth that will convict you. It's a clear case of self-defense, once we prove where the gun came from.

ELENA: I want to thank you, also, Don Leopoldo, for your lawyer friend and putting up the bail. I'll get you the money as soon as possible.

LEOPOLDO: Don't think about it, Doña Elena, it's the least I could do. And, don't you worry none about that money, that's what friends are for. Is there anything else you need? (*She shakes her head no. To* NORMA *and* LUZ.) I'll take these suitcases outside. (*To* ELENA.) I'll be outside in the car.

NORMA: Mami, we're ready.

LUZ: There's no need for you to remain here ...

ELENA: I've killed a man.

LUZ: You shouldn't think about things now, Doña Elena.

ELENA: I didn't sleep while I was in that cell. I had plenty of time to think things out. I'm not leaving. I'm staying right here.

NORMA: Mami, you can't be serious! We're not spending the night here. We're going to Doña Luz.

ELENA: This place is my home.

LUZ: Doña Elena, you don't have to make those decisions now. You have plenty of time to figure things out later.

NORMA: Please, Mami, I don't want to stay here.

ELENA: Where would we go?

NORMA: I don't know ... anywhere. You always said you wanted to leave this place. You were always trying to convince Papi.

ELENA: (*Fondly.*) That stubborn Max. I never could convince him. (*Almost in tears.*) But ... but, that's what I loved about him. He was my strength. Everybody drew strength from him. Once he had a mind to do something there was no way to change him.

NORMA: Mami, stop it! We can't stay here, this place is ugly now!

ELENA: (*Rising slowly and walking toward center stage.*) No, Norma, this place is filled with beautiful memories. This place is filled with your father. He's everywhere in this bodega. This bodega is also our home ... the home he built for us.

NORMA: Doña Luz, do something!

LUZ: There's nothing I can do, my child. Let's leave her alone for a while. Maybe she just needs to be alone for now. Come on, I'll buy you some coffee. (DOÑA LUZ *leads* NORMA *to the exterior door; as they exit* NORMA *stops at door.*)

NORMA: Do you want to get killed like Papi?!

ELENA: (*Motionless.*) I don't intend to get killed. I'm not letting anybody run me out of my home. I'm not running. (*Slow fade out. Spot.*)

First Class

by

Cándido Tirado

Characters

APACHE, warrior like. Tough with many scars. Early thirties to mid thirties.

SPEEDY, nice looking, smart. Early thirties to mid thirties.

Place: between two streets, like on Broadway. The set consists of a bench. Behind the bench there's a tree. A garbage can is placed at stage right and a lamp pole with a sign at stage left.

Time: Present.

Act One takes place in the morning. Act Two takes place in the early evening after it has rained.

ACT ONE

.... SCENE ONE ....

The siren of a police car is heard as the lights come up. We hear the chirping of birds. APACHE, who is wearing dirty jeans and sandals, is lying on the worn-out bench. A supermarket cart containing a black plastic bag with cans and bottles in it is chained to the bench.

APACHE: All right. All right. Shit. (*He gets up and angrily screams at the sirens.*) Turn the goddamn siren off, you fucking cops. Pigs! You aint no alarm. You think you're funny. (*To himself.*) Can't even let a man sleep. Shit. Shut the fuck up you fucking birds. (*He throws a can at the tree.*) All you do is shit all over the place. (*He goes behind the tree and pisses. Groans.*) Ahhhh! Pissing feels so good. (*Looks at the sun.*) Nine o'clock in the morning and ... (*Pauses.*) I'm going to fix his ass. (*He turns bottles upside down.*) Damn. (*Sings.*) I just want to celebrate another day of living. (*Picks up a bottle.*) I know you got some. (*Turns it.*) Hey, baby. Can't celebrate if I got nothing to drink. (*Sings.*) Just want to celebrate. (*Becomes more desperate, turning bottles and cans upside down with no luck, becomes angry and kicks the can.*) Fucking guys drank everything. They'll drink the damn Atlantic Ocean if you let them. Thirsty fucks. (*Searches his pockets for money.*) Damn, Sam. Twenty three cents and a Canadian nickel. Shit. (*He begins to put the bottles and cans into a plastic garbage bag. SPEEDY enters carrying a shoe bag. He's dressed to the T, but is wearing sneakers. Upon seeing APACHE he puts on a pair of sunglasses. He walks by APACHE.*) Yo, man. Got fifty cents you could spare? (SPEEDY *just stares at him.*) You know, want to get me something to drink. To wake up. You know!
SPEEDY: Get a job. (*When* SPEEDY *turns his back,* APACHE *sticks out his middle finger.*) I got you! (*Laughs.*)
APACHE: What? What?

SPEEDY: You didn't think it was me. You didn't think it was me.
(*Laughs as if to humiliate* APACHE.)
APACHE: You could become a whore and I'd know it's you.
SPEEDY: I could've tore your heart out and you wouldn't have
known it.
APACHE: I knew it was you. Just messing with your ass.
SPEEDY: Bull-dinky. How could you know? Ah?
APACHE: Uh ...
SPEEDY: Uh, uh.
APACHE: Your sneakers.
SPEEDY: (*Frowning. Disappointed.*) Shit. Damn sneakers. I
thought I had my baby alligators on. (*Pause. Takes off
sneakers and slips into shoes.*) Went by the apartment.
APACHE: So?
SPEEDY: The door was wide open.
APACHE: So?
SPEEDY: What do you mean, so? They are going to steal every-
thing. You're going to lose the apartment.
APACHE: I ain't staying there. It's your apartment, too.
SPEEDY: Where are you staying?
APACHE: The roach motel.
SPEEDY: You're staying there? Man, the roaches are bigger than
elephants.
APACHE: I tried catching one yesterday. She was fast. I named
her after you, Speedy.
SPEEDY: How you know it was a her? 'Cause you couldn't trap
her?
APACHE: I checked her body out after I step on her.
SPEEDY: You know what you are, Apache? A roach molester.
(*They laugh.*) So, what about the apartment?
APACHE: I don't want it, man. Where the fuck was you this whole
week?
SPEEDY: (*Feeling awkward.*) T.C. Being. Taking care of beeswax.
Business! You know? Business doesn't take a holiday. (*He
walks to the center of the stage. He moves around like a
model.* APACHE *stares at him.*) Apache, how do I look?
Do I look like myself. Think I could pass for a classy
dude? I look different, right?
APACHE: Yeah. A regular chameleon.
SPEEDY: (*Jumps on the bench.*) Right before your eyes, I've become a classy first class guy. (*Opens suit jacket.*) Armani,
bro. Five hundred hard ones. Bill Blass shirt. Fifty soft
ones. Paul Stuart tie. Ferragamo shoes. Seven hundred

and fifty smackaroos. Genuine baby alligators. Feel them.
Go ahead. They aren't going to bite you.

APACHE: (*Feels the front part of the shoe.*) Too tight!

SPEEDY: Seven hundred and fifty dollar shoes can never be too
tight.

APACHE: They are too tight.

SPEEDY: Bro. No offense, but what do you know about expensive
clothes? When that dude said "clothes make the man,»
he wasn't talking about you.

APACHE: All that shit is nice, bro. But don't forget where to find a
real bargain. You see this t-shirt? Seventy-five hard cents,
John's Bargain Store basement sale. The jeans you asked?
Two dollars and fifty cents. And these sandals are made
in Taiwan by real Taiwanese people. John's Bargain Store
throws away this junk special. Ninety-nine cents.

SPEEDY: You know the difference between you and me? (*Pause.*)
Money! (*Waits for reaction.*) With money you could live
first class. But without it, you can't afford to live.

APACHE: Some dumb chick is wasting her money on your good
looks and charm.

SPEEDY: (*Holding his crotch.*) Don't forget my eight and a half.
(*They slap each other five.*)

APACHE: Take them off. You can't scratch them 'cause they won't
take them back.

SPEEDY: What are you talking about?

APACHE: The shoes. The shoes. And don't sit on the bench with
those clothes 'cause they might get fucked up. We can give
all the clothes back and we'll get the money back. Then,
we could start our business.

SPEEDY: Run and Errand?

APACHE: Yeah. Bro, you're wearing our business. I had some
money under the mattress, but I had to spend it, you
know? But you're dressed like a lottery. You could be
the business manager.

SPEEDY: Apache.

APACHE: Yes, business manager?

SPEEDY: I don't want to be a business manager.

APACHE: What do you want to be, Speedy? You could be anything
you want. You're already half owner.

SPEEDY: I don't want nothing.

APACHE: Bro. You want to keep collecting cans? Full of spit and
germs? You don't know who put their mumble lips on

them. And only the devil knows where those lips have been and shit.

SPEEDY: Apache.

APACHE: Speedy.

SPEEDY: Apache.

APACHE: Speedy.

SPEEDY: Damn, man. Let me talk.

APACHE: Talk. (*Pause.*) I'm listening, but you ain't saying nothing.

SPEEDY: I'm trying to find the right words, okay?

APACHE: Okay, find them.

SPEEDY: Shut up!

APACHE: Okay!

SPEEDY: I can't be part of your business.

APACHE: Why not?

SPEEDY: I can't.

APACHE: Wait, wait. Don't just say you can't, with no excuse, and expect me to swallow the shit.

SPEEDY: You can't even read, Apache.

APACHE: I could read.

SPEEDY: Oh, yeah? Give me that business book you always carry with you. (APACHE *gives it to him.* SPEEDY *opens it to a page.*) Read this page. (*Pause.*) Read a paragraph. A sentence. A word!

APACHE: That's why you're here, man. That's your part in the business, bro.

SPEEDY: I can't. (*Pause.*) I'm leaving.

APACHE: Where the fuck you going? Mars?

SPEEDY: I'm leaving. For real, bro.

APACHE: Leaving ...

SPEEDY: Yeah. I'm getting the fuck out of here.

APACHE: Leaving what?

SPEEDY: This.

APACHE: This?

SPEEDY: This. This. Everything.

APACHE: Everything?

SPEEDY: Yeah, yeah. The bench, the island, the neighborhood.

APACHE: Me? (*Pause.*) When?

SPEEDY: Today.

APACHE: Today?

SPEEDY: Yeah.

APACHE: When you coming back?

SPEEDY: I don't know.

APACHE: I need a drink.

SPEEDY: Me too.

APACHE: The bottles are emtpy, the store is closed, the fricking birds shit all over the place and you're leaving. (*Pause.*) The guys drink everything in sight. They'll drink the Atlantic Ocean if you let them.

SPEEDY: Yeah.

APACHE: Where are you going this time?

SPEEDY: Boston.

APACHE: Where?

SPEEDY: Boston.

APACHE: That's where I thought you said.

SPEEDY: So why did you ask me again?

APACHE: I wanted to hear it again.

SPEEDY: Is there something wrong with your ears? You don't have to wait until Saturday to wash them.

APACHE: It ain't every day your best friend is leaving. The fucking guy you grew up with. The asshole you're closer to than your own brother.

SPEEDY: You don't have a brother.

APACHE: So what? (*Pause.*) You're my brother.

SPEEDY: Wait a minute. If I'm your brother, that makes you my brother.

APACHE: That's heavy, bro.

SPEEDY: Yeah. I mean. How many brothers have thrown cats off the roof to see if a cat had nine lives.

APACHE: And how many brothers have put clothes on a mannequin and thrown it off the roof?

SPEEDY: That fat man, what's his name?

APACHE: The Domino Champion?

SPEEDY: Yeah, yeah. The sucker got a heart attack and died. (*They laugh.*) That was fun.

APACHE: Yeah, the dummy went flying through the air and crashed on the domino table.

SPEEDY: Then, you took a quarter and threw it on his body. We shit bricks for a month.

APACHE: Talk for yourself! (*They laugh, then stop. They embrace.* APACHE *breaks it up.*) Don't want to dirty your clothes.

SPEEDY: Bro, I'll send them to the cleaners.

APACHE: (*Disgustedly.*) Boston?

SPEEDY: Uhuh!

APACHE: Boston.

SPEEDY: I left before.

APACHE: Park Avenue ain't leaving. Boston is far.

SPEEDY: Forty-five minutes by plane. When I get settled I'll send you first class tickets to come visit.

APACHE: I hate planes.

SPEEDY: First class train tickets.

APACHE: I hate trains.

SPEEDY: First class bus tickets.

APACHE: I hate buses.

SPEEDY: I'll send you a limousine.

APACHE: You know I hate limos.

SPEEDY: You're a first class pain in the ass. You know that? (*Pause.*) Apache. I want you to have my sneakers. (APACHE *just stares at him.*) Take them. They don't stink.

APACHE: (*Feels* SPEEDY*'s head.*) Are you okay. I think you got a fever. Yo, bro, you slept with your sneakers on. I used to try to take them off when you was asleeping, and you used to kick me.

SPEEDY: Take them. I'm serious.

APACHE: They don't fit me.

SPEEDY: Sell them.

APACHE: Sell your sneakers?

SPEEDY: I ain't wearing sneakers anymore.

APACHE: I never thought I see the day you hung up your sneakers.

SPEEDY: Guess what? You saw it.

APACHE: I'll keep them to show the boys. They ain't going to believe it.

SPEEDY: Those sneakers kept me out of a lounge in the Marriot. Embarrassing, bro. So Maurice bought me these shoes. That's where I stayed last night. A room so big you could have a rumble in it. First class all the way.

APACHE: You stayed in a hotel with a man?

SPEEDY: Yeah, no, not the way you're thinking. Business.

APACHE: Damn, Speedy. Don't tell me your cables are changing.

SPEEDY: I'm a man, okay?

APACHE: Anything you say.

SPEEDY: We went there to talk.

APACHE: Nobody goes to a hotel to talk.

SPEEDY: We had different rooms. It's only business.

APACHE: I believe you, sis. I mean, bro.

SPEEDY: Fuck you, okay? (APACHE *laughs.*) You're so fucking narrow minded.

APACHE: So are you in love with him?

SPEEDY: You fucking guy.

APACHE: (*Makes homosexual gestures.*) What he wants? You know, nobody gives you nothing for nothing.

SPEEDY: I knew you was going to do this.

APACHE: (*Making gestures.*) Do what, honeychild?

SPEEDY: He ain't a homo, okay?

APACHE: I never said he was.

SPEEDY: Fuck you, man. (*He leans against the light pole.*) He wants me to marry his daughter.

APACHE: I heard that one before.

SPEEDY: Could you just listen, man, without all this shit?

APACHE: Listen to what? Every time you fuck with rich people you get fucked.

SPEEDY: This time it's going to be different. I'm marrying into money.

APACHE: Everybody wants to marry a rich bitch, but nobody do.

SPEEDY: I am.

APACHE: She must be a dog, if her father has to find a man for her.

SPEEDY: (*Calmly.*) She's not a dog.

APACHE: So what's wrong with her. Come on, bro. You can tell me. She's fat. She's bald. She's got only one leg and her name is Ilene. She's blind out of one eye and can't see out the other. She's got one tit. Worse. She's got a flat ass.

SPEEDY: She's pregnant.

APACHE: And you're going to play daddy?

SPEEDY: Something like that.

APACHE: (*With irony.*) Hey, bro. (*Extends hand.*) Congratulations.

SPEEDY: Fuck you.

APACHE: You ain't shaking my hand? (SPEEDY *looks around as if he's waiting for somebody*.) My hand is catching a cold.

SPEEDY: I hope it gets frost bite and falls off.

APACHE: Then I couldn't ... (*Makes gestures of masturbation.*) How could I do it with no hands? Ah, bro?

SPEEDY: Lick yourself like a dog. (*He smiles. They shake hands.*)

APACHE: It's what you wanted? Right?

SPEEDY: First class all the way.

APACHE: (*Moving away. Puts cans in the plastic bag.*) What happened to the baby's father.

SPEEDY: (*Whispering.*) Her father is the father of the baby.

APACHE: (*Baffled.*) What? The baby is the son of the grandfather?

SPEEDY: No, no. (*Thinks.*) Yeah, that's it.
APACHE: All in the family. You fit right in.
SPEEDY: They love one another.
APACHE: So, father and daughter go shopping for a daddy.
SPEEDY: If they wouldn't want the baby, I wouldn't be in the
     position I'm in. But you got to swear never to repeat this
     to anybody.
APACHE: Bro. You could trust me.
SPEEDY: You got to swear.
APACHE: You don't trust me, man?
SPEEDY: Yeah, bro. I trust you with my life, but I don't trust your
     mouth. Your mouth has a mind of its own. A secret ain't
     safe with you. Swear it.
APACHE: You want me to swear?
SPEEDY: No. What the fuck have I been saying?
APACHE: Relax, too. I swear.
SPEEDY: I don't believe you. Swear on Mami's grave.
APACHE: She ain't been dead two weeks and you want me to swear
     on her grave.
SPEEDY: I didn't mean nothing by it.
APACHE: Fuck you, okay. Just fuck you.
SPEEDY: It slipped!
APACHE: I don't want to talk about her, okay?
SPEEDY: You have to talk about her sometime, man.
APACHE: What if I don't want to? Who's going to make me?
SPEEDY: It ain't your fault she killed herself.
APACHE: What the fuck are you saying? That it's my fault?
SPEEDY: Nah, man. I ain't saying that.
APACHE: It sounds like your saying it.
SPEEDY: I mean ... she committted suicide.
APACHE: You didn't even go to the fucking funeral.
SPEEDY: I'm sorry.
APACHE: Fuck you and your apologies. Say you're sorry to her.
SPEEDY: I would if I could.
APACHE: You don't give a shit about nobody but your goddamn
     self.
SPEEDY: I was T.C. Being. Taking care of business.
APACHE: Save your lame excuses. I don't want to hear it.
SPEEDY: I wanted to be there.
APACHE: Bullshit!
SPEEDY: I really wanted to.
APACHE: Bullshit, bullshit, bullshit!
SPEEDY: She was my mother, too.

APACHE: She wasn't your mother. You was a stray dog we found
and brought home.

SPEEDY: She had your blood, but that doesn't mean shit. She
talked to me, not you.

APACHE: Drop the shit.

SPEEDY: I'm not dropping shit.

APACHE: If you say another fucking word, I'm going to ...

SPEEDY: To what? Ah? To what? Kick my ass? You're going to
kick my ass?

APACHE: (*Retreating.*) Fuck it. It ain't worth it.

SPEEDY: Yeah, fuck it.

APACHE: All I know is that you wasn't there when I need help
with the cement cross I put on her grave.

SPEEDY: I felt something bad was going to happen. I felt it all
day.

APACHE: I don't want to hear it, Speedy.

SPEEDY: I'm walking up those dark steps and bang. A shot. Man,
I hit the ground. Survival, you know what I'm saying?

APACHE: (*Tries to open the lock on the chain, but cannot.*) Fucking
lock.

SPEEDY: I opened the door. I didn't want to but I did.

APACHE: I have to get the cans before the bums take them.

SPEEDY: At first I saw nothing. Then, I saw her hair. It was low,
close to the ground. I thought she was praying.

APACHE: Come on, you goddamn lock.

SPEEDY: I saw her.

APACHE: (*Screaming.*) The cans.

SPEEDY: Then, I saw the blood dripping from her long black hair.

APACHE: (*Grabbing* SPEEDY.) The cans. The fucking cans.

SPEEDY: Nooooo! I found her, goddamn it. Me! You didn't see
her like that. It was me! Then you get mad at me for not
going to the funeral. Fuck you!

APACHE: I saw her, too.

SPEEDY: Bullshit!

APACHE: (*Goes into his pants pocket and takes out a bullet.*) Look!

SPEEDY: What's that?

APACHE: The bullet.

SPEEDY: The bullet that killed Ma?

APACHE: Yeah.

SPEEDY: Let me see it?

APACHE: No.

SPEEDY: You saw her?

APACHE: I came in from the roof after you ran out looking for help.

SPEEDY: While Mami was lying there, you started looking for the bullet that killed her?

APACHE: No, man. I went to throw up. It was in the toilet.

SPEEDY: Make a hole in it, put it on a chain and wear it around your neck.

APACHE: I don't want nobody to see it. (*Pause.*) How could this little shit kill somebody?

SPEEDY: Speed, man. How fast it goes.

APACHE: It's death. It just don't wear a hood.

SPEEDY: I wonder what were Mami's last thoughts?

APACHE: I don't know.

SPEEDY: The bullet knows. (APACHE *looks at the bullet and with a quick gesture puts it in his pocket. Pauses, looks at* SPEEDY, *goes to cart.*)

APACHE: Got to get my cans.

SPEEDY: You ain't waiting with me.

APACHE: Cans wait for no man.

SPEEDY: Bro. Come on. It's my last day.

APACHE: You want me to lose my cans because you're leaving?

SPEEDY: Just half an hour. Half an hour.

APACHE: No.

SPEEDY: I'll pay you not to collect cans.

APACHE: If I don't collect them, somebody is going to take over my garbage cans.

SPEEDY: How much do you want? (*Takes wallet out.*)

APACHE: Are you going to pay me for the rest of my life not to collect cans? No, right?

SPEEDY: Twenty-five. (*Pause.*) Fifty. (*Pause.*) Seventy-five. (*Pause.*) Hundred. You drive a hard bargain.

APACHE: I don't want your money.

SPEEDY: Look, look. How many cans you got to collect before you make a hundred dollars?

APACHE: (*Immediately.*) Two thousand.

SPEEDY: (*Surprised.*) You knew that?

APACHE: I know my cans.

SPEEDY: I'm giving you cash money.

APACHE: I got to go.

SPEEDY: (*Takes the plastic bag.*) Can't leave without your bag.

APACHE: Give me that shit.

SPEEDY: (*Running behind the bench.*) You can't catch me.

APACHE: (*Tries to catch him, he can't.*) Don't play games.

SPEEDY: Say you're staying.

APACHE: Speedy.

SPEEDY: Apache.

APACHE: Don't fuck with me, man.

SPEEDY: I want you to stay. Homeboy. Please.

APACHE: (*Pause.*) Okay. Just give me that bag. (*They sit.*)

SPEEDY: Here's your bag.

APACHE: Thanks. (*They sit in silence. SPEEDY smells his hand, then he puts his hands by* APACHE's *nose.*) What the fuck? (APACHE *moves way from* SPEEDY, *who follows him.*) Stay away from me.

SPEEDY: Smell it.

APACHE: Get the fuck out of here.

SPEEDY: Come on, bro. Smell it.

APACHE: Fuck you.

SPEEDY: You don't like the smell of love juice?

APACHE: Not from your hand.

SPEEDY: (*Smells his hand again.*) Uh. Uh. Uh. There's nothing like the smell of love juice early in the morning. Love juice. From cherry, cherry and cherry. Had three cherries last night at the same time. Maurice bought them for me. We had coke and shit. Wild night. You think anybody ever fucked a million girls?

APACHE: How the fuck would I know?

SPEEDY: I want to fuck a million beautiful, rich ladies. (*Pause.*) You like ugly women.

APACHE: What do you want, I'm ugly.

SPEEDY: Pretty chics look at you all the time.

APACHE: They look at my scars and cross the street.

SPEEDY: Women love scars. Why do you think I gave myself this one? (*Shows the scar on his arm.*) They kiss it. Rub their bodies on it. Has anybody licked your scars?

APACHE: No.

SPEEDY: Bullshit. Brandy did. She was a freak.

APACHE: She just wanted to fuck my brains out.

SPEEDY: Why did God give you that joy stick for? Use it and never look back.

APACHE: I want to know who the fuck I'm sleeping with.

SPEEDY: When we were kids you used to steal porno magazines from the candy store and we used to beat our meats like crazy. Did you meet any of those girls? Where did I go wrong, bro? Where? I should've taught you how to rap

the chicks to get out of those magazines. Damn, I feel
really bad.

APACHE: Speedy. Fuck off.

SPEEDY: Nah, man. It's my fault. A girl killer like me not passing
my talent, big talent around. Forgive me, Apache. Can
you forgive me?

APACHE: Get out of my face.

SPEEDY: See, Apache. Chicks have a weakness. (*Grabs his crotch.*)
Johnson here. You know why chicks are chicks? Because
they don't have one of these. And they are always looking for one. You know who Freud is, right? He said that
women got this thing he called Johnson jealousy. And
Freud was a hip dude. The man was a coke addict when
everybody thought that coke was that thing you drink.
I bet Maurice's daughter, Susan, came on to him. That
Johnson jealousy shit. Oh, man, look at that sweet thing
walking by. (*Looks into the audience.*) Hey, babe, what's
happening? What?

APACHE: She said, if you don't know, not to talk to her.

SPEEDY: You tough, ain't you? I love a challenge. Huh! Huh!
Huh! Don't walk too fast, I want to enjoy the rear view.

APACHE: She's embarrassed, man. Red like a tomato. (*He's getting cans out of the garbage can.*)

SPEEDY: She's hot! Excuse me. Are you wearing a bra? Look
at those melons bounce. I want them to bounce into my
hands. What. What, wait I got to get a pen. 660-2525.

SPEEDY: (*Disinterested.*) I'll call you sometime.

APACHE: What's your name?

SPEEDY: Don't worry about it. Yeah, bye. Too easy! Remember,
Apache, everybody is naked inside their clothes, especially
women. Why don't you try it? There's another chick
there. Wow!

APACHE: Leave me alone!

SPEEDY: Try it once, that's all.

APACHE: I got better things to do.

SPEEDY: Don't be scared, man. Girls don't bite unless you want
them to.

APACHE: Do Millie bite?

SPEEDY: That chick is whacked. Too serious for me. She's as
much fun as you are.

APACHE: Are you going to say goodbye to her?

SPEEDY: Hell, no.

APACHE: Millie is nice.

SPEEDY: Nice and poor. What can she offer me? A welfare check? Shoeless kids. Food stamps. She's even missing a tooth. She's a girl like any other. You know what your problem is? You respect girls too much.

APACHE: I just don't see what she sees in you.

SPEEDY: You like Millie. You like Millie.

APACHE: No, I don't.

SPEEDY: I know you do. You don't even breathe when she comes around. Take her, bro. She's my gift to you.

APACHE: If I want her, I'll go after her myself.

SPEEDY: Bro. Bro. Don't take it like that. All I'm saying is that you could go out with her if you want to. You got uncle Speedy's permission. You and her make a nice couple.

APACHE: Speedy, shut the fuck up. Ah, shit!

SPEEDY: You cut yourself again? How many times I told you not to collect bottles? Always collecting broken bottles! For what? To cut your hands? You can't put broken bottles back together.

APACHE: It's a knife cut.

SPEEDY: Knife cut? What happened?

APACHE: You're leaving, so forget it.

SPEEDY: What do you mean, forget it?

APACHE: Forget it.

SPEEDY: Just tell me what happened?

APACHE: Grizzly did this.

SPEEDY: (*Backing away.*) Oh.

APACHE: Lucky he found me and not you.

SPEEDY: Fuck that big white motherfucker.

APACHE: He wants to cut your balls off. What you do to him?

SPEEDY: Nothing.

APACHE: That bear was angry, man.

SPEEDY: I didn't do nothing to him. I did it to his woman.

APACHE: You fucked Grizzly's babe?

SPEEDY: She's a fox, man. What's a fox doing with an ugly bear?

APACHE: You better learn to keep that ding-a-ling inside your pants before somebody cuts off your bells.

SPEEDY: She came on to me. I didn't know who the bitch was. I gave her the time of her life, then she runs and talks about it.

APACHE: Don't worry about it. I kicked his ass.

SPEEDY: Grizzly is crazy. He spends more time in jail than out here.

APACHE: He ain't crazy. He's stupid. Imagine, him coming here
and telling me he's the new owner of this island. I told
him over my dead body, fool. And he swung at me. I
ducked under his punch and, pang! I hit him square in
his balls.

SPEEDY: (*Jokingly.*) His babe told me his balls were small. They
must've been hard to find.

APACHE: My eagle eyes zero in on those suckers and double him
over, then I kneed him in his face.

SPEEDY: I would've paid anything to see the ear on the floor.

APACHE: Then I gave him the Apache stump. Right in his ribs.
(*Stomps ground.*) His boy jump on my back.

SPEEDY: Midget?

APACHE: Yeah, yeah. And I started to beat Midget's face too.
And every time I hit him I told him, "This is my island.
This is my island. This is my island." Grizzly got up and
went to stab me in the back, I turned around and put my
hand up to block it. It ain't that big ... (APACHE *looks
at the cut.* SPEEDY *wants to see it.* APACHE *moves hand
away.*)

SPEEDY: Let me see it.

APACHE: I'm okay.

SPEEDY: You might need stitches.

APACHE: Now you're a fucking doctor?

SPEEDY: (*Backing away.*) You better be careful. Grizzly goes after
people in the night. You have to listen for his footsteps
in the dark.

APACHE: Let him try it. I'll put a whipping on his ass he'll never
forget.

SPEEDY: I should've been here.

APACHE: I didn't need you.

SPEEDY: It was my fight.

APACHE: You wanted to fight Grizzly?

SPEEDY: Yeah. I mean ... I could hold my own.

APACHE: Right.

SPEEDY: What the fuck is that supposed to mean?

APACHE: Grizzly would sweep the ground with you.

SPEEDY: (*Takes out a knife.*) I'd cut him to pieces.

APACHE: Bro. I hope you know how to use that shit.

SPEEDY: I don't want you fighting my fights anymore. I could
take care of myself.

APACHE: Okay, if that's what you want.

SPEEDY: (*Cleaning his fingernails with knife.*) You think I'm a
    punk. I know you think that. I knew it for a long time.

APACHE: What are you on?

SPEEDY: You didn't let me join your gang.

APACHE: You was our rabbit.

SPEEDY: Why didn't you let me walk the line?

APACHE: You wanted to get initiated? To get hit by bats and
    chains?

SPEEDY: Why not? Every gang member got initiated but me.

APACHE: An asshole could've hit you in your legs. Anybody could
    fight, but nobody ran like you, man. It was beautiful. You
    would go to the other gangs and say "your colors are for
    faggots." And they would chase your ass right into our
    traps.

SPEEDY: (*Picks up chain.*) Then, you would take care of them.
    You stood in the middle of the rumble and took on any-
    body and everybody. A perfect fighting machine. A fuck-
    ing gladiator. This chain got blood from everybody who
    joined the gang but me. The gang would form two lines
    while holding chains and bats, bottles, and the new mem-
    bers had to walk through the midddle until they got to the
    other side. I never knew how that felt.

APACHE: Okay, bro. I'm going to initiate you right now. (*Gets his
    chain.*)

SPEEDY: Get the fuck out of here.

APACHE: Let me do it.

SPEEDY: And let you mess up my silk shirt?

APACHE: So, stop crying. I'm tired of hearing that shit.

SPEEDY: You don't understand.

APACHE: I understand. You want to get initiated.

SPEEDY: Fuck you. And stay away from me. (*He sits on the bench
    and a splinter rips his pants.*) Fucking bench. Fucking
    bench. (*He kicks it.*)

APACHE: What the fuck are you doing?

SPEEDY: The fucking bench ripped my pants.

APACHE: You don't have to kick it, man. I told you not to sit on
    it.

SPEEDY: I'm going to burn the son-of-a-bitch. (*He tries to kick
    the bench again but* APACHE *pushes him away.* SPEEDY
    keeps trying until he gets tired.*) Don't put your dirty
    hands on my clothes.

APACHE: Leave the bench alone then.

SPEEDY: Of all the traffic islands around here, you got to hang out
    in the worst. Raggedy, shit stained, piss smelling. Two
    blocks from here there's a cement bench and a steel one
    in four blocks. You can sit there and not worry about a
    splinter all day.

APACHE: Listen, you tender thing. Nobody asks you to come
    around here. You don't do nothing here but destroy what
    we got. You think you're too good and shit. Always criti-
    cizing and never putting up. Look, you broke the bench.

SPEEDY: I'm going to break it to pieces before I'm gone.

APACHE: Over my dead body.

SPEEDY: That's a way.

APACHE: You better go with your fairy godfather before you get
    me mad.

SPEEDY: Get mad. I don't give a shit.

APACHE: Maybe he'll make you a gold bench with a couple of
    rats.

SPEEDY: It was mice not rats in Cinderella.

APACHE: What the fuck do I care? In her life there was mice and
    in yours rats.

SPEEDY: She didn't have a life. She's a fictional character.

APACHE: You're so smart. You know so much. You always knew
    when to run from a fight. You're a brain. And whenever
    our gang went straight and got some gigs, you knew how
    to leave everybody flat. You're a genius.

SPEEDY: I wasn't the only one who left people flat. You don't
    know what I'm talking about? (*Pause.*) The night you left
    me in the car? Remember?

APACHE: I thought you was dead.

SPEEDY: You panicked.

APACHE: Bullshit.

SPEEDY: Our great leader ran scared and I paid with two years in
    jail.

APACHE: I thought you was ...

SPEEDY: Nobody pays you to think.

APACHE: Nobody told you to steal a Rolls Royce. That's why you
    ended up in jail.

SPEEDY: You wanted to steal a Chevy. You got no class.

APACHE: You ain't shit.

SPEEDY: At least I got my good looks. You got no school, no
    brains, no looks.

APACHE: Your fairy godfather is going to fuck you real good.
    When he don't need you no more, he's going to spit you

into a first class toilet bowl.

SPEEDY: I made it, Apache. Apache. I made it into the first class world. First class baby cakes. I'm going to own a Rolls Royce. (APACHE *finds a can with beer and drinks*.) Hey, give me some beer.

APACHE: (*Grabs his crotch*.) Drink some of this.

SPEEDY: Fuck you, man. Just a sip. My lips are dry.

APACHE: I don't give a shit.

SPEEDY: Come on, man.

APACHE: Stop begging.

SPEEDY: (*Aggressively*.) Just give me a sip.

APACHE: You're too good for this beer.

SPEEDY: Cut the shit.

APACHE: (*Ironically*.) I'm just looking out for my buddy. If Maurice sees you drinking garbage can beer, he might leave without you. (SPEEDY *goes for the can. They struggle with it. Beer spills on* SPEEDY. APACHE *pushes him away*.) You ain't drinking my beer.

SPEEDY: Shit. I should kick your ass for wetting my suit.

APACHE: When you're man enough, try it.

SPEEDY: I ain't afraid of you.

APACHE: You're so full of shit, your eyes are turning brown.

SPEEDY: If I wasn't dressed, I'd kick your ass.

APACHE: You got a better chance of turning into a woman.

SPEEDY: (*Goes to hit* APACHE, *but stops*. APACHE *overreacts*.) Don't get scared, bro. (*Laughs*.)

APACHE: Fuck with me and you go to Boston in a wheel chair.

SPEEDY: Not as brave as you used to be. Before, you wouldn't blink if a gun was pointing at your head. (*He fakes a hit,* APACHE *doesn't move*.) Now, that's the Apache I used to know. Fearless.

APACHE: Stop playing games with me.

SPEEDY: (*Jokingly*.) I'm so scared. (*He fakes hitting* APACHE *again,* APACHE *grabs his wrist*. SPEEDY *tries to pull away but can't*.) Want to dance? (APACHE *releases him.* SPEEDY *starts laughing*.) Remember when we were kids. All the kids made a circle around you and called you Frankenstein and the one you caught, you beat up? (*Begins to encircle him, walking like Frankenstein*.) Frankenstein. Frankenstein. Frankenstein. (*As he walks he swings his arms nearly hitting* APACHE, *who's staring forward angrily.* SPEEDY *hits him.* APACHE *grabs him by the collar*.) Come on, man. You are fucking up my suit.

(APACHE *throws him on the bench.*) Ouch! (*He gets up quickly!*) You and this bench got something in common. You're both a pain in the ass.

APACHE: You would know about pain in the ass.

SPEEDY: You better be careful, boy.

APACHE: The gang knows what you are.

SPEEDY: Who cares what the assholes think?

APACHE: They didn't call you our rabbit. They called you our bunny. If you know what I mean ...

SPEEDY: Every time they want to know a girl, they come to me.

APACHE: Homos know girls, too.

SPEEDY: I ain't a faggot.

APACHE: In jail you gave up your ass if somebody raised their voice.

SPEEDY: I was gang raped. Like we used to do to Debbie.

APACHE: Debbie liked it. Maybe you did too.

SPEEDY: (*Taking knife out.*) Take that back.

APACHE: Put that knife away before you get hurt.

SPEEDY: Take it back.

APACHE: You know what you are. (SPEEDY *goes after* APACHE, *who puts the garbage can between them.*)

SPEEDY: Running?

APACHE: (*Tries to break a bottle.*) Plastic shit.

SPEEDY: You're dead, Apache. (*Swings knife again.* APACHE *pulls back and grabs the chain.* SPEEDY *backs away.*)

APACHE: Now we're even steven.

SPEEDY: I'm not scared.

APACHE: The first thing I'm going to teach you about fighting is not to talk so much. Put the knife down.

SPEEDY: Fuck you.

APACHE: You don't want that little pretty face of yours all cut up, do you?

SPEEDY: You touch my face and I kill you.

APACHE: Cute things like you shouldn't be playing with knives, you cheap whore.

SPEEDY: At least I don't collect people's garbage for a living.

APACHE: I'm going to punch you in your eye so you could see it coming, whore.

SPEEDY: Don't make me say it, Apache. I'm warning you.

APACHE: Say what, you faggot whore?

SPEEDY: Your mother was a whore.

APACHE: The best whore in the world.

SPEEDY: Is that why you locked her in the apartment and she couldn't get out. (*They dance around.*) She was the best blow-job giver around.

APACHE: Oh, yeah?

SPEEDY: They said she was the best blow-job giver around 'cause she didn't have any teeth. I bet she's giving the devil one right now. She couldn't go to bed without her milk bottle. (APACHE *drops the bottle.*)

APACHE: Come on. Come on. Die like a man! (SPEEDY *drops his knife and charges* APACHE. APACHE *grabs him by the lower back and squeezes him.* SPEEDY *has* APACHE *by the neck.* SPEEDY *is in a lot of pain and lets* APACHE *go.*)

SPEEDY: Kill me, Mami is already dead because of you. (APACHE *throws* SPEEDY *in the garbage can. A horn is heard.* SPEEDY *gets out and cleans himself off.*) I'm glad I'm leaving this nothing. (SPEEDY *starts to leave but stops, he looks at* APACHE, *picks up his knife and exits.* APACHE, *who's been looking down, looks at* SPEEDY *leaving, picks up the sneakers and is about to throw them when we hear a car door slam.* APACHE *puts the sneakers on a branch of the tree.*)

APACHE: (*Screams.*) I don't need you. I don't need your stinking ass. Don't come back. Your shoes are too tight. (*End of first act.*)

ACT TWO

The sound of thunder is heard. Lightning lights up the island, then back to black. Lights up. This is the same set as in Act One. The bench is more worn out and is missing a couple of planks, which lie underneath the bench. On the backrest the name Grizzly is written with spray paint. The garbage can is overflowing with garbage. It's early evening. And it has been raining. A man with a dirty raincoat and hemless pants is lying on the bench. He coils up into a fetal position. APACHE *enters pushing a full shopping cart with a sign on the side, "Run an Errant." He's dressed cleanly. Jeans, T-shirt, shoes, vest and a blue handkerchief around his neck. His hair is in a pony tail. In the cart he has a bottle of beer in a paper bag. He waits impatiently, he drinks. Looks at his watch.*

APACHE: Hey, man.
SPEEDY: (*Without looking up.*) Ah?
APACHE: You seen this guy come around here?
SPEEDY: Nuh, nuh.
APACHE: A rich guy, you know? In a Rolls Royce. Rich guy with
    a big head.
SPEEDY: (*Sniffs now and throughout the rest of the play, as a coke
    addict.*) Hey, man, got a dollar I could borrow?
APACHE: Do I look like welfare? There's a lot of cans in the
    garbage. (*Pauses. He takes out a dollar and gives it to
    him.*) Here.
SPEEDY: Surprise. Fooled you. (APACHE *looks stunned by*
    SPEEDY'*s appearance; he looks burnt out, broken down.*)
    Don't you recognize me? It's me, Apache.
APACHE: I know who you are. (*They are both surprised by each
    other's appearance. Pause. They stare at each other.*)
SPEEDY: Look at you. (*Pause.*) First class. (*Pause.*) Shit. (*Pause.*)
    Clean. (*Pause.*) You are very becoming in a pony tail.
APACHE: (*Looks at watch.*) What do you want?
SPEEDY: Hey, hey, you got a watch.
APACHE: Two dollars.
SPEEDY: Cheap time. (*Laughs.*) Get it? Cheap time?
APACHE: Why, you want to see me?
SPEEDY: It's been a long time. (*Laughs.*)
APACHE: Not long enough.
SPEEDY: Five months is a long time between brothers.
APACHE: You're not my brother. And it's been six months.
SPEEDY: (*Uneasy.*) Time flies, changes everything and it crashes.
    (*Makes sound of explosion.*) Where are you going?
APACHE: I'm splitting.
SPEEDY: Please, man, don't go.
APACHE: Next time you come to visit, don't come.
SPEEDY: Man, sit down.
APACHE: I don't want to see your face, Speedy.
SPEEDY: (*Grabbing him.*) Please, man.
APACHE: No. Goddamn it. No! Let me go.
SPEEDY: (*Pleadingly.*) Stay five minutes. Five minutes. (*Angrier.*)
    Five minutes! Five fucking minutes!
APACHE: Okay. Five minutes and that's it.
SPEEDY: I need to talk to you.
APACHE: We got nothing to talk about.
SPEEDY: We do. We do. (*Reaches out his hand to give him five
    but* APACHE *doesn't respond.*) We do.

APACHE: I don't want to hear what you got to say.

SPEEDY: I need help.

APACHE: I know that. That's why you're here. You need help. What's new? The same story. Same ending, right?

SPEEDY: This time it's serious.

APACHE: I don't want to hear it.

SPEEDY: (*Scream.*) Listen to me. (*Pause.*) Please.

APACHE: Listen to what? You need a place to hide. I ain't giving it to you. Just go back to wherever the fuck you came from.

SPEEDY: I can't go back. Maurice wants me dead.

APACHE: Your fairy godfather want to kill you? I told you, you fuck with the rich and end up in a toilet bowl. Didn't I tell you?

SPEEDY: You did. You did. And I fucked up, man.

APACHE: You shouldn't have left.

SPEEDY: Fuck this "shouldn't" shit.

APACHE: You got yourself in this mess. Now face the music.

SPEEDY: The only music I'm going to hear is his bat banging against my knees. Man, they want to break my knees before he kills me.

APACHE: Break your knees?

SPEEDY: Yeah.

APACHE: He must be playing around. He ain't going to break your knees.

SPEEDY: (*Raises his pants to his knees.*) Look. Look. It's swollen. He tried but I got away.

APACHE: So you can't run no more?

SPEEDY: What do you mean, I can't run? I always can run. I'm going to show you that I'm still fast like lightning. Like a bullet.

APACHE: You don't got to show me nothing.

SPEEDY: I want to. I want to. Say go. Say it. (*Gets in running stance.*)

APACHE: Go.

SPEEDY: See. I'm back already. Zoom. Say go again.

APACHE: I said it already.

SPEEDY: Serious as ice. Say go again. I'll run to the end of the block and back. Time me, okay? Okay?

APACHE: Okay, go.

SPEEDY: No, no. Get on your mark, get set, go.

APACHE: (*Reluctantly.*) Get in your mark, get set, go. (SPEEDY's feet get tangled up and he falls.)

SPEEDY: (*Sits on the ground cleaning his shoes.*) I scratched my baby alligators. Shit.

APACHE: You can't run with alligators, man.

SPEEDY: (*Angrily.*) Baby alligators!

APACHE: You're sneakers are hanging on the tree. (*Points to them hanging.*)

SPEEDY: Fuck those funky sneakers. (*He extends a hand to* APACHE *to get some help getting up, but* APACHE *looks the other way and drinks from his beer.* SPEEDY *stares at* APACHE, *then gets up slowly. He limps noticeably.*) If I'm going to die, I'm going to be wearing classy shoes.

APACHE: Even if they don't fit?

SPEEDY: That's right. (*Pause.*) I need some money. Maurice will find me here. All I need is two hundred dollars. Could you lend them to me? (*Pause.*) I'll give you four hundred back. Five hundred. A thousand. Anything you want. Ah, Apache? What do you say?

APACHE: I ain't got it.

SPEEDY: Bullshit! Look at you. You got to have some money. I saw the sign on your cart. For twenty blocks I saw your flyers, "Run an Errant." How much you pulling down a week? A grand? Two grands?

APACHE: Enough!

SPEEDY: Enough to lend me two hundred?

APACHE: Not that much.

SPEEDY: Why are you lying to me, Apache? I bet you got the gang working for you.

APACHE: It's just me, man. Nobody else. It's my business. I run it. I do the work.

SPEEDY: That's dumb.

APACHE: Then, I'm stupid.

SPEEDY: The more the people, the more the money.

APACHE: I ain't depending on nobody.

SPEEDY: Oh, yeah? You depended on the wrong dude for this sign.

APACHE: What are you talking about?

SPEEDY: Errand isn't spelled like that.

APACHE: Like what?

SPEEDY: With a "t."

APACHE: Are you sure?

SPEEDY: Yep. It's with a "d."

APACHE: I look like an asshole pushing this cart around.

SPEEDY: Next time you get somebody to write for you, make sure they know how to spell.

APACHE: I wrote it.

SPEEDY: You wrote the sign?

APACHE: That's right.

SPEEDY: Bullshit.

APACHE: Bullshit?

SPEEDY: Yeah. Bullshit.

APACHE: (*Pushes* SPEEDY *to the pole.* APACHE *reads with great difficulty.*) De ... po ... depo ... sit. Deposit ... lit ... lit ... ter. Litter. Deposit litter ... in ... con ... tai ... contai ... ner. Container. (*He says it to himself quietly.*) Deposit litter in container.

SPEEDY: (*Reads sign to make sure* APACHE *read it.*) Hey, bro. Nice trick. Now, you're going to stand on one leg.

APACHE: I read it.

SPEEDY: Somebody read it for you and you memorized it. Admit it.

APACHE: I'm learning how to read.

SPEEDY: (*Takes book from* APACHE's *back pocket and opens it to a page.*) Read this.

APACHE: Getting your ... business star ... ted.

SPEEDY: You memorized that page too. (*Changes pages.*) Read this page.

APACHE: Man ... man ... age ... ment. Management tech ... ni ... ques ... for the ...

SPEEDY: (*Closes book.*) You memorized the whole book.

APACHE: See. I don't need nobody for nothing. Not even you.

SPEEDY: That's coool. I dig where you're coming from.

APACHE: Good.

SPEEDY: (*Goes to cart.*) Hey, man. Anything to eat in here?

APACHE: No. (SPEEDY *starts to look in the bags.*) Hey, get your hands out of there.

SPEEDY: I'm just looking for something to eat.

APACHE: (*Moves cart away from* SPEEDY.) I told you there ain't nothing to eat there.

SPEEDY: Cement? You're delivering cement and plants?

APACHE: I deliver a lot of stuff.

SPEEDY: I bet it's some wierdo who wants to see if plants could grow in cement. Do you deliver coke?

APACHE: No drugs.

SPEEDY: You should. You be rich like that. (*Snaps fingers.*) Man, Maurice had the best coke I ever had. The best without a doubt, man. There was coke everywhere, everywhere. Like rain, you know? Maurice used to give me coke whether I wanted it or not.

APACHE: You stole the man's coke. That's why you're running from him.

SPEEDY: Nah, man. I've never been crazy about coke, although I could use a couple of hits right now.

APACHE: You fucked his daughter?

SPEEDY: Man, you think I'm going to fuck my shit up for a babe?

APACHE: You did it a million times, Speedy.

SPEEDY: No, man. I didn't touch her. I swear. I swear. She was like this. (*Makes gesture of a big belly with his hands.*) She was my friend. And I didn't touch her. Maurice raped her. Her own father. You know what I thought, you know? She had something for her father. That she wanted him or something. But she hated him. She hated the mansion. She called it jail. Once I was talking to her and he locked me up in the basement. Big ass basement with a pool table. Sauna and shit. That's when he tried to break my knee. So I let her out of jail. And we ran through the forest. She had this huge belly and she was running. I took her to a friend's house and she had the baby. She named him Little Speedy.

APACHE: This is the first time you don't think with your dick.

SPEEDY: And I fucked everything up. You know, Apache, I didn't want her to end up like Ma.

APACHE: Ma wasn't in jail.

SPEEDY: She was. She was. She told you to put her in jail because you were ashamed of her. But she said that you were in jail, too. Your shame put you in jail.

APACHE: Being a whore is nothing to be proud of. Everybody looked at me and said, "your mother is a whore."

SPEEDY: Nobody dares say that to you.

APACHE: They used to yell it in their thoughts. "Your mother is a whore." I could read their little minds ... then, they walked away laughing at me. (*Pause.*) The Domino champion always laughed when he saw me.

SPEEDY: Was he banging Mami?

APACHE: When you was in school he used to come up and act like the apartment was his. He came in my room and turned the volume in the T.V. real high. Then, he went

into Mami's room and when he finished his business with
Mami, he came back into my room, turned the volume
back down and put a quarter on top of the T.V. That's
why I threw a quarter at him when he got the heart attack.

SPEEDY: That's no reason to lock her up in the apartment. She
hated being locked up. She hated elevators.

APACHE: I wasn't locking her in. I was locking the assholes out.

SPEEDY: Same difference.

APACHE: She was old, man. She was old. An old whore got
no business in the streets. She didn't have no business.
People laughed at her, too. (*Pause.*) I'm making her a
house.

SPEEDY: A house for Mami? Where?

APACHE: The cemetery.

SPEEDY: You mean a mausoleum.

APACHE: Whatever. It's big. For three caskets. It ain't got a door.
Lots of windows. Open. Plants everywhere.

SPEEDY: So these cement and plants are for the mausoleum?

APACHE: Don't touch them ... I'm making this big cross on top
of the house. The biggest fucking cross in the cemetery.

SPEEDY: All the money you made you put into the mausoleum.

APACHE: Not all. Had to buy me some clothes. I don't know
why, but people that go to the cemetery dress good. I
don't know why. Nobody ain't going to judge them. Even
dead people wear good clothes. But they don't wear shoes.

SPEEDY: (SPEEDY *cleans his shoes.*) Take me to see her grave.

APACHE: Why?

SPEEDY: What do you mean, why? I want to see it.

APACHE: No.

SPEEDY: Why not?

APACHE: 'Cause I don't want to.

SPEEDY: Okay. So tell me where it is.

APACHE: No. You should've gone to the funeral.

SPEEDY: Could you forget about the funeral?

APACHE: I forget about the funeral and you forget about the grave.

SPEEDY: You don't want me to see her grave because you're jealous.

APACHE: (*Patronizingly.*) Yeah, I'm jealous of a piece of shit like
you.

SPEEDY: I used to talk to her while she was alive and now you
want to keep her death to yourself. I got the right to see
her grave.

APACHE: You got the right to get the fuck out of here and leave me alone. (*Starts checking* APACHE*'s pockets.*) What the hell are you doing?

SPEEDY: The bullet. Mami's bullet.

APACHE: (*Moving away.*) Get off me.

SPEEDY: Where is it? (APACHE *shows him the bullet in a necklace.*) Give it to me. You don't have to show me her grave. Just give me the bullet and I'll get the fuck out of your life for good. I'll leave right now.

APACHE: Hell no.

SPEEDY: (*Tries to take the bullet from* APACHE*'s neck.*) Give it to me. Give it to me. I want it. Give it to me. (SPEEDY *pauses. He hears something. He lets* APACHE *go.*) Footsteps! He's here and he's not alone.

APACHE: I don't hear anything.

SPEEDY: I hear them. Just listen.

APACHE: Nothing.

SPEEDY: What kind of gang leader are you? You used to hear footsteps from our enemy gangs blocks away. Go get the gang. We'll kick Maurice's ass. Send him back to Boston in a wheel chair. Yeah! If he comes, I'll slow him down for a few minutes. (*Takes out knife.*)

APACHE: The gang ain't going to come.

SPEEDY: That's right. They don't give a shit about me. (*Gets chain and gives it to* APACHE.) Here! Initiate me. The gang is mad. I wasn't initiated. Do it, so you can tell them I'm part of the gang now.

APACHE: They ain't coming, anyway.

SPEEDY: I'll fight with them. I'll be a member.

APACHE: They ain't coming, Speedy. I ain't their leader anymore.

SPEEDY: Once a leader always a leader.

APACHE: I stopped leading.

SPEEDY: Why?

APACHE: 'Cause I wanted to.

SPEEDY: Bullshit. Something happened.

APACHE: Nothing happened.

SPEEDY: This is Speedy here. Nobody bullshits better than me and I know when somebody bullshits me.

APACHE: They wanted to have a rumble and I didn't want to.

SPEEDY: Yeah? . . .

APACHE: That's it.

SPEEDY: They never went against you before.

APACHE: There are lots of islands. Ain't no difference between one and the other. An island ain't no reason to fight.

SPEEDY: Who wanted to fight you for the island, Apache? (*Pause.*) Who? Who, man? Grizzly! Don't tell me Grizzly took this island from you.

APACHE: This is his island.

SPEEDY: And you didn't fight him for it? You didn't fight him? I can't believe it!

APACHE: It ain't ours.

SPEEDY: 'Cause you didn't fight for it.

APACHE: I'm busy.

SPEEDY: Busy hanging out with dead people. You rather hang out in a cemetery than on your island?

APACHE: In a cemetery there ain't no problems. No noise.

SPEEDY: 'Cause everybody is dead.

APACHE: Dead people don't fight.

SPEEDY: And they don't fuck either. (*Hears a noise which* APACHE *reacts to.*) You hear that?

APACHE: No.

SPEEDY: (SPEEDY *is more and more nervous.*) I saw you, man. You became a warrior for a second.

APACHE: If you need help, call the cops.

SPEEDY: Call the pigs? The flatfoots? They'll probably beat my head in for asking for help. Like they beat your head in for doing nothing. Who are you? Mr. Upright Citizen?

APACHE: Just do what the fuck you want.

SPEEDY: Help me fight them.

APACHE: You mean, you want me to fight them.

SPEEDY: Nah, man. I'll help.

APACHE: You never helped me fight nobody. Everytime I went to help you, I ended up doing all the fighting. And I got the scars to prove it. I ain't fighting no more.

SPEEDY: Does that mean you're not going to help me?

APACHE: I ain't protecting your ass.

SPEEDY: You're scared!

APACHE: Anything you say.

SPEEDY: Chicken! (*Cackles like a chicken.*) What's the matter, you chicken without the gang? You always had little balls. You're bigger than me, but I got bigger balls.

APACHE: Is that why you never fought?

SPEEDY: It's the price you pay when you got big balls. Got to protect them. You never had to worry about your little balls. You either fight or I'll yell out you got little balls.

APACHE: I guess I got little balls.

SPEEDY: Apache got little balls. Apache got little balls.

APACHE: (*Grabs him.*) Shut the fuck up.

SPEEDY: Get your paws of me. (APACHE *releases him.*) You better.

APACHE: You better run.

SPEEDY: Run?

APACHE: Leave.

SPEEDY: They're going to catch me, asshole. It might as well be here. On our island. Excuse me. My island. Speedy's island. I like the way it sounds.

APACHE: Why do you want to look for trouble?

SPEEDY: I'm not looking for trouble. Trouble found me.

APACHE: (*Takes money out of his pocket.*) Here. Fifty dollars. It's all I got.

SPEEDY: I don't want it.

APACHE: Take it.

SPEEDY: Keep it for your cross.

APACHE: (*Throws it at him.*) Take the fucking money.

SPEEDY: It's too late for money, Apache. It's too late. Too fucking late. (*Throws money back at* APACHE *who starts to pick the money up.*)

SPEEDY: You look so little picking that money up.

APACHE: I worked hard for this. If you don't want it, I'll take it.

SPEEDY: Always thinking of yourself.

APACHE: Me?

SPEEDY: No, you.

APACHE: Look who's talking, Mr. Me.

SPEEDY: The great leader must have it his way. You lost Mami. You lost the gang. Your business sucks. And you're losing me.

APACHE: I can't live for weak people.

SPEEDY: You're the weak one.

APACHE: (*Sarcastically.*) Yeah, right.

SPEEDY: If you're so strong ... (*Spits on the ground.*) ... pick this up. Come on, man. Pick it up.

APACHE: Fuck you.

SPEEDY: If you're so strong, why are you hanging out with skeletons? In grave yards and shit? You are all alone, man. Nobody wants to hang with you.

APACHE: Who you got, Speedy? You got nobody.

SPEEDY: At least I know it. You're too stupid to know it. (*Pause.* APACHE *drinks from his beer.*) Can I get a sip from that beer?

APACHE: No.

SPEEDY: You owe me a sip, man.

APACHE: I owe you nothing.

SPEEDY: Is that right?

APACHE: That's right.

SPEEDY: How about when you were surrounded by that gang and I ran and got help.

APACHE: Once. You helped me once. But it wasn't shit. When that wild husband came after you with a machete, who kicked his ass?

SPEEDY: That was shit. He couldn't catch me, anyway. When you got shot my blood kept you alive.

APACHE: I told the doctors that I didn't want your blood. Anyway, when you was in jail I took you cigarettes.

SPEEDY: I took you to Park Avenue.

APACHE: I picked you for my stickball team when nobody else wanted your ass.

SPEEDY: I shared my clothes with you.

APACHE: I showed you how to fire a gun.

SPEEDY: I shared my money.

APACHE: I shared my mother.

SPEEDY: I ... I ... I shared everything with you. You owe me.

APACHE: I owe you shit. You owe me.

SPEEDY: Fuck you. Every fucking woman you had I gave to you. Every single one.

APACHE: Bullshit.

SPEEDY: If it wasn't 'cause of me, you wouldn't know what pussy is. You're scared of women.

APACHE: Anything you say.

SPEEDY: Name one you got on your own. Let's hear it. There ain't none.

APACHE: Millie.

SPEEDY: My Millie with the missing tooth?

APACHE: Yeah. Poor Millie.

SPEEDY: Poor or not, she's mine. You couldn't wait until I left so you could stab me in the back. I can't fight for her if I ain't here.

APACHE: I ain't fighting for her.

SPEEDY: You know you're going to lose her, you ugly fuck.

APACHE: She ain't yours. She don't belong to nobody.

SPEEDY: I want her back. Get ready for a fight you ain't going to
    win.

APACHE: No.

SPEEDY: You're scared.

APACHE: I ain't scared.

SPEEDY: Scarry cat. Scarry cat.

APACHE: I'm tired of broken bones. And tired of scars.

SPEEDY: (*Punches him in the chest.*) Fight. Then, she's mine.
    (APACHE *gets the cart.*) She feels sorry for your ugly ass.
    That's why she fucked you. (SPEEDY *stops the cart.*) You
    ain't going nowhere until we clear this shit up.

APACHE: There ain't nothing to say.

SPEEDY: You backstabbed me in my back and you have nothing
    to say?

APACHE: Get out of my way.

SPEEDY: What are you going to do about it?

APACHE: You don't look in shape to fight. If I breathe on you,
    you'll fall.

SPEEDY: With your bad breath. Breathe on me. (*Holds his nose.*
    He pushes cart on APACHE.)

APACHE: You're sick, man. You need a doctor, man.

SPEEDY: After I get through with you, you're going to need a
    doctor.

APACHE: You look fucked up.

SPEEDY: There ain't nothing wrong with the way I look. Look at
    my shoes. Fu-ra-ga-mo. They cost more than everything
    you got on. I look good.

APACHE: I got to go. You know where I live.

SPEEDY: No, man. (*Stops the cart again.*) I don't want you to
    touch her again. I fucked her first. She loved it. "Ay,
    papi. Ay, papi. You're so big inside of me." (*Pause for*
    reaction.) See, she ain't your woman. If anybody said shit
    about my woman, I'd kick his ass.

APACHE: She's more to me than just a fuck. Millie was there for
    me. When I told her about Run an Errant, she said, let's
    do it. Not like some people I know. I ain't going to let
    you talk about her like if she's trash or something.

SPEEDY: Are you going to stop me? (*Laughs.*) She kisses your
    scars when you make love?

APACHE: She makes love to me like a man, not a monster.

SPEEDY: She loved my scar. She licked it. Put it between her legs
    and rubbed against it. When she makes love to you, she
    thinks about me.

APACHE: You know what she said about your love-making?

SPEEDY: It was great, right?

APACHE: You didn't even know she was there.

SPEEDY: She was there. I know. (*He moves as if he's fucking with a girl while holding the garbage can.*)

APACHE: You was doing gymnastics or something.

SPEEDY: Yeah. I pump the shit out of them. They love it.

APACHE: You never touched her.

SPEEDY: I'm lying on top of her.

APACHE: You never kissed her.

SPEEDY: I'm there to fuck, not kiss. I know my business. Oh, yeah. Millie, baby. I'm coming deep inside.

APACHE: (*Desperately.*) You was too busy looking at yourself in the mirror.

SPEEDY: I like looking at myself when I do it.

APACHE: That's what she thought.

SPEEDY: What? She loved it. (*Pause.*) She didn't like it?

APACHE: She never made love to you again.

SPEEDY: I didn't want to.

APACHE: She didn't want to.

SPEEDY: (*Screaming, trying to regain pride.*) She's lying.

APACHE: She ain't got nothing to lie for.

SPEEDY: That's how they are. When you do it to them they love it, then they talk bad behind your back. (*Pause.*) She really said I wasn't a good lover?

APACHE: Yeah.

SPEEDY: Fuck her. There's hundreds of women who love the way I do it. The footsteps are getting closer. Take me with you. You hear them? (*Grabs* APACHE *who turns around and pushes* SPEEDY, *who falls to the ground.*)

APACHE: No.

SPEEDY: My knee. My knee. I think I broke it.

APACHE: You full of shit.

SPEEDY: (*He's on his knees.*) I'm joking. It was a joke. Come on, man. Don't leave me alone. I'll change. I'll be everything you want me to be. Help me this time. (APACHE *turns around.*) Don't turn your back on me. (SPEEDY *takes his knife out. He runs to* APACHE *and raises the knife over his head and he's about to strike* APACHE. APACHE *turns around slowly and looks at* SPEEDY's *eyes as if saying, "Kill me, brother."*) See what you're making me do? You see? (SPEEDY *falls to the ground in a fetal position.* APACHE *stares at him, undecided about his next action.*)

APACHE: Come on, man. Get up.

SPEEDY: I'm a fuck up.

APACHE: Get up from there.

SPEEDY: Just leave, man. Just leave. It's not your problem.

APACHE: Get up, then I'll leave.

SPEEDY: No. I'm scared.

APACHE: (*Sits and places* SPEEDY*'s head on his lap.*) There's nothing to fear, Apache is here.

SPEEDY: Like when we were kids?

APACHE: Yeah.

SPEEDY: Apache, you think I'm a man?

APACHE: Just be what you are.

SPEEDY: Apache, I didn't give my ass up in jail ... I didn't. You know how roosters fuck chickens? With their beaks they push the chicken's head down to the ground, then the roosters climb on their backs. That's what happened to me. Five roosters climbed on my back and pressed my head with their arms. I'm their chicken.

APACHE: Forget about it.

SPEEDY: You can't forget when they take your manhood away. They laughed and laughed. They had seconds, and they laughed. You think I'm a man? Ah, Apache?

APACHE: It takes more than a tight asshole to be a man. (*He gives* SPEEDY *some of his beer.*) You're going to be okay.

SPEEDY: Apache.

APACHE: What?

SPEEDY: You think there can be brothers without a mother?

APACHE: Yeah.

SPEEDY: I miss Mami ...

APACHE: Me too.

SPEEDY: Remember how nervous she would be before a rumble?

APACHE: Drink. (*Gives* SPEEDY *more beer.*)

SPEEDY: Man, she would worry!

APACHE: Shh!

SPEEDY: She waited by the window until we got home. (APACHE *is trying not to cry.*) We have to keep her grave clean. You know what I mean?

APACHE: (*Sniffs and drinks.*) Yeah.

SPEEDY: 'Cause Mami knew how to keep the house clean, you know, Apache?

APACHE: Yeah. (SPEEDY *falls asleep.* APACHE *begins to sob. He can't control it anymore. The loud sound of a garbage can being overturned is heard.* SPEEDY *wakes up and crawls underneath the bench.*)

SPEEDY: You heard that? (APACHE *doesn't give him a response.*) Apache! (*Pause.*) Did you hear that, man? Apache ... They are getting closer. You hear me? Apache ... Are you okay? (*Pause.*) You're crying! You can't cry now. Listen to those footsteps. Grizzly is with Maurice. It's time to fight, not cry!

APACHE: I shouldn't have locked her in. Locking her in was like pulling the trigger.

SPEEDY: It's okay. It's over.

APACHE: It ain't over. It ain't never over.

SPEEDY: There's nothing you can do. You just can't think away what happened. It happened!

APACHE: Maybe it didn't happen. Ah, Speedy?

SPEEDY: It happened. It happened, man. It happened. Mami is dead.

APACHE: Because of me.

SPEEDY: She loved you, man. Everything was Apache for her. Apache this. Apache that. She loved you so much.

APACHE: She had no reason to love me.

SPEEDY: She's probably looking at you right now.

APACHE: Hating me.

SPEEDY: Loving you.

APACHE: No.

SPEEDY: You hear that? They are getting closer. (APACHE *takes out bullet and caresses it.*) Throw away the bullet.

APACHE: No.

SPEEDY: Throw it away, man. There they are, Apache. They're coming to get us. The bullet.

APACHE: No. (SPEEDY *crawls out and grabs the bullet. They struggle for it and* SPEEDY *gets it. He throws it away.*) Noooo! Maaaamiiiii!

SPEEDY: Are you okay? Ready to fight? I'll fight too, Apache. This time I'm with you. You and me together. Nobody can whip us when we're together, right? I can't be wearing these shoes. (*He goes to the tree and gets his sneakers. As he's putting them on he talks to* APACHE.) You know, Apache, we got to fight them and get our island back. Nobody is going to tell us what to do in our island. Right, Apache? Kick their ass. (SPEEDY *tries to give* APACHE *the chain.*)

APACHE: (*Jumps and grabs* SPEEDY *by the neck.*)   Mother-
    fucker. (*He continues to squeeze* SPEEDY*'s neck and
    presses* SPEEDY *to a kneeling position.*)
SPEEDY: Apache ... I'm not the enemy. It's them, man. It's
    them, bro! (APACHE *releases* SPEEDY *who looks at him.*
    SPEEDY *gets up. He picks up the chain and a couple
    of planks. He offers the chain and a plank to* APACHE.
    APACHE *looks at* SPEEDY *and takes them.*)
APACHE: This is my last fight.
SPEEDY: And I ain't running no more. Are you ready to fight?
APACHE: Yeah ... (*Black out. End of Play.*)

Midnight Blues

An Original Two Act Drama

by

Juan Shamsul Alam

Characters

JACKSON, a mental case, pathetic, selfish, full of guilt. A womanizer, drunk. Once a strong, cheerful man.

EVA, vindictive, insecure, eccentric. A woman who slowly has weakened through the years.

JOE, poet, rebellious, a loner and drunk.

BOBBY, gay, a lover of art. Insecure, self-expressive. Inferiority complex.

LINDA, attractive, self centered, naive. Forcefull and unhappy.

ANNA, once a healthy child. Abused, somewhat slow. Brain damaged. Limited speech.

ACT ONE

.... SCENE ONE ....

*The setting is a basement apartment turned into a duplex some-
where in the southeast Bronx. Scenes are played in the kitchen,
living room, bedroom and in the hallway that leads to an upstairs
apartment. Family pictures decorate most parts of the walls, which
are light green. The furniture is modest: a sofa, end tables, lamps,
cocktail table, two chairs. On a corner to the left is a bookcase with
a phone, a few books, a picture of President Reagan and Nancy on
the middle shelf, a bottle of rum, a radio, and on top is a tin sil-
ver box the size of a small imported candy box. All exit and enter
through the kitchen.*

*As the lights come up, a man, JACKSON VEGA, enters from
the kitchen; his appearance is gentle, but sickly. He's dressed in a
light blue suit, black shoes, white shirt, open at the neck. JACKSON
looks out of breath as he holds his chest. He moves into the living
room, confused. He stops and removes his jacket, then lays it over
one of the chairs by the sofa. He crosses to the radio on the bookcase
and he turns it on to easy-listening music. He stands away from the
radio, looks up to the top of the case, his eyes fixed on the tin box.
As he reaches for the tin box his hands begin to tremble. Clutching
the box, he carefully brings it down and walks over to the sofa. He
lays down, resting the box on his chest, and closes his eyes.*

*The sound of a door closing in the kitchen is heard, then the
rustling of packages. EVA, JACKSON's wife, appears. She's dressed
in a flowered print dress, and white sandals. In her hand she carries
a handbag and two newspapers. As she crosses into the living room
she discovers JACKSON on the sofa, curled up in a fetal position.*

EVA: Jackson, is that you?

JACKSON: Yes.

EVA: You didn't go in?

JACKSON: No.

EVA: What's wrong?

JACKSON: Nothing.

EVA: Are you sure?

JACKSON: I'm fine.

EVA: But you're laying there.

JACKSON: Just tired.

EVA: Did anyone try to hurt you?

JACKSON: No, sweetheart.

EVA: Muggers?

JACKSON: Nothing like that.

EVA: Are you sick?

JACKSON: (*Sitting up.*) Just beat.

EVA: What's the matter?

JACKSON: When I left you at the store, I tried to walk up Tiffany Street. I got as far as Fox Street. The pain hit me again in my chest. (*Rubbing his hands.*) I couldn't make it any farther. I couldn't pull myself outta the neighborhood.

EVA: I think you're coming down with something.

JACKSON: I don't know.

EVA: You want cough medicine?

JACKSON: I don't have a cough.

EVA: It's starting again, you were getting better.

JACKSON: I know, I know.

EVA: (*Sitting next to him.*) You wanna see a doctor?

JACKSON: (*Moving away from her.*) Nah, it's a lotta trouble, lotta waiting around. Plus I don't like when they tell you to pull your pants down, bend over, then with the finger, bam! Right into the calzón.

EVA: Could it be the cigarettes?

JACKSON: I don't think so.

EVA: Who's at the store?

JACKSON: Eddie.

EVA: Are you getting hot and cold flashes?

JACKSON: Just pressure in my chest.

EVA: You have to slow down.

JACKSON: And the headaches ...

EVA: You want a midol?

JACKSON: (*Smiles.*) ... And the gas.

EVA: You need to exercise.

JACKSON: I do when I get a chance.

EVA: You need a lot of rest.

JACKSON: I'll rest. Let's see, maybe I'll get the strength to go back to work.

EVA: Forget the store.

JACKSON: Oh, I don't know.

EVA: (*Trying to lay* JACKSON *down.*) Lay down.

JACKSON: What are you doing?

EVA: You need to lay down and get rest. (*Trying again to lay him down.*) Come on.

JACKSON: Oh, Eva. I don't know what to do. I'm so scared.

EVA: Ssshh! Look. I'll get you a glass of milk and medicine.

JACKSON: I don't need any. (EVA *pulls on the box.*) That's all right.

EVA: You don't need that right now.

JACKSON: Honey, please. I need to hold it.

EVA: Jackson, why?

JACKSON: Peace of mind. I wanna look at it. It's part of me.

EVA: If that's what you want. (*She gets up, crosses over to a chair, and sits.*) It's part of me too.

JACKSON: Don't get mad.

EVA: Who me? Never. Burnt fortune, that's what it is. That's what Joe always says.

JACKSON: A life of work.

EVA: All gone into the past.

JACKSON: Always present with me.

EVA: Us!

JACKSON: Right, my love. (*They both look at each other for a long while.*)

EVA: Why don't you let Joe run the store for you?

JACKSON: Joe?

EVA: Before you explode, listen first.

JACKSON: Okay.

EVA: He knows the business.

JACKSON: I guess so.

EVA: He's young, you're old.

JACKSON: But wiser.

EVA: You're not active like before.

JACKSON: (*Smiles.*) Remember that time when Joe sold the wrong pair of navy pants to the fat lady? He sold her a size fourteen and she was more like a forty eight. She came back into the store fuming mad and chased Joe around the store? (*They both laugh.*) She kept wacking him with the pants until I came to his rescue. (*More laughter.*) I don't know, Joe running a store?

EVA: I think he's ready.

JACKSON: Yeah, ready to sell everything half price.

EVA: (*She laughs.*) Then we would lose everything.

JACKSON: That's not funny. (EVA *gets up and goes to the kitchen.*) I tried with that boy. He calls himself a poet. Ha! Only

God knows what he is. He should be committed somewhere. He's ungrateful. His mouth doesn't help him either.

EVA: (*By the kitchen entrance.*) What do you expect? You wake
up with one of those attitudes, then you take it out on the
poor man.

JACKSON: What did you call him? A man? Don't make me laugh.

EVA: Face it. He's not a boy. What is it with you? You wanna
drive everyone away from here?

JACKSON: (*Popping up from the sofa.*) No! No! No! I don't
wanna do that. For crying out loud! I care for them.

EVA: You have a funny way of showing your love.

JACKSON: Look, Eva, all I said to him was, "Could you please
hurry it up in the bathroom," then I said, "You're not the
only one here." And what happens? He comes storming
outta the bathroom, slamming doors, throwing things here
and there, all over the damn place. Now tell me, do I have
to put up with his temperment? Do I? I shouldn't. I'm
the parent here, not him!

EVA: Calm down, take it easy.

JACKSON: He makes me this way, my love.

EVA: Why don't you give him the chance to prove himself. You
know how they are at that age.

JACKSON: A chance for him to kill me?

EVA: He loves you.

JACKSON: You call that love.

EVA: And what do you want? He's taken his ways from you.

JACKSON: Just the same, he's gotta clean up that act of his. One
minute he's one way, the other minute he's another. (*Going back to the sofa and sitting.*) How many times have I
asked Joe to come down to the store and work with me,
how many times? I tol' 'im I'd teach him the stock, work
him up to manager, I tol' 'im he can run the store. The
same way I taught Bobby.

EVA: (*Coming out of the kitchen with two club sodas.*) Maybe he
wants his independence.

JACKSON: Hey! He's free to do what he pleases.

EVA: (*Handing him a soda.*) Here.

JACKSON: It gives me gas.

EVA: Good, take it.

JACKSON: (*Taking the soda.*) I can't explain it. Here I am,
third generation, Joe is fourth. My grandfather came

from Puerto Rico, with my grandmother, both were simple peasants. They worked hard. They never asked for
nothing. No one ever took welfare in my family. What
they got, they got it by working hard for it. The same goes
for my father, George. He worked and worked. No com-
plaints. That poor man never took a vacation, he would
go to work sick. Pop was scared he would lose his job.
Pop saved every cent he ever made so that he would have
something to pass on to his kids.

EVA: Some are fortunate. I never had a family. I don't even have
a family Bible. Nothing. Just you, and whatever is left of
my children.

JACKSON: Who knows if we have them?

EVA: At this point only God knows. (JACKSON *drinks his soda.*)

JACKSON: Know whaaaa ... (*Popping up from the sofa, coughing,
he grabs his chest, barely able to talk.* EVA *stands there
glaring at* JACKSON, *motionless. He reaches out to* EVA
gasping.) Pump ... the pump ... please ... help me ...
(*A few beats and* ANNA, *a fifteen year-old, comes into the
livingroom, clutching a doll and* JACKSON'*s pump. She
tosses it to him.* JACKSON *grabs the pump and pumps
the precious air into his lungs.* ANNA *shuffles her way
towards* EVA, *and clings to her mother's skirt.*) Oh God!
Thank you Anna. (*He moves towards her, she pulls away
behind* EVA.) What's the matter?

EVA: Jackson.

JACKSON: Hunh?

EVA: Feel better?

JACKSON: Yes, now I do.

EVA: Go lay down in the room.

JACKSON: (*Patting his chest.*) I thought that was it. I felt I was
going. What a lousy way to go.

EVA: Try laying down.

JACKSON: Okay, in a while. (EVA *leads* ANNA *towards a table
where a set of curtains are lying.* EVA *begins to sew as*
ANN *looks on.*) I didn't know Anna was here? Why did
you leave her here by herself?

EVA: I wasn't gone long.

JACKSON: It's dangerous, you know that.

EVA: She's a big girl Jackson. Fifteen.

JACKSON: She's still a baby.

EVA: She has to learn to be independent.

JACKSON: Well, I guess you know what's best. Maybe I should go to the store. I feel better now.

EVA: Jackson, get the store outta your head. Eddie knows the prices.

JACKSON: Eddie doesn't know where his ass is, he thinks it's in his head.

EVA: Jackson, today is Bobby's birthday.

JACKSON: I know.

EVA: I think I'll go to church and light candles for the kids, and light one big one for Bobby.

JACKSON: I don't think he likes me anymore.

EVA: I miss him so much.

JACKSON: He wasn't like that when he was a kid.

EVA: He would bring me presents.

JACKSON: We got along great.

EVA: He never forgot me, Mother's Day, Christmas, Valentine's Day, Easter.

JACKSON: We'd go to the baseball games, boxing, football, basketball.

EVA: Young, so young. (*Wipes tears away.*) Poor baby, my poor boy ...

JACKSON: Where did Joe say he was going?

EVA: Just around.

JACKSON: Around where?

EVA: He just said around.

JACKSON: That could be any place, around the house, corner, block, world?

EVA: To Edgar Allan Poe Park.

JACKSON: For what?

EVA: To find inner peace, he said.

JACKSON: He's an American, not Chinese. It's inner nothing. You know, I really think deep down inside he hates me.

EVA: He never told me.

JACKSON: That's two people he hasn't told.

EVA: I'm going to get Anna ready. I'm going to church, light a few candles.

JACKSON: Good. Light a few for me too.

EVA: Before I go I wanna make sure everything is all right.

JACKSON: Looks fine to me.

EVA: When Joe comes back, please don't argue.

JACKSON: I won't if he won't.

EVA: Just don't.

JACKSON: Honey ...

EVA: Say you won't argue.

JACKSON: I'll try not to.

EVA: Good. I'm going shopping when I come out of church.

JACKSON: I need a box of cigars.

EVA: What else?

JACKSON: Newspapers.

EVA: Should I fix you some food before I go?

JACKSON: No, I'm fine. I'll find something.

EVA: Do you want your pills?

JACKSON: I know where they are.

EVA: Anything else?

JACKSON: My love, go already.

EVA: Look, I can cook something in five minutes.

JACKSON: Hon, go to church already.

EVA: You want me to tell Father Quail anything?

JACKSON: Tell 'im I've been too busy with gas to go to mass.

EVA: Nothing else?

JACKSON: No. (EVA *takes* ANNA *by the hand and crosses into the bedroom.* JACKSON *picks up the tin box and stares at it, gently rubbing the top of the box. Lights come down.*)

.... SCENE TWO ....

The lights come up on JACKSON *sleeping on the sofa with the tin box on his chest. A blue light reveals* BOBBY *dressed all in white, standing in front of the sofa, looking at* JACKSON *with his back to the audience, looking very pale, as if he were a dead person. He begins to sing to* JACKSON. JACKSON *slowly sits up.*

BOBBY: (*Reciting.*) Set me free, I'm in the light of dawn. Gotta get away from the house of mourn. Set me free, set me free. Oh, set me free. Set me free, don't mourn no more I hate for her to mourn, so set me free, set me free, set me freeee ...

JACKSON: Bobby!

BOBBY: Hey, Dad.

JACKSON: Hey, Dad? What happened to the hugs?

BOBBY: Come on, I'm too old for that.

JACKSON: Too old?

BOBBY: Yeah. Hey, where is Joe?

JACKSON: Around.

BOBBY: Where?

JACKSON: Looking for himself, who knows, I don't.

BOBBY; You never change Pop.

JACKSON: (*Smiling.*) You either. Hey, you wanna eat?

BOBBY: Why would I wanna eat?

JACKSON: Why would anyone wanna eat? To get fat.

BOBBY: Do I look like I need to eat.

JACKSON: You need a few pounds here and there. You look dead.

BOBBY: Where's Mom?

JACKSON: In the room getting Anna ready for church.

BOBBY: Why aren't you going?

JACKSON: Church. I hate church. It puts me to sleep when Father Reagan preaches. And I had a feeling you were going to show.

BOBBY: That was thoughtful of you.

JACKSON: Hey, I might be getting up in age. One thing, the Vegas never forget.

BOBBY: What's that?

JACKSON: They never forget. They have good memories. Oh, happy birthday.

BOBBY: You almost forgot. (*They both laugh.*)

JACKSON: Hey, I'm not perfect. (BOBBY *moves out of light into the hallway.*) Hey, Bobby! Where'd you go?

BOBBY: (*From hallway.*) I'm in here, be right out!

JACKSON: Come on, hurry it up, don't leave me here talkin' to the air. Bobby, Bobby.

BOBBY: (*He comes back into the living room waving his bat.*) Who am I?

JACKSON: Ruth of the Yankees.

BOBBY: Much later.

JACKSON: Robinson?

BOBBY: Naw.

JACKSON: Mantle? Mays? Bobby Knight?

BOBBY: Yaa hot!

JACKSON: Nettles? Jackson? Oh I can't take it, my heart.

BOBBY: You give up?

JACKSON: (*Defeated.*) Yes, yes, yes. I'm exhausted, I can't take it. Who is it?

BOBBY: ME!

JACKSON: You had me sweating.

BOBBY: You gave up, Dad. See how easy it was.

JACKSON: I had no choice. I was running out of names, faces, bodies.

BOBBY: We all have to give up something.

JACKSON: No, Bobby, I disagree. We must hold on.

BOBBY: Dad, you have pushed us all out of your life. How can anyone hold on? Your drinking ...

JACKSON: I stopped that.

BOBBY: Give it up, set them free.

JACKSON: They're free to do what they want.

BOBBY: Mommy won't go unless you give up one or the other.

JACKSON: She can't have both. When I go ... (*He shows him the box.*) ... this goes with me.

BOBBY: If I were you, I would take it and spread it across the city, and let it be the will of the spirit to set itself free ...

JACKSON: Bobby.

BOBBY: Yes.

JACKSON: Why did you leave?

BOBBY: I had no decision in the matter.

JACKSON: You did, Bobby, you know you did.

BOBBY: You were always in control. (*He lays his bat down.*)

JACKSON: Was I? ... (*Flashback.*)

BOBBY: Yes, look. (*He points towards the kitchen. A young man appears. His name is* JOE. *He shadow-boxes.*) See. (BOBBY *joins in the shadow-boxing.* JACKSON *gets up from the sofa as he looks on.*)

JACKSON: Come on, let's go, let's see some action here. Let's see what you sissies can do. (BOBBY *and* JOE *become teenagers again.*)

BOBBY: I be Duran!

JOE: No, man, that ain't fair.

BOBBY: Then I won't fight.

JOE: Yesterday, you was Rocky Marciano, then Ali, and Leonard. Today I wanna be Duran, and you better not try to be him. You always wanna be what I wanna be. Just be yourself.

BOBBY: You see, Dad, he wants to beat me up again.

JACKSON: He doesn't want to beat you up. Stop acting like a little fag. Be a man, not a girl.

BOBBY: Then can I be Duran, Dad?

JACKSON: If it's gonna make you macho.

JOE: Oh man! That ain't right! I picked Duran first.

JACKSON: Look, both of you! Shut the hell up and fight!

JOE: I don't feel like it now.

JACKSON: Look, Joe, don't make me mad. You don't wanna see me mad. (*He pulls out his cigar and pairs* BOBBY *and* JOE *off.*) You two ready?

BOBBY: Yeah.

JACKSON: Lets go. (BOBBY, *raising his hands, circles* JOE. *He jabs at* JOE. JOE *stands there with his hands down.*) Come on, Joe! (BOBBY *gives* JOE *a shot below the belt.* JOE *goes down.* BOBBY *jumps up in triumph.*) You see! You beat 'im. (*Lights fade on* JOE.)

BOBBY: That was below the belt.

JACKSON: So what! You won, that's what counts. Never give up.

BOBBY: But I don't like to fight. I never did.

JACKSON: It's part of life. We all have to fight in life. For survival. (*He lays back down.*)

BOBBY: You always wanted me to be a figure of your imagination. (*He picks up the bat.*) I think Mom is coming out. I don't want her to see me. I wanna surprise her. (*As he walks out of the blue light, the light fades.*)

JACKSON: (*Jumps up yelling.*) Bobby! Bobby!

EVA: (*She enters the livingroom applying lipstick.*) Did you hear me, Jackson?

JACKSON: What happened?

EVA: I said we're ready to go. I heard voices, are the children home?

JACKSON: Children?

EVA: Oh, never mind. (*She drops the lipstick in her bag.* ANNA *enters the living room dressed for church, she clutches her doll under her arm, and grabs hold of* EVA's *arm.* EVA *begins to exit.*) Look, you get hungry, there's chicken in the bottom of the regrigerator. Open up a couple of cans of whatever you want to go with the chicken. I'm gonna buy a dress I saw in the catalog. You know, something cheap for the weather. It's too bad you didn't open up a women's clothing store instead of that army-navy store. Now I have to go all the way downtown and spend money on a dress. Well, I guess money was meant to be spent. (*She blows him a kiss and exits with* ANNA.)

JACKSON: (*He shakes his head.*) The way she spends money. I'm glad I opened the kind of store I have. I'd be bankrupt by now. To think, we've been married for over twenty years. (*He shakes his head. He gets up and goes over to the chair and picks up the newspaper. He then sits back down on the sofa and scans through the paper. He stops and lays back down, placing the paper on the side and the tin box back on his chest. Jackson falls back to sleep. The only sound in the house comes from the radio. Lights fade.*)

.... SCENE THREE ....

The lighting in the house is about noon, a few hours have passed. A man appears in the living room from the kitchen. He's dressed in an olive trench coat, white sailor cap pushed down over his head, green army pants, and black combat boots. His name is JOE. He moves in the apartment swiftly, goes into the bedroom, then back out into the living room. He crosses over to the bookcase and feels around and steps back to see that the box is gone. JOE goes over to JACKSON, he looks to see if JACKSON is awake. He tries to take the box away, but can't. He goes over and turns the radio off, then makes his way back and stands over JACKSON. He shakes his head and takes a seat in the chair. JOE moves in face length towards JACKSON, he stares. JACKSON moves, dropping the newspaper and box on the floor. JOE pulls back. JACKSON sits up and picks the box up from the floor, he wipes it off with his shirt sleeve, turns and is surprised by JOE's presence. JOE hunches.

JACKSON: What the hell is wrong with you? You think you're a
          ghost? How long have you been sitting there?
JOE: Not long.
JACKSON: What's that supposed to mean?
JOE: A while?
JACKSON: (*He gets up holding on to his box.*) You look like crap,
          Joe.
JOE: I feel like it too.
JACKSON: Ya smell like it. (*He walks over into the kitchen with
          the tin box.*) You're wasting your time. It's not that easy.
          Don't try it. I know what ya thinking. Ya can't take it
          from me.
JOE: I wouldn't bet your life on it.
JACKSON: You're not going to get it that way.
JOE: I won't give up.
JACKSON: (*Opens and closes the regrigerator. He enters with juice
          in one hand and the tin box in the other.*) They all tried
          and failed.
JOE: I'll just try harder.
JACKSON: Is that right?
JOE: I think so.
JACKSON: Don't kid yourself.

JOE: I won't.

JACKSON: How is it out there?

JOE: Hot. Real hot.

JACKSON: Almost eighty-five?

JOE: Something like that.

JACKSON: Then, why you wearing that coat and hat? (*He crosses in front of* JOE.) I mean, you look stupid, crazy. Who do you think you are, looking like that? (*He sits down on the sofa.*) I don't know what to do with you.

JOE: Where's Mom?

JACKSON: Went shopping.

JOE: She's been doing that a lot.

JACKSON: What else is there to do? (*He drinks the juice.*)

JOE: Play bingo.

JACKSON: That's all I need.

JOE: Always complaining.

JACKSON: Why shouldn't I? Money comes in one hand and out to her hand.

JOE: She's your wife.

JACKSON: That's no excuse.

JOE: It's on the contract.

JACKSON: What stupid contract you talking about?

JOE: The one you signed when you married.

JACKSON: Who are you, Perry Mason?

JOE: Nobody.

JACKSON: That's right, you can say that again.

JOE: From nothing you can get something.

JACKSON: You are a pity. You shouldn't walk the street like that. You look ... I don't even know how you look. Why wear that dirty thing.

JOE: You never know when it's gonna rain.

JACKSON: No time soon.

JOE: I did a lot of walking today.

JACKSON: Walking where? (JOE *gets up from the chair and walks over to the center of the livingroom.*) Well?

JOE: I walked around.

JACKSON: Can you be more specific?

JOE: I walked over to Hunts Point.

JACKSON: (*Strokes the box.*) For a job?

JOE: No. I went to watch the produce men unload. Bobby, Linda and me used to go there and watch the men work. They used to give us fruit.

JACKSON: You get any today?

JOE: It's tough today. No one wants to give away anything.

JACKSON: Isn't that telling you something?

JOE: People are starving?

JACKSON: No. It means get your act together. You're not far from the bottom.

JOE: I've seen the top. It smells like the bottom, just different cologne. (JACKSON *throws his hands up and shakes his head.*) I went by the center where you used to take me and Bobby to box. (*He walks towards the bookcase. He picks up the boxing trophies and holds them up.*) Bobby and I won these for you, remember? (*He tosses both trophies to* JACKSON *one at a time.* JACKSON *catches them and begins to polish them on his shirt.*) We were bloody for that one. I had a black eye, and Bobby had a broken nose. You were in your glory. Took us to the pizza shop and bought a big pie. I never forget Mom's expression when you brought us home. (*He gleams.*) She had a holy fit. My god, I thought the world was going to end. She was crying, "My babies, my babies, you stupid, look what you let happen to my babies." Then she grabbed us and took us to the hospital. (*He crosses over to the center of the living room.*) And then I walked as far as Yankee Stadium, I found a rail and sat down to think.

JACKSON: You know how to think?

JOE: You know I sat there and I couldn't figure it out. Why did you have us walk from here all the way to the stadium?

JACKSON: I could have saved you a lot of walking and thinking. All you had to do was ask. I did it to save carfare.

JOE: There were times when Bobby would cry, complain of the pain in his little legs.

JACKSON: (*He gets up.*) He came out like your mother. A wimp. What I wanna know is what are we gonna do with your mother. She spends too much. (*He crosses into the the kitchen.*) I have to pay rent, buy food, gas, electricity, pay my employees, and the rent in the store. Joe, (*He comes out eating a banana.*) I'm not getting help nowhere else. (JOE *reaches into his back pocket and pulls out a pint of gin.*) Look at you! Like a goddamn bum. (JOE *unscrews the top and drinks from the bottle.*) Why do that, huh?

JOE: Kills the pain in my brain.

JACKSON: Ya gonna drink, be civilized.

JOE: What's civil to you?

JACKSON: Drinking out of a freaking glass.

JOE: You want a glass?

JACKSON: I have my own, thank you.

JOE: (*He shakes his head.*) Fine, sir!

JACKSON: Knock it off.

JOE: What am I doing, Pop?

JACKSON: Don't play mister innocent with me.

JOE: Okay! I'll play it your way.

JACKSON: (*He walks over to the chair.*) You know what I want from you.

JOE: Lay down and die.

JACKSON: Don't say that! Don't ever say that! All I want, Joe, is for you to get it together. Then come work for me.

JOE: When I'm ready I will.

JACKSON: When, when the last ounce of life is gone out of me?

JOE: (*He points at the tin box.*) When you give that up.

JACKSON: That's when I give up part of my life.

JOE: You gave up part of your life a long time ago.

JACKSON: Are you here to torment me?

JOE: No, I'm here to celebrate Bobby's birthday tonight. Yesterday's clock is today's being, tomorrow's clock will be in the past.

JACKSON: Then why don't you pass outta here and let me have some peace of mind?

JOE: If life continues at this pace, what will be of the human race? (*He takes another shot.*)

JACKSON: Who gives a damn!

JOE: Damn? Slam, bam, you said it. (JACKSON *moves over to the sofa.*) You have to get rid of the bomb. It keeps ticking, and ticking away, destroying us little by little. (JACKSON *grabs the box.*) It has made us strangers. Mother against daughter, father against son, brother against sister. Strangers.

JACKSON: You're the only strange one here. (*He gets up and slowly walks over to* JOE.) I have tried to give of myself. Extend myself backwards. You ... you turn away as if I were a disease. Your mother is the same way. I try to help her along and all she does is shop, shop, shop! What is she shopping for?

JOE: For time.

JACKSON: Who's time?

JOE: Time to reminisce of the dear and departed. Life is like a rose, once plucked, it dies a slow death. Wilts away like Mommy's nerves.

JACKSON: My nerves flew away a long time ago.

JOE: Like the eagle flies so do I. (*He takes a drink.*)

JACKSON: (*Waves his hands.*) This whole thing does not make any sense.

JOE: Cents, since, sense. Which has more value?

JACKSON: You and your stupid poetry. You stand there like a fool and call yourself my son. Let me tell you something. All those ... those papers you saved up that you call poetry, and all those things you call plays ... You call yourself writing for the people. Well, this people here was the one who took all those papers that were written in pencil and pen, and I put it all in the can and lit it up with a flick of a Bic! How do you like that! It was me! Not Anna, me, you jerk. How do you like that one, Son?

JOE: (*He takes another drink.*) Son? Sun? One who obeys, one who shines. (*He points to his head.*) It's all up here, Pop. (*He smiles.*) You ain't burnt that yet.

JACKSON: (*He shakes his fist at* JOE.) You contemptible good-for-nothing. (*He walks back to the sofa.* JOE *tries to control his giggle.* JACKSON *takes a seat.*) You are very foolish.

JOE: Man. (*He begins to move about the living room.*) He who represents male. Male offspring of Wo, that connects to Man, who brought forth man, is wo-man. (*He stops.*)

JACKSON: You cheap bum.

JOE: Rum, fun, bum, run ...

JACKSON: Bastid. (*He begins to cough.*)

JOE: Play, say, hay, bay, slay ...

JACKSON: (*He stops coughing, upset.*) Get out! Get out of my sight!

JOE: Sight, bite, might, fight. (*He exits to the bedroom.*)

JACKSON: What kind (*He coughs.*) of son are you! You're suppose to take care of your sick father, ya bum! (*He lays back down and craddles the tin box. Lights fade.*)

.... SCENE FOUR ....

Flashback. Lights come up in the living room. The whole family is together. JACKSON *is playing cards with* JOE *and* LINDA. EVA, *sitting in a chair, combs* ANNA's *hair.* BOBBY *is reading a play in another chair.*

JACKSON: (*Lays his cards down and starts laughing.*) I'm out.

JOE: So am I.

LINDA: (*Tosses her cards.*) You two gotta be cheating.

BOBBY: (*Looking up from the book.*) Sore loser!

LINDA: I never win with these two. What else can I think?

EVA: Find another game to play.

JOE: Yeah, like go play with yourself.

EVA: Stupid.

JACKSON: Come on, Bobby, put that book down and play a hand of five-cards stud.

BOBBY: No, no. Not for me. I don't want any part of your card games.

EVA: (*She finishes combing ANNA's hair.*) Let's see how my little princess looks? (ANNA *stands up and models for* EVA.) Look at my pretty little doll. Go show Daddy. (*She walks over to* JACKSON.)

ANNA: How do I look, Daddy?

JACKSON: (*He grabs her.*) Beautiful! (*He gives her a kiss.*)

EVA: Be careful. I spent a lotta time with her hair.

JACKSON: (*To* ANNA.) Ah, are you going to be my star when you grow up?

ANNA: Yes. And I'm going to buy everyone in the family a house and ... and everyone a car too.

JACKSON: (*He sends* ANNA *off. She sits next to* JOE.) What a kid, huh? Kids today, they all think big. I never had enough time to think when I was a kid. It was work from morning till night. A little school when I could get it. (EVA *gets up and sits next to him.*) But, we made it, huh, baby?

EVA: (*She kisses him.*) Making it is not that important to me. What is of value is to have us all together as a family. When I think of my mother, how she left, abandoned me. She left me like that on the church steps. (*She wipes her eyes.*) A father I never knew. Growing up in a home. I gotta go wash the dishes. (*She gets up and wipes her eyes.*)

BOBBY: Ma, I got it, I'll wash them.

JACKSON: Let her do it, Bobby. Washing dishes is not for men.

BOBBY: It's no big thing.

ANNA: Daddy, are you taking me to the zoo tomorrow?

JACKSON: If you are a good girl.

ANNA: I wanna see the lions and tigers.

JOE: And, you can see Linda too. (LINDA *throws a small pillow at* JOE. *Everyone gets into the game.* ANNA *becomes the monkey in the middle until* ANNA *catches the pillow.*

They all grab her and show their affections. EVA *exits to the kitchen, followed by* LINDA *and* ANNA.)

JACKSON: Boy, I'll tell you, Bobby ...

BOBBY: Yes?

JACKSON: Why don't you, me and Joe go to a ball game next week?

BOBBY: I don't know, Dad. I got a lot of homework. My last year of high school is no fun.

JACKSON: One day off won't hurt.

JOE: Take the day off, Bobby.

BOBBY: Let's see.

JACKSON: (*To* JOE.) That boy is going to be a genius. Really. Hey, Bobby, wha'cha reading?

BOBBY: A play.

JACKSON: (*To* JOE.) See. We have a person who reads plays. You should do the same thing. Be like your brother.

JOE: Plays stink. I don't understand them. And poetry, with all the crap about roses are red. I know they're red. So what?

JACKSON: What's the play about, Bobby?

BOBBY: It's called "Boys in the Band."

JACKSON: Ah, about music?

BOBBY: Yeah, Dad.

JACKSON: You plan to join a band?

BOBBY: (*He looks directly at* JOE.) Someday.

JACKSON: What'cha gonna learn to play, the trombone ... (*He gestures with his organ.*) ... or the organ? (*He and* JOE *burst out laughing.*)

BOBBY: (*Shakes his head.*) You two need to be committed to a joke farm. (JACKSON *and* JOE *continue to laugh as the lights fade.*)

.... SCENE FIVE ....

The lights come up slowly. JACKSON *sits on the sofa staring out. The sound of the door closing. The sound of foot steps, a young woman appears at the archway of the kitchen, she twirls a set of keys, she's dressed in a white summer dress, with sandals to match; a brown straw bag dangles in her hand. Her name is* LINDA. *He calls out.*

JACKSON: Eva, is that you?

LINDA: (*Crossing over to* JACKSON.) Hi, Papi. (*She leans down and kisses him, then pats the box.*) Papi, you're still the same as I left you last time. I hear you don't do anything but lay around.

JACKSON: Forget me for now. (*He sits up.*) Where the hell you been? You came alone? Where is what's-his-name, your husband? He lets you walk the streets alone like that?

LINDA: (*She sits next to* JACKSON *on the sofa.*) Me and him had a fight. He didn't want me to come. I told him I wasn't going to miss Bobby's birthday. He called me ridiculous, so I gave him a left hook and knocked him right out.

JACKSON: (*Laughing.*) That's my girl. See, what I taught you didn't go to waste.

LINDA: Believe me, I don't care. I walked out just like I am, with nothing, and I don't care if I never see him again. I'm tired of him, anyway. Sick of the whole relationship. What the hell does he work for? The man is always broke, he is hardly ever home. I'm gonna have to give up my apartment, we can't afford it. He never pays rent. How can you live without paying rent? There were days I would go hungry, left without energy to do anything. Look at me. I'm getting thin like a skeleton. I can't go on like this. All my money goes on rent, no food, very little food. There has to be another woman, could be my next door neighbor, I don't trust her, she's too pretty. Papi, what should I do? I'm so confused. Should I leave him and come back home? (*She rubs the tin box.*)

JACKSON: You wanna come back, its up to you. You have a key. I could never turn my little girl away.

LINDA: You are wonderful. (*She leans over and hugs him. She gets up and crosses into kitchen.*) This whole thing with Hector has been one big pain.

JACKSON: The man is a complete jerk.

LINDA: (*She opens the refrigerator.*) He's jealous that my father has his own business, your own duplex apartment in the Bronx.

JACKSON: I wouldn't call this a duplex.

LINDA: You have two apartments, this and the second floor.

JACKSON: It's not a duplex. All I did was build a pair of stairs from this floor to the one upstairs.

LINDA: (*She enters with a chicken leg and a beer.*) Papi, it's a duplex and that's that. (*She walks over to the sofa.*) You want some chicken?

JACKSON: Naw, eat , you need it more than me.

LINDA: Dad, you gotta eat. Move around and walk. Take long walks. What is it, your heart?

JACKSON: It's everything.

LINDA: How is it upstairs, the same?

JACKSON: Curtains. All the rooms have new curtains. And they don't match.

LINDA: Curtains are curtains. It doesn't matter if they match or not. (*She picks up her bag.*) I'm going up. (*She hurries out down the hallway.*)

JACKSON: Linda! (*He shakes his head. He lies back down, placing the box on his chest.*) None of them care for me. (*He sits up and places the tin box on his lap and begins to stroke it. Lights fade.*)

.... SCENE SIX ....

Lights come up. A few beats and BOBBY *appears. He enters the living room.* JACKSON *sits there looking out.*

BOBBY: (*Peeved.*) Dad! Why did you let Linda go upstairs?

JACKSON: I tried to stop her.

BOBBY: She almost saw me.

JACKSON: I'm sorry.

BOBBY: (*Apologetic.*) It's not your fault. She's just a nosy body.

JACKSON: She's still your sister.

BOBBY: I know, I know. (*He points at the box.*) I see you still have the remains of the past.

JACKSON: It's what keeps the family together.

BOBBY: No, Dad. That's what's holding you back. You don't do anything anymore. You carry that box everywhere you go. Even your employees are talking. You can't keep this up.

JACKSON: What can I do? I'm trying to preserve our sanity.

BOBBY: You're doing a poor job.

JACKSON: What would you know? You come in and out around here. You have your faculties intact, the rest of us are on the edge.

BOBBY: Dad, you're holding on to dirt. Nothing more.

JACKSON: You might as well call it garbage.

BOBBY: Why not trash?

JACKSON: You're sounding like Joe.

BOBBY: He's my brother.

JACKSON: Speaking about him, what the hell is he doing in the room? Joe!!

BOBBY: Ssshh! I don't want to be seen. (*He begins to walk.*)

JACKSON: Where are you going now?

BOBBY: For a walk, dearie.

JACKSON: Watch your mouth. And don't get lost like your mother does.

BOBBY: Byeee. (*He exits out the kitchen. Lights fade.*)

.... SCENE SEVEN ....

JACKSON: (*He calls out.*) Joe! Hey, Joe!

JOE: (*From bedroom.*) Whadaya want, Pop?!

JACKSON: Whadaya doin' in there?

JOE: Looking.

JACKSON: Looking for what?

JOE: Looking over some pictures. (*He appears at the bedroom doorway.*)

JACKSON: I wanna talk. Come out here and talk.

JOE: About what?

JACKSON: You, me, life. The whole situation here. Who knows until we talk?

JOE: We need a new picture album.

JACKSON: What's wrong with the one we have?

JOE: Pictures are old, and the thing is falling apart. Like everything around this joint.

JACKSON: So what do you want?

JOE: Take new pictures and buy a new album ... new furniture, the whole works.

JACKSON: Eva does the picture taking around here. And the buying. We need things, she'll get them. (LINDA *enters from the hallway drinking her beer.*)

LINDA: Joe! (*She runs to him, giving him kisses and hugs.*) Let me look at you. (*She stands back.*) You look better since I last saw you.

JACKSON: Lies!

LINDA: You gained weight.

JACKSON: Crap!

LINDA: How's life?

JACKSON: Boring!

JOE: Will you knock it off, Pop?

JACKSON: No consideration for the truth.

JOE: (*To* LINDA.) How's Hector?

LINDA: Oh, please don't ask. (*She walks over to the sofa and takes a seat.*) He's turned into a real shithead. What about you? You have a girlfriend, wife, woman?

JOE: I'm working on it.

JACKSON: Who the hell would want you? (*Chuckles.*)

LINDA: Daddy, cut it out.

JACKSON: Well, look at him.

LINDA: I don't see anything wrong.

JACKSON: His whole appearance is out of place.

LINDA: It's not what you wear that counts. Still writing, Joe?

JOE: Yes.

LINDA: Any plays?

JOE: Three.

LINDA: Three! Great! What are the names, in case you sell them I can brag about you to my friends.

JOE: I have one called "Sopa," the other is called "Gimbambó," and my third is "Chuleta."

LINDA: The names make me hungry. Is that what it's supposed to do?

JOE: My statement is food.

LINDA: Can I read one of them?

JOE: (*He shakes his head.*) They're all up here. (*Points to his head.*)

LINDA: Who's gonna see it, how you gonna sell it? You plan to put it on paper?

JOE: Whoever wants to buy or use any of my works will have to hire my head. I can't trust anyone with my masterpieces. Especially certain people who love to destroy and steal my creations.

JACKSON: (*He pops up from the sofa.*) Destroy, yes! Steal? You gotta be outta your freaking mind. (*He walks over into the kitchen, holding on to the tin box.*)

LINDA: He's getting worse.

JOE: So am I. With his crap.

LINDA: No change.

JOE: As you can see.

LINDA: What do we do?

JOE: I'm planning. He doesn't leave it unguarded. He takes it with him everywhere.

LINDA: We have to lure him away, distract his attention. Mommy called me up and said she won't have it in this house one more day. She wants to put it where it belongs, especially today.

JOE: I tried to get him into the bedroom. He won't bite.

JACKSON: (*From the kitchen.*) I know you're talking about me. I feel it.

LINDA: No, Daddy.

JACKSON: (*He enters with a beer.*) I know you're lying. You lie. You got it from your mother.

LINDA: Don't drink too much, you know how you get.

JACKSON: Yes, Mother. (*He walks over to the sofa.*)

LINDA: Eat! (*The sound of the door closing in the kitchen, everyone's focus is on the kitchen.* EVA *and* ANNA *enter the livingroom with two shopping bags.*) Mommy! (LINDA *hugs* ANNA.)

EVA: I'm so tired. (*She lays the bags down.* LINDA *goes over and hugs* EVA.) How are you doing, Linda? My feet are killing me.

LINDA: What you get, Ma?

JACKSON: I'll be broke before the year is out.

EVA: (*Hobbles over to the sofa.*) Bring the bag over. (*She sits down.* LINDA *brings her the two shopping bags.*) I bought the curtains I wanted, a pillow for my bed. The other one I have sinks in, so I got a new one. (*She pulls the items out of the bag.*) A dress I wanted, and shoes, a slip, a lamp. Oh, I went to the church and lit five candles. (*She looks* JOE *over.*) Did you take a bath? I don't like the way you are looking. When you get a chance, go take a bath. I know you're a big boy, but you're still my baby. I was on Thirty-Third street, almost near Penn Station and I saw this man I swear looked a lot like you. (*She pulls out a plant.*) He was walking down the street pushing a shopping cart. He had all these things in it. Like his clothes and personal things. He put a lot of protection on it. You weren't downtown were you? I mean, this man was dressed like you, the same face and all that. The poor man wanted to enter the station with his cart, but this cop wouldn't let him in. I feel so foolish. You know what I did? I thought he was you. So I was calling out, Joe! Joe! I thought you didn't hear me, so I went up to this man and pulled his arm almost off. When he turned around, I was so ashamed to see it wasn't you. The man was cursing me out for no reason. Joe, you better take a bath, change your clothes, 'cause I don't want that to happen to me again. (*She pulls out a dress and stands placing the dress to her body.*) Isn't it pretty? (*She smiles. Smile fades.*) My God,

something just passed my mind. That man could have
killed me. Worse, I coulda got raped. (*She nervously sits.*)

JACKSON: In broad daylight in Penn Station? Don't be silly.

EVA: People get excited in the day too.

LINDA: Ma, you see someone who looks like Joe, ignore him.

EVA: What if one of them is him?

JACKSON: Just keep walking.

EVA: (*She cradles the dress.*) You know, in church when I was
praying I was getting chills. I felt like someone, something
was praying with me.

JACKSON: Bad vibes in the church. Too many sinners go to
church.

EVA: You should go sometime.

JOE: You could be a medium, Ma.

JACKSON: More like a large.

LINDA: Pop, he means a person who can contact spirits.

JACKSON: What does he know about that? Always talking about
spirits, monsters, and UFOs. Grow up, Joe. (*He takes a
seat.*)

EVA: What did he say? He didn't say anything.

JACKSON: That's his problem. He never says nothing that makes
sense around here.

JOE: Look who the hell is talking. Can't hold a conversation without arguing. You're the cause for everything wrong around
here. It starts with Mommy, then Bobby, me, Anna, and
Linda. We all end up with the "Midnight Blues" around
here.

JACKSON: (*Pops up from the chair.*) Yeah, go ahead, blame me!
Blame me for your own stupidity!

LINDA: Dad, don't argue.

JACKSON: (*To* EVA.) That boy is sick.

JOE: You! You're the sick one.

JACKSON: You wish I was! I know your kind. Take, take. Take it
all when I'm gone.

JOE: I don't want nothing from you. NOTHING!

JACKSON: Liar!

EVA: Not today, please, it's Bobby's birthday.

JOE: I'm sick of him!

LINDA: Joe, please!

JOE: (*To* JACKSON.) All the things you have, you can take them
and stick them ...

EVA: (*She produces her dress and she shows it around.*) Look! Look!
I bought a dress, see, see how pretty ...

JACKSON: Don't ever ask me for nothing, you creep!

JOE: I don't need nothing from you but peace of mind. (*He takes a hold of his head.*)

EVA: *Puñeta! Carajo!* Stop it!

LINDA: Papi, you're sick, come on, huh.

JACKSON: Sick!

EVA: (*Wild eyed.*) It has to stop. I can't take this shit, Jackson!

LINDA: Fight! Fight! Argue, that's all we do!

JACKSON: He's gonna come on hands and knees begging, they all do. And when he does, I'll spit on him.

JOE: Who gives a shit!

LINDA: You think Bobby would like this, what's going on?

JACKSON: Ass! (*He grabs his chest and coughs.*)

JOE: Die! You piece of crap!

LINDA: Daddy!

JACKSON: You'll beg, Joe! Begging! Like a wounded dog! (ANNA *holds her head, lets out a scream that vibrates throughout the house. They all freeze and focus on* ANNA. *Lights come down slowly.*)

ACT TWO

.... SCENE ONE ....

Lights come up in the living room. The set and scene are the same as Act One. Jackson is sitting on one of the chairs, rocking back and forth rubbing the tin box. He smiles and rocks. He stops to listen as he moves slowly towards the kitchen. BOBBY *appears from the kitchen.*

JACKSON: Where have you been? I'm a sick man. Nobody cares about me. Your mother's upstairs with Linda, hanging curtains again. Joe went out. What is this? And then you, you forget me. All of you like gypsies, moving, moving, never in one spot. Forgetting me.

BOBBY: How long have you been down here by yourself?

JACKSON: Too long. Eva made dinner. You wanna eat?

BOBBY: You know I don't eat.

JACKSON: Everybody eats except me. They don't care. Left my
    food over there in the kitchen.

BOBBY: Should I bring it to you?

JACKSON: It's cold by now. It's been sitting in there for two damn
    hours. I don't wanna eat anything in there. Who knows
    what these gypsy brujas put in my food. It's a conspiracy,
    that's what it is. And I told them so.

BOBBY: You shot your mouth off again, didn't you?

JACKSON: That's not nice to say, Bobby.

BOBBY: Dad, you're not going to heal the way you're going. You
    gotta learn how to get along with others.

JACKSON: Don't you think I try?

BOBBY: No.

JACKSON: Well I do.

BOBBY: Not hard enough.

JACKSON: It's a big joke with them.

BOBBY: Learn to blend in.

JACKSON: With them?

BOBBY: Yes.

JACKSON: They never do anything right.

BOBBY: You're talking perfection.

JACKSON: (*Searching for words.*) Take you, for instance. All I
    wanted from you was happiness.

BOBBY: I thought I gave you that.

JACKSON: You turned on me, Bobby.

BOBBY: No I didn't.

JACKSON: (*Getting up.*) You did what you wanted to do.

BOBBY: I had to find myself.

JACKSON: For what?

BOBBY: To learn why I was feeling the way I did.

JACKSON: Don't give me that.

BOBBY: I needed to go my own way, Dad.

JACKSON: And find what?

BOBBY: Life.

JACKSON: Your life is here, your life is our life.

BOBBY: It's not the same. What about my friends?

JACKSON: Bobby, you hurt me.

BOBBY: I had feelings too. And so do my friends.

JACKSON: Friends. You call them friends. Oh, come on. Bobby,
    please be realistic, will you. The store is your friend, your
    family, everyone in there is a friend.

BOBBY: I could have never found happiness there. The taunting
    from you, your workers. You always humiliated me in

front of them. You tell me sit, I would, stand, I did. I was
your robot.

JACKSON: I had to do that. I didn't want them to think I was
giving you special privileges.

BOBBY: I was destroyed. The names, Dad, the names killed me.
Drained every bit of breath from me.

JACKSON: Why worry about names?

BOBBY: Sissy, fag, queer. How many times I got down on my
hands and knees, Papi, and begged you to treat me like
everyone else at that store. You did it here in front of
Mommy, Linda, Joe.

JACKSON: I did it to toughen you up.

BOBBY: Saying things like that to a boy of seventeen, it only makes
you weak. (*He turns his head towards the hallway, as he
slowly walks away. A few beats.*)

JACKSON: You didn't try. You just didn't try. (BOBBY *turns,*
JACKSON *calls out.*) Wait. Please. (BOBBY *comes back.*)
Bobby, what about the time ... Like the time just before
you decided to leave us? I bought you and Joe tickets to
a Mets game. I was tired, but I knew it was your birthday
and I drove all the way out to Queens and got you those
tickets. I came home, handed you the tickets. You didn't
know what it was for. You totally forgot that we had set
that day to go see the Mets play. You had made other
plans with those friends of yours. That tore me up inside.

BOBBY: That was then, this is now, Dad.

JACKSON: Who are you now? Joe? With the poetic nonsense?
That's another thing. I wish you never taught him none
of that crap. He drives us up the wall with it.

BOBBY: It's the only beauty he has left that was given to him by
me.

JACKSON: It's still baloney to me.

BOBBY: Pop, why did you bring us into this world? (*He wipes his
eyes.*) You can't expect us all to be molded into Jackson
Vega. We're all different when entering this world.

JACKSON: You're lucky you're here. Some don't even make it.

BOBBY: I died a long time ago. (*Silence fills the air. Pause.*) I
gotta go. I need to rest now, I'm really tired.

JACKSON: Don't go, stay.

BOBBY: I must.

JACKSON: (*Sympathetic.*) Will you come back down, talk some
more, look after me? I feel so lonely.

BOBBY: If I can make it. (*He walks off, disappearing down the hallway. A long beat as* JACKSON *watches* BOBBY. *He then crosses into the bedroom. A beat, then* EVA, ANNA *and* LINDA *enter the living room from the hallway.* EVA *stops when she finds that* JACKSON *is gone.*)

EVA: What happened to him?

LINDA: Maybe he went out.

ANNA: Ah-ah. Bah-Bah.

EVA: Jackson! (*The sound of a toilet flushing.*) Jackson!

LINDA: Ma, be nice, okay?

JACKSON: (*He enters the living room.*) You called me?

LINDA: We thought you went out.

JACKSON: Where? (*He crosses over toward the sofa.*)

LINDA: Anywhere.

JACKSON: I had to relieve myself.

LINDA: Ma has something to tell you.

JACKSON: (*He turns.*) If it's nonsense, I don't wanna hear it. (*He sits.*)

EVA: (*To* LINDA.) You see?

LINDA: Dad, will you please stop being so hard?

EVA: Forget it, you don't have to defend me. (*She and* ANNA *head for the bedroom.*) He's the one that starts around here.

JACKSON: Starts what?

EVA: (*Stops and turns.*) Agitates.

LINDA: Ma, Dad! (*Enter* JOE *from the kitchen into the living room. He's in a stupor from drinking. He looks around at everyone.*) Joey?

JACKSON: Look at him, sad gypsy with sad melodies. Never know when he's coming or going in life.

JOE: (*He claps.*) Beautiful. You'll be a poet yet. Unhappy burden of life, he who ... who siphons plasma which sustains life. (*As he walks across the room to the other side.*)

JACKSON: Listen to that? You see, Eva, you see what you brought into this world?

EVA: (*At doorway of bedroom.*) No, what am I supposed to see?

JACKSON: Nothing, a big zero stands there before me. Yap, yap, yapping away like excreted gas!

EVA: (*Ignores him.*) Linda, could you please help me with the things on the sofa? (*She crosses over towards sofa.* LINDA *follows. They both begin placing the things* EVA *bought in the bag.* JOE *walks over to a wall opposite* JACKSON. *He pulls a pint of gin from his trench coat.* JACKSON *eyes him.* JOE *wipes his mouth with his sleeve,* EVA *and*

LINDA *ad lib as they cross into the bedroom with the shopping bags.* JOE *stares at* JACKSON, *he then breaks into a big smile as he shakes his head. He does this a few times,* JACKSON *becomes annoyed.*)

JACKSON: You see a circus on my face? (JOE *shakes his head no.*) So what the hell are you smiling about? (JOE *hunches.*) Why don'cha get outta here, staring at me, go stare at the wall somewhere. (JOE *nods, then exits through the hall.* JACKSON *begins to cough.* ANNA *appears at the doorway, her doll dangling by her side. As* JACKSON *watches* JOE *disappear, he shakes his head.* JACKSON *turns to see* ANNA, *he smiles and slowly moves towards her.* ANNA *pulls back.* JACKSON *stops. They stare at each other a couple of beats.*) Sweetheart, come to Daddy. (*She shakes her head.*) Daddy is not gonna hurt you. Where's your dolly? (*She produces her doll.*) Nice dolly? What's her name?

ANNA: Dada.

JACKSON: That's a nice name. Does she talk to you?

ANNA: (*Nods.*) Dadi-dalk do mah.

EVA: (*Calling from the bedroom.*) Anna! Anna! What are you doing out there? (EVA *and* LINDA *appear at the door way.*) What are you doing here? (*She leads* ANNA *into the bedroom.*)

JACKSON: (*Filled with emotion.*) I only wanted to communicate with her. Why she do that?

LINDA: (*As she walks over to him.*) She's afraid.

JACKSON: I'm trying, Linda. All I want is forgiveness. I want her love. That's all I want. (*He wipes his eyes.*) I know I don't have that much time left. The little I have I'd like someone to love me. (*He begins to cough, then he keels over.*)

LINDA: Daddy! (*He continues to cough.*) What is it? (*He gets up and points over towards the sofa. He holds on to* LINDA, *she helps him over to the sofa.*) Take it easy. (*He lays down, putting his feet up.*) Papi, take those shoes off. (*She helps pull them off. He stops coughing.*) Lay back, take deep breaths. (*She tries to take the box away.*)

JACKSON: No, leave it.

LINDA: Gimme, I'll put it up.

JACKSON: No, leave it right here where I can see it.

LINDA: But don't you feel uncomfortable with that all day?

JACKSON: I want it right here.

LINDA: It's no good for you.

JACKSON: When you learn how to control your life, then you can give me advice.

LINDA: Just trying to help.

JACKSON: I don't need it.

LINDA: (*She picks up the newspapers and dumps them on* JACKSON.) Hell with it. Okay, that's how you want it. (*As she starts off.*)

JACKSON: Go ahead. I know you people are out to get me.

LINDA: It's not true. (*She turns.*)

JACKSON: Look at me. All this paper.

LINDA: Please.

JACKSON: What do you call this all over me?

LINDA: Paper, plain newspaper! (EVA *comes into the living room.*)

EVA: What's going on out here?

LINDA: Nothing, Ma, go back inside.

JACKSON: She's nuts, Eva, take her with you.

EVA: What are you doing to him, Linda?

LINDA: Nothing.

JACKSON: (*Points to paper.*) You call this nothing?

EVA: I was in the room and I heard you two arguing.

LINDA: Go back inside, finish sewing your curtains. We wasn't arguing.

JACKSON: You were so.

LINDA: I was not!

EVA: And what are you doing now?

LINDA: Yelling.

EVA: Then don't yell!

JACKSON: Will you two shut up, please!

EVA: I don't want you two arguing and that's it. (*She exits.*)

LINDA: (*She taps his leg.*) Move your leg.

JACKSON: I don't feel like it.

LINDA: (*Loud whisper.*) Will you move your damn leg.

JACKSON: There's chairs all over the place. (*As he points.*) One there and there.

LINDA: (*She moves his legs and sits; he props his legs on her lap.*) Papi, I wanna talk.

JACKSON: What do you want to say? You women never have anything to say.

LINDA: What about Joe?

JACKSON: He doesn't have anything to say either.

LINDA: He's a man.

JACKSON: He's an exception. I don't know what he is. He didn't come out like me. (*She massages his foot, he occasionally jumps when she touches a tender spot.*)

LINDA: I remember when I used to do this for you when you would come home from work. "Linda!" You would call out and I would come running. "My feet need a rub, they feel like lead," you'd say. I used to hate it. I used to tell you your feet smelled like cheese. (JACKSON *laughs and so does* LINDA.) I'll eat any cheese except limburger cheese, it reminds me so much of your feet. (*She continues the massage.*)

JACKSON: Is that a nice thing to say? Do you massage Jerk's feet?

LINDA: Who is Jerk?

JACKSON: That half husband of yours.

LINDA: (*She slaps his foot.*) No, I don't. I never had the feeling. There was no affection there. I try to love Hector. Why is it so hard for me to love?

JACKSON: Because he's a complete sap.

LINDA: I'm serious. I mean I can't explain why I don't fully love him, like other women love their husbands.

JACKSON: I should go down to the store.

LINDA: Can you just listen once?

JACKSON: Why are you telling me all this?

LINDA: Because you are my father. Mommy's too caught up in her sewing.

JACKSON: Why you married him?

LINDA: To get away from here. Maybe I did love him. I must've. I married him.

JACKSON: With all the money I spent, I hope to God there was some kind of feeling there.

LINDA: Could it be that I never got it to give? When I was a little girl I never really felt loved by you. You bought me things and that was fine for an hour or two, but I could never say that you actually took a minute of your time to give me a real fatherly hug, a caress, the warmth of a father.

JACKSON: (*Removes his feet and sits up.*) That's the way it is. I didn't write the book. Sons shall be loved by their fathers and daughters by their mothers.

LINDA: Who's book? Archie's comic book? The laws of Jughead?

JACKSON: Can't remember, it was so far back.

LINDA: I felt left out.

JACKSON: Why should you feel like that? You are part of this family.

LINDA: Daddy, don't you know anything except chaos?

JACKSON: I'm perfect. I didn't come to you for favors.

LINDA: Go ahead throw it in my face. I knew it was coming.

JACKSON: You threw it in mine! (EVA *enters the living room.*)

EVA: I'm all through. (*She walks over and takes a seat in one of the chairs.*) You see how nice and peaceful it is without the yelling. I was able to put all my things away without distraction. I hate to be distracted. I lose things when that happens. I end up putting them away and never finding them again. I must have a hidden treasure, hidden away somewhere among the lost. How I hate to lose something that's irreplaceable. I'm glad we're not poor, well not poor, poor. If I were, I'd be dreaming about all the things we have. If I were you, Linda, I would get a divorce. Find someone who will spend money on you, not you on him. You don't need a man who can't do for you. I told you he was no good for you. When I met Hector I could see he was one of those, the kind who doesn't care. It's plain to see, look at his eyes. They're small and he wears a moustache. It's men like that that never succeed. (JOE *enters from the hallway and finds a spot on the wall in the living room to lean on.*) Joe, you look like you need rest. Why don't you go upstairs and rest before I cut the birthday cake?

JOE: I just came from upstairs.

EVA: Then go back up. Sleep.

JOE: I'm fine. (*He pulls his gin out of his pocket.*)

EVA: I was telling Linda she should re-marry.

JOE: You should do the same. (*He unscrews the gin cap.*)

EVA: I can't, I'm married to your father.

JOE: And she's married to Hector. (*He takes a shot.*)

EVA: Somewhere I lost you.

JACKSON: Haven't we all?

LINDA: How old is Bobby now?

EVA: Last year he was eighteen, nineteen.

LINDA: What a shame.

EVA: Jackson, are you comfortable? You want a blanket?

JACKSON: Just fine. (LINDA *gets up and moves towards the bookcase.*)

EVA: What about tea? Piece of pie? I bought a nice lemon pie. Why don't you have a piece, Jackson?

JACKSON: I know where it is. (*He takes his box into the kitchen. LINDA turns on the radio to Latin music.*)

EVA: How about you, Joe?

JOE: I'm chilled.

EVA: Linda, you want pie?

LINDA: I don't eat before going to bed.

EVA: I don't blame you. You can have nightmares when you don't digest properly.

JACKSON: (*Sticks head out from kitchen.*) If you knew that, why did you offer me? (*He goes back in.*)

EVA: You didn't eat dinner. (LINDA *turns the radio up and dances in place. She moves out to the center of the living room, dancing to the beat. She goes up and grabs* JOE's *arm, he holds back,* LINDA *pulls him out until he gives in.* JOE *awkwardly dances with* LINDA *who can hold her own.* EVA *watches.* LINDA *then dances over to* EVA *and pulls her out of the chair,* EVA *shaking her head,* LINDA *insisting.* EVA *gives in as she dances a pachanga to the music. The music comes to an end.* JACKSON *enters the living room and makes his way over to the radio, he turns it off.* JOE *leans on the wall.* JACKSON *sits on the sofa.* EVA, *out of breath, nearly staggers over to a chair and sits.*)

LINDA: Too loud?

JACKSON: Yes.

EVA: (*Gaining her breath.*) Oh, my goodness, I'm so out of breath. I remember a time when I used to spend all my weekends with the girls from my job dancing at the Paladium. I met your father dancing there. He was a good dancer. All the women loved to dance with him. He would come to pick me up in his white Cadillac. We were the best dressed couple in the whole place. Oh and the bands, they were real good, very good. I used to always love to see Tito Rodriguez. Oh my God, he was so handsome, and his voice could melt many hearts. And for the mambo they had Tito Puente, Patato, Machito and Bobo. They would have us dancing all night. After we got married we went a few times, until I got pregnant with Joe, then we went less and less. And the store kept us away too. Jackson, maybe one day soon you can take me out to one of those dances again. I'll buy a new black dress with red heels, and a red bag to match the shoes. (JOE *sings into his bottle out of tune "Eleanor Rigby."*)

JOE: Eleanor Eva, picking the rice at the church where her wedding had been, all the lonely people, where do they all belong.

JACKSON: Hey, John Lennon, knock it off!

JOE: (*Agitated.*) You pushing me? (*He moves about the living room.*) You are pushing me!

JACKSON: Pushing you where? You drunk!

JOE: (*He moves about the living room.*) There, here, everywhere. I'm bouncing off the walls, rolling on the floor into corners and cracks. Spacing, man, nowhere, because of you. It's space man for me here, rolling and rolling around, the planets moving in the speed of light ready to burn out! I'm not burning out, man. Life is mellow yellow. (*He darts out into the hallway and disappears.*)

EVA: What was all that about?

JACKSON: You asking me?

EVA: I think it's the clothes. You have to get him new clothes. Clothes make a difference.

JACKSON: Nothing can help him. He's in space, you heard him.

EVA: I pray he lands some day.

JACKSON: Right on his ass.

LINDA: I'm going to see if he's all right.

EVA: Go ahead, Linda, and make sure he doesn't mess up the curtains, they're brand new. (LINDA *nods and exits.*) My poor kids.

JACKSON: Well who's at blame? It's all your fault.

EVA: How is it my fault?

JACKSON: You baby them too long. I told you it would ruin them.

EVA: Look, I did the best I could. I raised them while you were out there whoring with other women, don't tell me I never did a good job. They don't even know what kind of man I had to live with. Coming home drunk, abusing us. Don't put it all on me.

JACKSON: Let's drop this.

EVA: But you brought it up.

JACKSON: Well, now I just would like to drop it, forget it.

EVA: You never want to face the facts.

JACKSON: Facts? Huh. (*He takes a drink of beer.*)

EVA: The truth.

JACKSON: You want truth? I'll give you truth. Joe is an idiot. Linda spends all her time dancing in discos looking for her perfect man. And Bobby ...

EVA: You shut up! Don't you dare talk about Bobby.

JACKSON: I hope you don't ruin Anna.

EVA: You already did.

JACKSON: That's it. Leave me alone! Get out!

EVA: Oh, the truth hurts. It gets into your skin, right down to the blood, straight into your bones.

JACKSON: You evil, evil woman.

EVA: You made me like this, Jackson. I was never like this.

JACKSON: Whoa ... Give me a break, okay? I wouldn't have been in this predicament if it weren't for you and your voodoo friends—burning candles, putting garbage in my food.

EVA: It was one great loss of my money. If I would've known what kind of beast you were going to turn out to be, I would have never wasted my time.

JACKSON: (*Gets up, so does* EVA. *She moves far right as he moves towards the bookcase. He takes the rum and belts down a large swig.*) I should've walked out on you the first time you told me that lie.

EVA: What lie?

JACKSON: The time you told me you were pregnant.

EVA: I told you that four times.

JACKSON: Don't get smart Eva. You know what I'm talking about. Eight months after we met, one Fourth of July night.

EVA: I made up for it, didn't I?

JACKSON: You don't get the point, do you?

EVA: What point?

JACKSON: That you told me a lie, just so I would marry you.

EVA: I didn't want to lose you. I loved you. I let you touch me. I was never touched before. My friend, Tonia, she told me that once a man does what you did to me, they leave you. But I've told you this before.

JACKSON: Yeah, and my heart is still sad for you.

EVA: Jackson, I tried to make you the best wife a man could have, didn't I? (*No answer.*) I kept a lot of things in ... when I carried Linda ... and (*He grabs her head.*) the woman after woman you had ...

JACKSON: Lies!

EVA: You know it's true.

JACKSON: More lies!

EVA: Jackson, how many times have we argued about those women?

JACKSON: Crap.

EVA: I have proof.

JACKSON: Yeah, sure. (*He takes another drink.*) Proof, ha!

EVA: Letters, Jackson. Letters I've saved through the years. Just in case you would ever try to hurt me with a divorce. Letters and notes I found in your clothes.

JACKSON: Eva! For God's sake! Get outta here! (*He takes a drink.*) Get outta my face!

EVA: You want to deny it, fine, you wanna drink yourself into a stupor, okay.

JACKSON: Look, take you and your lying self outta my face. Now I see why you never had parents. Who the hell wants a liar!

EVA: Oh yeah! (*She darts into the bedroom.*)

JACKSON: And don't come back out, liar! (*He laughs.*) You looney bird! You tuna! Bobby, Bobby, where are you? (BOBBY *appears from the kitchen.*)

BOBBY: I'm here.

JACKSON: Talk to me, son. I need you to talk, ease my mind.

BOBBY: I don't want to get involved.

JACKSON: In what?

BOBBY: You and Mom.

JACKSON: But it concerns you.

BOBBY: Just the same.

JACKSON: Come on. (EVA *comes barging out.* BOBBY *disappears.* JACKSON *seems confused.* EVA *confronts him with a handful of letters and notes.*)

EVA: You see, you sonavabitch! (*She throws a letter at him.*) Pick it up! Pick the damn thing up. (*He leans down and picks the letter up, he pulls the letter out of the envelope.*) And I have more here from (*She reads off names.*) Carmen, Julia, Jenny, Sonia, Elba, Ray, Ray? (*To* JACKSON.) A letter from your brother. (*She tosses it at him.*) You kept yourself very busy through the years. (*She takes a seat.*) I never asked for much, just that you be a husband and a good father, that's all ... that's all. I brought them here into this world for you, for us, Jackson. (*He looks over at her.*) Set the memory free, bury the past, that's the way it should be. Not like a prisoner in a box.

JACKSON: No! Never! Never, never! (*He runs over to the box and cradles it.*) Get out! Out, out, out! (LINDA *enters from the hallway, excited.*)

EVA: What?

LINDA: It's Joe.

JACKSON: What happend to him?

LINDA: He's up there stroking the curtains and he's crying, Ma. I didn't know what to do. (EVA *moves into the bedroom. To* JACKSON.) I was up there all this time talking to him. Daddy, come upstairs and talk to him.

JACKSON: I can't.

LINDA: Daddy, please talk to him, I'm scared.

JACKSON: Linda, I can't go up there. Don't force me.

LINDA: What if he does what ...

JACKSON: No! Don't say it!

EVA: (*She exits out of the bedroom with water and a white candle.*) Where is Anna?

LINDA: With Joe. She's crying.

EVA: I don't want Anna to go through this again. Send her down.

.... SCENE FOUR ....

JACKSON: All the candles and water will never save anything around here. (*He grabs a hold of his head.*) Ahhh!

LINDA: Daddy.

JACKSON: Pounding, the boom, boom, boom.

LINDA: You want water or something? (*She turns into the kitchen.*)

JACKSON: It comes and goes. (*He checks to see if it's clear, then scoots into the bedroom.* ANNA *comes from upstairs and stands by the hallway with her doll.* JACKSON *comes out of the bedroom with a handful of letters and notes. He carefully hides them under his pillow and turns to see* ANNA. *She backs up and runs upstairs.* LINDA *comes out of the kitchen with a glass of orange juice.*)

LINDA: Daddy, you can't go on like this. You gotta go to a hospital. Get a thorough check up. (*The phone rings,* LINDA *goes for it. She hands him the juice.*)

JACKSON: You have to take it in the bedroom, the receiver doesn't work. (LINDA *darts into the bedroom for the final ring. Out to* LINDA.) I bet it's what's-his-name. (*He gets up with his box and tries to pull himself towards the hallway. He listens out. The lights dim as we see a flash back of* BOBBY *and* JOE. JACKSON *listens as* BOBBY *helps* JOE *with his poetry.*)

BOBBY: You got it Joe.

JOE: You think so?

BOBBY: Yeah. Let me hear it again.

JOE: (*He begins to read his poetry.*) Love. I gaze upon those sweet thighs, so soft, I wish they were mine. The form of your lips are for many to kiss, as I embrace you in my mind, I know you will never be mine, but I dream of the day when I can wisk you away. To my dome called love.

BOBBY: Listen, it's good. It needs a little work, but you have a general idea of what poetry is all about. And that's what counts.

JOE: Thank you, Bobby.

BOBBY: For what?

JOE: Well, for showing me the beauty in words. For taking time out to teach me how to read better than how I used to read.

BOBBY: Reading comes easy for some, hard for others. You happen to fall into the others.

JOE: The thing is Pop knew how hard it was for me in school. He didn't take the time to help me out with my problem.

BOBBY: You know how Pop is with his macho image. (JACKSON *enters.*) Hi, Dad.

JACKSON: (*Insulted.*) Don't Dad me. Wha', you didn't think I heard you talking about me? You thought I heard Joe with his faggoty poems that you taught 'im? Let me tell you something, I don't want that crap in my house.

JOE: Hey, Pop.

JACKSON: You shut up. You can't teach an idiot how to read. (JOE *lowers his head. To* BOBBY.) I'm warning you, Bobby, I don't want this in this house. You wanna recite about butterflies and flowers, then take that to those daffodil friends of yours.

BOBBY: I'm sorry you feel this way.

JACKSON: There is no sorrys or maybes 'round here. You're either male or female, 'cause I don't need that crap around here, around the girls. You understand?

BOBBY: Why are you so uptight about what I am? Maybe there is something hidden in you you're scared might come out. (JACKSON *hauls off and slaps him.* BOBBY *runs off,* JOE *runs off after him.* JACKSON *stares as the lights come back up and we see him in the present. He listens as* LINDA*'s voice carries. A blue light comes up behind* JACKSON. BOBBY *appears. A beat.*)

BOBBY: What are you doing?

JACKSON: (*Startled.*) Don't do that.

BOBBY: Do what?

JACKSON: Creep up on me like that.
BOBBY: I can't help it.
JACKSON: I'm sorry, I'm a little jittery.
BOBBY: Stop drinking.
JACKSON: Don't try to run my life.
BOBBY: You're unreasonable, I'm leaving.
JACKSON: Fine, go with the rest of the dead beats. (BOBBY *enters the hallway,* JACKSON *turns to him.*) No wait! I'm sorry. Bobby! Wait, Bobby!
LINDA: (*Enters the living room towards* JACKSON.) Daddy?
JACKSON: Yeah, what!
LINDA: I heard you calling for Bobby.
JACKSON: I was calling for your mother. (*He staggers back to the sofa.*) Was that who I thought it was?
LINDA: Hector?
JACKSON: Who else? (*He sits.*)
LINDA: Yes.
JACKSON: I don't want that jerk calling here anymore. You stay here, we'll have new rules. No jerks calling here.
LINDA: (*Moves slowly towards a chair.*) I'm going back home.
JACKSON: You gonna what? After you came to me with a sob story? I open my arms to you, give you my home? You're going back?
LINDA: I don't know what to do, Daddy. He's over there crying for me. I feel so bad. He's really not that bad.
JACKSON: Linda, I need you I'm a sick man.
LINDA: What about Mommy?
JACKSON: What can she do? Pour holy water on me, burn candles. Set my ass on fire.
LINDA: Daddy, he's my husband.
JACKSON: I'm your father.
LINDA: I know.
JACKSON: Is he more important than me?
LINDA: I never said that.
JACKSON: I never thought I would see the day you would stand in front of me like this.
LINDA: Like how?
JACKSON: Put some stranger in front of me.
LINDA: Daddy. (*She walks over towards him.*)
JACKSON: Stop where you are.
LINDA: (*She stops.*) Oh, come on, Dad.
JACKSON: Just remember who took care of you when you were a baby. Who fed you ...

LINDA: I know ...

JACKSON: Bought your clothes ...

LINDA: You're right.

JACKSON: Paid for your education ...

LINDA: All right!

JACKSON: What can he give you that I never gave you, huh?

LINDA: Love.

JACKSON: Wise up.

LINDA: I did.

JACKSON: Going back to him will make you dopey.

LINDA: I don't think so. Coming back here woke me up. There's nothing here for me anymore. (*The sound of* EVA *chanting as she gets closer.* EVA, ANNA *and* JOE *enter the living room.* EVA *with a lighted candle and smoking a cigar.* JOE, ANNA *walk behind, assisting with the sprinkling of Florida water.* EVA*'s evangelical maneuver echoes through the house as they move from wall to wall, then center.*)

EVA: In the name of the Lord, bless this home of evil!

JACKSON: You're the one who needs to be blessed.

EVA: Lord, take whatever evil there is away from us!

JACKSON: Do a Michael Jackson and beat it outta here!

EVA: Lord, listen to this sick man.

JACKSON: Yeah, listen to me, Lord!

EVA: Lord, deliver us from evil in the name of the Almighty Powers!

JACKSON: It's too late for you, nothing can help you.

EVA: Out! Out! Out! (*She shakes.*) Out!

JACKSON: A bunch of jerky nuts!

LINDA: Daddy, don't, it's not right to make fun.

EVA: I feel it! I feel it! Lord, in your powers help rid us of this man!

JACKSON: (*Pops up from the sofa with his tin box and moves towards* EVA. *She blows smoke in his face.*) Take that garbage outta my face!

EVA: Listen to him, Lord!

JACKSON: I'm warning you, Eva! So help me!

EVA: In the power invested in me I say out from here!

JACKSON: Joe! Get her outta here now!

LINDA: Daddy. She's not harming anyone.

JACKSON: She's on my nerves!

EVA: Bless my children! Bless Joe, Linda, Bobby and Anna!

JACKSON: So help me, you don't get outta here, I'll throw you out! You and the likes of you.

EVA: (*She blows smoke in* JACKSON's *face.*) Clean this man of
    his sickness!

JACKSON: (*He grabs the cigar from her mouth and the candle from*
    ANNA.) I warned you!

EVA: Sacrilege!

JACKSON: Sackmyass!

JOE: Give it back to her.

JACKSON: No!

EVA: I curse you seven times seven, may you be unhappy for the
    rest of your stinking life.

JACKSON: Oh, blow your cigar up your ass! (*He walks back over*
    to the sofa.)

EVA: (JOE *sits* ANNA *down, he goes over to* EVA *and puts his arm*
    around her.) Why, Joe, why does he do this to me?

JOE: Ma, don't let him get to you.

EVA: (*Upset.*) I did it to clean the house of evil. And for Bobby's
    birthday tonight. (EVA *enters the kitchen followed by* JOE.
    ANNA *looks on puzzled.*)

LINDA: (*Intense, walks over towards* JACKSON.) Big man. What
    a big man.

JACKSON: Don't get involved in this, Linda.

LINDA: That's my mother, whadaya mean!

JACKSON: This does not concern you, Linda.

LINDA: When you hurt Mommy it does.

JACKSON: Your mother is very ill upstairs.

LINDA: Oh bullshit!

JACKSON: (*He jumps up.*) Linda! I told you this is none of your
    business. Your business is with your wimpy husband.

LINDA: Before you were singing a different song.

JACKSON: That's right!

LINDA: I'm glad I don't live here anymore.

JACKSON: So what the hell you doing here?

LINDA: When I'm ready to go, I'll leave.

JACKSON: (*He waves her off.*) You're not worth it. (*He sits.*
    LINDA *stares at him.*) Keep looking at me!

LINDA: I'm trying to figure out how I ever got you for a father.

JACKSON: Look you, go take that look somewhere else. I mean
    it, tramp!

EVA: I heard what you called her!

JACKSON: Ah, shut up! Who's talking to you?

EVA: Linda, don't pay any attention. Come to the kitchen.

LINDA: No, I'm fine right here.

JACKSON: I think you better listen to her.

LINDA: I don't hear nothing! (*She shakes her hips.*)

JACKSON: Keep it up. (*She shakes her hips again. He lays the box down and jumps up from the sofa.*) Look at you, why don't you give me a little respect?

LINDA: I'll give you the same respect you gave Mommy.

JACKSON: Don't make me mad.

LINDA: Am I supposed to tremble?

EVA: Linda!

LINDA: What?!

EVA: Leave that man alone.

JACKSON: I'm not that man! I'm a husband around here. Don't you all forget that.

LINDA: What a husband.

JACKSON: I'm more of a husband than that worm you got.

LINDA: At least he's not a pig who abuses his wife!

JACKSON: You slut! (*He jumps up and slaps* LINDA.)

LINDA: You bastard! (EVA *hurries out of the kitchen with a birthday cake with lighted candles,* JOE *and* ANNA *are by her side.*) I hate you!

EVA: What happened! (*She sets the cake on top of a small table.*) Huh? What?

LINDA: (*Sobbing.*) He slapped me!

JOE: You hit her?

JACKSON: That's right. And I'll do it again.

EVA: Why don't you go out there and slap one of those women of yours.

JACKSON: Shut up, Eva.

EVA: No! I'm tired of it, damn it. I'm tired of you abusing my children every time you drink.

JACKSON: Quiet!

EVA: I won't. Look at him. You know why he's sick?

JACKSON: Eva.

EVA: It's all the women he runs around with. They never give him a break to rest. This is what I have to put up with. (*She begins to cry.*) Hiding it from you kids, making him look like a saint. (*She breaks down.*) I'm so tired. (JOE *tries to comfort her, she pulls away.*) You sonavabitch! I would've left you a long time ago, if I had a family to go to. Because of you I don't know what to do. You always had me in the house with babies, cooking and cooking! I hate it! I hate you and your lies!

LINDA: (*Sobbing.*) What's she talking about?

JACKSON: The lady is nuts. She doesn't know what she's talking about. Joe, look at her, she's a sick woman. Linda, you know your mother's sick. (JOE *and* LINDA *are lost as they blankly stare at* EVA.) You see, look at her, she needs our help.

EVA: I don't need anyone's help. (*She feels taken.*) I like the way you turn things around.

JACKSON: I don't know what you're talking about Eva?

JOE: Ma, maybe you need rest?

EVA: I don't. I don't! (*She folds her arms as she searches through her mind.*) He knows.

JOE: Knows what, Ma?

EVA: He knows what he's done to me.

JOE: Me, let me put you to bed. (*He walks over, she backs away.*)

EVA: No! All of you are trying to run me crazy. I know it.

JOE: Ma, no.

EVA: But I can prove it.

JACKSON: You're tired, Eva, go lay down.

EVA: (*To* JACKSON.) You started all this!

LINDA: Ma, calm down.

EVA: Wait you want proof? (*She swiftly moves into the bedroom.*)

LINDA: I can't take this. All of this is driving me insane.

JACKSON: (*To* JOE.) Now you know what I've been going through. (*He moves in between* JOE *and* LINDA.) Eva, are you all right?

JOE: Ma!

EVA: (*She breaks to the bedroom entrance and braces herself tearfully.*) Where are they, Jackson?

JACKSON: Where is what?

EVA: You know what. I can't find them.

JACKSON: Eva, what the hell are you talking about? You got me confused here.

EVA: The letters, notes!

JACKSON: This woman is disturbed, demented.

EVA: You're trying to erase the truth. Driving me to insanity.

JOE: Ma, please cut it out.

EVA: You're taking his side, aren't you?

JOE: I'm not on nobody's side.

EVA: (*Grabs her head.*) There were letters. I put them there myself. He saw them.

JACKSON: I never saw nothing.

EVA: You did, you did! (*Enters back into the bedroom.* JACKSON *follows and stands by the entrance.*)

JACKSON: Eva, will you please cut these childish games?

EVA: Where are they! (ANNA, *getting up, moves towards the sofa and reaches under the pillow.* JACKSON, *catching a glimpse of* ANNA *yells out.*)

JACKSON: Get away from there you! (ANNA, *frightened, screams, dropping the letters on the floor.* EVA *scrambles out of the bedroom.* JOE, LINDA, JACKSON *and* EVA *make a dash towards* ANNA *and the letters.* LINDA *takes* ANNA *in her arms to calm her.* JOE *picks up a handful of letters.*) Put 'em back, Joe!

EVA: No, read them! (*She leans down and sifts through the letters as* JOE *reads. She hands* JOE *a special one.*) I got that one in 1972 from the Board of Health.

JACKSON: (*Setting the box down, goes over and snatches the letters out of* EVA's *hand.*) You call yourself a wife, a mother, gimme that, Joe. (*He staggers over to* JOE. JOE *backs away.*) Come on, Joe.

JOE: (*Throws the letter at* JACKSON's *face.*) You're worse than scum!

JACKSON: Don't talk to me like that, I'm your father!

JOE: (*As he walks about and around* JACKSON.) Mr. Almighty, Mr. Clean, cleaner than clorox bleach. The rigid man. My persecutor, our example. The man of conscience, the tyrant. You put that poor woman into hysterics to save your soul. Damn you! While you lived a life of filth and lust. You are a sad man. Mr. Jackson Vega.

JACKSON: (*Raising his hand.*) Cut it, Joe!

JOE: No! (*He walks up to* JACKSON.) You wanna hit me! You had me believe that you were concerned about her, about us. (JACKSON *brings his hand down.*) You had the nerve to ask me why she was acting strange. Man, can't you see! You drove her that way. Are you too dumb to know why, hasn't it penetrated yet? (JACKSON *backs up.*) Don't back away from me! (*He pokes him.* JACKSON *stops.*) You've hurt us all. Poor Anna can't talk because of your drunken ways.

JACKSON: It was an accident. I slipped on the stairs carrying her. She fell out of my arms.

JOE: But you were drunk! And what about Bobby! We all know you killed him!

JACKSON: Noooo!

JOE: Yes!

JACKSON: Not true! (*He grabs his head.*)

JOE: You killed him when you put him out in the street because he had AIDS. You let him die homeless in the street, like a stray dog. (LINDA *goes over to* EVA, *who is embracing herself.*)

JACKSON: (*He lets out a wail as he falls to his knees.*) Please, please, no more. (*He sobs.* ANNA *picks up the tin box and opens it.*)

JOE: You're nothing but a big lie! (ANNA *walks slowly with the box open towards* JACKSON *as* EVA, LINDA *and* JOE *watch.* ANNA *pours the ashes on the floor in front of* JACKSON. *He gives out a loud wail.* ANNA *runs to* JOE's *side.*)

JACKSON: Noooooo!!! What have you done!

JOE: Dreams, Pop, just dreams. You can't hold on to something that's not there.

JACKSON: No, no, no, no! (*He tries in vain to scoop it up.*) Oh, Bobby, Bobby!

JOE: (*Yells out.*) Bobby, you got 'im on his hands and knees. I wish you could see him!

JACKSON: (*He slowly look up.*) Get out of my house now! All of you, get the hell outta here! I don't need any of you. (JOE, ANNA *walk over to* LINDA *and* EVA.) I said get out! (*He rubs ashes on his face.*)

JOE: (*To* LINDA.) Can you go back home?

LINDA: Yes.

JOE: You have room for us?

LINDA: I'll make room.

JOE: Let's go, Ma.

EVA: My clothes, what about my things?

JOE: Material, Ma, just material. (*While* JACKSON *sobs on his knees,* JOE *takes* ANNA *by the hand and leads* EVA *and* LINDA *out. As they begin to exit,* ANNA *pulls away and makes a run for her doll that's propped up in one of the chairs. She hurries out looking back at* JACKSON.)

JACKSON: (*Looks up.*) I don't need you! You need me! (EVA, LINDA, ANNA *and* JOE *exit through the kitchen. A beat, then* BOBBY *appears from the hallway.*) Bobby! Oh, Bobby! (JACKSON *points to the ashes,* BOBBY *looks down at the ashes.*) Gone.

BOBBY: Soon it'll turn to dust.

JACKSON: Bobby, why, why?

BOBBY: You planned it that way, with your bickering, pettiness and your myopic view of your own stinking little world. (*He starts to walk out.*)

JACKSON: Where ya going?

BOBBY: With Mom, it's late.

JACKSON: Why?

BOBBY: I have to.

JACKSON: Do you?

BOBBY: I do.

JACKSON: You going to leave me alone?

BOBBY: Dad, you've always been alone. (BOBBY *exits through the kitchen.*)

JACKSON: Don't leave me, come back! (*He folds his arms and rocks as he bites his lip, fighting back the tears. The boyishness comes out of him.*) Don't leave me here alone in the dark. I'll be good. I promise. I won't do it again. I'll be nice. Let me out, I won't hit. (*Lights come to a slow fade as he curls up into a fetal position.*)

Ariano

by

Richard V. Irizarry

Characters

ARIANO, a Puerto Rican man in his early thirties. Extremely charming and intelligent. His good looks are icing on the cake. He has legitimate businesses, real estate, as well as a numbers operation. He is definitely upward-scale. His wings, however, are made of wax.

DOLORES, Ariano's wife. She is a nurse and also in her early thirties. Blindly in love (obsessed?) with her husband. She shares her husband's better qualities. She loves her son Serafín, very, very much.

SERAFÍN, Ariano's son. He is eight. He is fragile and somewhat intimidated by his father, who keeps sending mixed signals as to the shape of their relationship. He loves his mother dearly, but it is his father who holds the emotional key.

CLARA, Dolores' closest friend. She will frequently hold a lighted match to Ariano's "wings." Very independent, she has made an impressive career as a fashion designer. Her close relationship with Serafín is such that he calls her "Titi" (Aunt). She lives in Ariano's brownstone, below them.

CRYSTAL, the woman that Ariano has paid to have his child. She is a free spirit, very sharp and very independent. Unlike Dolores, she takes no crap from Ariano. Crystal is very attractive, but more importantly, she is a blond and she is blue-eyed.

DOÑA HERNÁNDEZ, she has seen Ariano grow from a child to a man. Ariano's mother's was her best friend. She made a deathbed promise to watch over Ariano, guide him. She is lively and sharp and traditional in her thoughts and deeds. She is in her early sixties.

SOLDIER, Ariano's "go-fer." He enjoys the money and prestige that comes from being associated with Ariano, yet he is very jealous. A punk, he'd probably be more dangerous as an adult, had he the brains necessary to live that long.

Notes on Casting

Ariano is a play that deals with the racial ambiguities and prejudices that are rife within the Puerto Rican community. It is suggested, then, that in casting this play an effort be made to reflect "the rainbow" that is the Puerto Rican. Ideally, and in keeping with the logic of the play, Doña Hernandez should be the "lightest-skinned" of all the characters. Ariano should be somewhat light-skinned, with Dolores a bit darker. Serafín should be the darkest of the group. Clara should also be light-skinned and Soldier should be equally as ambiguous.

Notes on Dialogue

The use of Spanish throughout the play should not intimidate a monolingual audience, as no information is lost in not being a Spanish-speaker. The Spanish merely echoes or repeats the English phrase it is associated with. This is how the New York Puerto Rican communicates and fuses both cultures.

ACT ONE

.... SCENE ONE ....

At rise, the stage is in complete darkness. Dissonant music is heard. Lights up slowly on the sleeping ARIANO. He is slumped over his desk. He mumbles. His sleep is restless. He fidgets as if in the throes of a nightmare.

ARIANO awakens with a sudden start. He seems terrified, disoriented. Lights up full reveal that he is in a laundromat and that he is not alone. DOÑA HERNÁNDEZ hovers over him, concerned. Synchronically with ARIANO's awakening, the dissonant music dissolves into an old Puerto Rican bolero that comes from a radio on ARIANO's desk.

ARIANO's laundromat is a small modern space that is equipped with the latest hardware. The off-white walls take on a sickening glow from the rows of white, fluorescent lighttubes on the ceiling. The floor is done in a checker-board pattern of black and white tiles. On the back wall is a large colorful map of the island of Puerto Rico. A potted palm stands underneath. ARIANO's desk sits in a corner in a makeshift office he has set up.

ARIANO is dressed in an expensive, European grey suit. The jacket is placed over the back of his chair. He has a white shirt with a perfectly coordinated tie. His shirt-sleeves are rolled up, revealing an expensive watch. DOÑA HERNÁNDEZ is always dressed simply but traditionally feminine.

ARIANO: Serafiiiin!

DOÑA HERNÁNDEZ: *M'ijo, ¿qué?* It's only a dream. You had a bad dream! (*ARIANO is still shaken. He looks around and then at her. He takes her hand.*)

ARIANO: Wooo! (*Beat.*) Wow! Did I fall asleep on you, Doña? (*Beat.*) I'm so sorry.

DOÑA HERNÁNDEZ: (*Interrupting.*) Ay, sorry for what, Ariano? Come on!

ARIANO: I feel embarrassed.

DOÑA HERNÁNDEZ: (*Laughing.*) You'll live.

ARIANO: (*Distant.*) Yeah. I guess I will. (*There is a long uneasy silence.*)

DOÑA HERNÁNDEZ: That bad, eh?

ARIANO: It'll go away. It's only a dream.

DOÑA HERNÁNDEZ: (*Interrupting.*) Did you see falling teeth?

ARIANO: No.

DOÑA HERNÁNDEZ: White horses?

ARIANO: (*Amused.*) No. No white horses either.

DOÑA HERNÁNDEZ: (*Crossing herself.*) You're safe then. No death! (*Pause.*)

ARIANO: I dreamt with Serafín. (DOÑA HERNÁNDEZ *lets out a sigh of frustration and walks away. But she cannot refrain from commenting for more than two seconds.*)

DOÑA HERNÁNDEZ: You know something? ¿Sabes qué? (*Beat.*) NO! (DOÑA HERNÁNDEZ *gives herself a light slap across her mouth.*) Deja quedarme callada. Min' my own business.

ARIANO: DOÑAAAAAAAAAAAA!

DOÑA HERNÁNDEZ: Why say anything? You must like torturing yourself, pues sigueeeee.

ARIANO: They were bothering him in that school again.

DOÑA HERNÁNDEZ: And that's your fault?

ARIANO: Maybe I shouldn't have changed him ...

DOÑA HERNÁNDEZ: (*Interrupting.*) Ahhhhh! Ahora llegaste.

ARIANO: It's an excellent private school! The best!

DOÑA HERNÁNDEZ: Oh siiii! ¡Siiiii! Muy "high-fidelity" que tiene que ser, me supongo.

ARIANO: He deserves that much from me at least!

DOÑA HERNÁNDEZ: A-hah. Y te apuesto que he's the only Puertorriqueño in the whole school right?

ARIANO: There's another kid who's black. Serafín says they pick on him too.

DOÑA HERNÁNDEZ: ¡Pues seguuuuuro! For them it's all the same: black, Puerto Rican. ¡Hasta los chinos meten ellos! No, no, no, es que in those schools, lo que hay son un chorro de racists! They all prejudice.

ARIANO: Ay, I don't know what to do ya.

DOÑA HERNÁNDEZ: Y total, es ignorancia, ignorance! If they only knew—m'ijo, you come from the whitest town on that island, el pueblo más blanco que viene siendo San Sebastián! Okay? El Pepino tiene gente rubia, red hair, blue eyes—look at your mother. ¡Una mujer blanca, elegante! Claro, es un poco racista también y come mierda, stuck-up! What's wrong con estos americanos es que they all think we're black. Prieto!

ARIANO: Thank God, Mommy's not around to see any of this shit.

DOÑA HERNÁNDEZ: No. She's not around, que en paz descanse, but I am! And I am sure that she is very relaxed in heaven, knowing that I'm here watching over you. I told you from the beginning, when all this started, leave things the way they are. No te vuelvas loco, don't go crazy. Things will work themselves out for the best. They always do. Did you listen? No! Right away you change Serafín's school, buying him things like crazy, you redecorate your house—Dolores is going to get suspicious. She's not stupid. Esa sí que no es bruta.

ARIANO: Yes, Ma-Ma! (DOÑA HERNÁNDEZ *slaps him softly over the head, then kisses the spot.*)

DOÑA HERNÁNDEZ: (*Echoing.*) Yes, Mama? Hmmpht! ¡Hazme caso! Listen to me and you won't go wrong. ¡Porfiao! (DOÑA HERNÁNDEZ *returns to her laundry, inspecting it as she speaks.*) Qué jurutungo, tanta confusión. Your generation—I don't understand. Always so confused, tanta mierda ... y hablando de mierda ... (DOÑA HERNÁNDEZ *picks out a pair of underwear that she holds up to the light.*) ¡Y sigue con las jodías manchas! ¡Ay, dame paciencia Padre Celestial!

ARIANO: What's the matter?

DOÑA HERNÁNDEZ: I love him dearly! But if that husband of mine doesn't hurry up and drop dead soon, then I will!

ARIANO: Oooooh! Sounds serious.

DOÑA HERNÁNDEZ: You know, Ariano, I look at you. "Now there goes a clean man," I say to myself. Immaculate looks. You take care of yourself, you have pride. Anyone can tell just by looking at you that you are a man who keeps his underwear clean. You don't have to answer sí, I already know the answer. (DOÑA HERNÁNDEZ *continues inspecting all the underwear she can find.*) All the same! Look! Look! I get tired, uno se cansa! Sixty-two years old y mira, still scrubbing shit stains out from underwear. I am sure that this was not my intended destiny, pero quizás, cuando uno nace para ser bestia ...

ARIANO: You're not an animal. Stop saying that!

DOÑA HERNÁNDEZ: Don't get me wrong. Juancho is a clean man. Yes, my husband has always been very clean. Decir lo contrario sería mentir. He combs his hair, brushes his teeth, puts cologne, pero este viejito, ay bendito! He's

old. He loses control sometimes. (*Beat*.) ¡Pues, qué puede
hacer uno? Seguir con mi cruz ¿verdad? ¡Eso es todo!

ARIANO: Come on. It's not that bad. Just put them through
again.

DOÑA HERNÁNDEZ: Ooooh! Es que I have to! No tengo reme-
dio. He won't put them on like this. ¡Me los bota! (DO-
ÑA HERNÁNDEZ *starts pouring all amounts of detergent
into the machine. She is, as usual, exaggerating.*) Oh no!
He wants the super whiteness and the super brightness
like on T.V.! If not, olvídate, un escándalo. ¡Se enciende!
¡Dime tú si ese viejo no es un listo! I'll be goddammed
if I'm going to spend half of my social security on underwear para el viejo zángano ese! (DOÑA HERNÁNDEZ
now takes the bleach and empties it into the machine.) Pu-
rity is pain!

ARIANO: ¡Doña!

DOÑA HERNÁNDEZ: ¡Qué diantre! Que se le sancoche. He
don't need them anymore anyway.

ARIANO: Bendito Doña. De verdad, you want que Juancho es-
tire la pata ya? (*A danza comes on over the radio and
ARIANO exploits the opportunity to distract DOÑA HER-
NÁNDEZ's temper. He begins to dance with her.*)

DOÑA HERNÁNDEZ: Of course, I don't want him dead. Pero
que no se cague encima, concho.

ARIANO: (*Laughing.*) Ay, Doña. You kill me, you know that?
You are too much.

DOÑA HERNÁNDEZ: Ssssshhh! I want to hear the music. (A-
RIANO *and* DOÑA HERNÁNDEZ *dance a few seconds.*
DOÑA HERNÁNDEZ'S *mind is traveling backwards. She
sighs.*) Ay, Ariano. Los tiempos de antes. Those times
are gone forever. (*She stops abruptly. She is choking back
tears.*) Ya, ya, pues ...

ARIANO: What's wrong? Heeey ... ¿Qué pasa?

DOÑA HERNÁNDEZ: Na', m'ijo, na' ... perdón. (*She laughs
nervously, reassuringly.*)

ARIANO: Doña ...

DOÑA HERNÁNDEZ: Too far back. Too many memories.
(*Pause.*) Still there. (*Pause.*) Forty years in this country y mira, aquí lo tengo ... right here. (*She points to her
gut.*) ¡Maldita sea esa jodía isla!

ARIANO: Hey, hey. Come on. You know you don't mean that.
Doña? (*Beat.*) You know, the first time I went ... God!
That island! (*Beat.*) I was only ten. Just me and Mommy

together. We got there at 4 a.m. The KI-KI-RI-KI special!
I had never seen Mom so nervous. Pa' decirte, she even
threw a small peíto getting off the plane.

DOÑA HERNÁNDEZ: ¡Ay, fo!

ARIANO: ¡De verdad! I opened my eyes wide y a toa' boca I said,
"MOMMY!" "Sssshhh!" she whispered. "Cállate! Es que
estoy nerviosa. I'm nervous!" She played it off so cool.

DOÑA HERNÁNDEZ: Ay, cómo se recuerda de su mama, bendito. (DOÑA HERNÁNDEZ *then kisses him on top of
the head.* ARIANO *is too involved in the memory to miss
a beat.*)

ARIANO: We didn't even stop at the hotel first. She made the cab
driver stop at the first stretch of beach we passed. She
grabbed my hand and made a bee-line for the water! She
had to drag me, practically, 'cause I was so scared. Hell,
it was pitch black! Do you know that she left me there!
She let go of my hand and kept running herself. "¡Vente!"
she cried out. "Come on!"

DOÑA HERNÁNDEZ: And you just stayed there! Cabeciduro
como siempre. Stubborn!

ARIANO: Hell no! I ran right after her. (*Beat.*) I could hear her
splashing in the water. (*Pause.*) I ran towards her voice
until I reached her. She started splashing me, she was
laughing. Then she dunked me. I freaked out, you know.
I said, whoa, what's up? Mom stopped laughing. She was
looking at me now. Serious. Even in the dark I could see
her face because she was so close. She was trying not to cry
but I knew she wanted to. Then she started taking sand
from under the water and she started rubbing me all over
with it: my face, my arms, my hair. "This, this is yours.
This is where we come from!" Then she held me. And I
held her. And we both started crying como dos pendejos.
(DOÑA HERNÁNDEZ *pulls* ARIANO *into her arms and
caresses him gently.*)

DOÑA HERNÁNDEZ: Some children only get toys, bicycles, ra-
dios. What a lucky young man you were, to get a whole
island!

ARIANO: (*Elated.*) Oh, Doña! It was the most beautiful thing I
had ever seen. Green palms. A blue sky ... bluer than
any I'd ever seen, with water to match! And that yellow,
yellow sun! Always in the sky! Always warm! (ARIANO*'s
mood becomes one of anger.*) Somebody lied to me, Doña.
Somebody had let me believe for all those years that the

world was ugly. And I cried plenty of times because I felt I was part ... of that ... ugliness ... my God ... the dreams ... Serafín ...

DOÑA HERNÁNDEZ: (*Interrupting.*) Nah, nah, nah. Ssssshhhh!

ARIANO: But don't you see? The dreams ... It's the same thing.

DOÑA HERNÁNDEZ: We went through that already. Vamos, vente. Dance. ¡Baila conmigo ven!

ARIANO: This place is bad, Doña.

DOÑA HERNÁNDEZ: Ay, m'ijo. Think only good thoughts. Forget all that.

ARIANO: It makes you do strange things. (*They dance a short while, working through the melancholy and beginning to enjoy themselves. A young Puerto Rican boy appears at the door, unnoticed by either* ARIANO *or* HERNÁNDEZ. *He is manicure-neat in appearance, but defiantly in the street mode of fashion. His hair is blown back straight and sprayed into place. He carries a large and loud radio. The boy looks on cynically. He suddenly gets the idea that it is his duty to liven things up a bit and he clicks on the radio, which is already fixed at an ear-shattering decible. The music is pure conga, timbales and drums. It swallows the dulcid tones of* ARIANO's *danza while scaring both* DOÑA HERNÁNDEZ *and* ARIANO.) Shut that off, goddammit! (SOLDIER *obliges after a challenging two or three seconds. He laughs hysterically.*)

SOLDIER: Yo, bee. Hittin' on the viejas too?

DOÑA HERNÁNDEZ: ¿A quién tú llamas vieja?

ARIANO: Apologize now!

DOÑA HERNÁNDEZ: ¡Contéstame, pila 'e mierda! Who you calling "old lady?"

SOLDIER: (*Laughing.*) Yo, chill! Don't take it so personal. It was a joke. (ARIANO *goes to* SOLDIER *and takes the radio.* SOLDIER *resists at first but surrenders, knowing better.*) When I leave I'm taking it! (DOÑA HERNÁNDEZ *returns to her laundry.*)

DOÑA HERNÁNDEZ: Estos zánganos que vienen de la calle ni saben limpiarse el fondillo y quieren faltarle el respeto a uno.

ARIANO: I told you to apologize.

SOLDIER: All right, all right! (*Beat.*) Hey, señora ... (DOÑA HERNÁNDEZ *looks at him.*) Sorry, okay?

DOÑA HERNÁNDEZ: (*Calmly.*) Go to hell.

SOLDIER: Yo! What be with the females today? Damn! First I
    got my mom poppin' junk all up in my face, then I go
    to your lady's crib and she start's breaking my hump ...
    and yeah, by the way, Crystal said she needs some bucks
    quick, so I don't know, it's up to you. (SOLDIER *goes to*
    ARIANO *'s desk and commences with his irritating habit*
    of playing with whatever is on it. ARIANO *did not like*
    the reference to CRYSTAL.) So Arrie ... What you think
    about the hair, bee?
ARIANO: What happened to the 'fro?
SOLDIER: (*Irked.*) Curls, my man. I got good hair. I ain't no
    cocolo kinks, like some people.
ARIANO: (*Interrupting.*) If you got some business for me then get
    to it! If you don't ...
SOLDIER: What's all this hostility, bro? (SOLDIER *puts his arm*
    around ARIANO*'s shoulder.* ARIANO *shrugs it off and*
    SOLDIER *plays the rejection off very cooly.*) Come on,
    for real. What you think about the new look?
ARIANO: What was the matter with the old one?
SOLDIER: Shiiiiit! The old one was P.R.! This here new shit be
    G.Q.! And this is just the beginning!
ARIANO: Whatever you say.
SOLDIER: Naw! Word up! I noticed the diff'rence. People look
    at me diff'rent now. I'd be gettin' all these hostile looks
    before. People bein' scared a me an' shit, thinkin' I was
    prob'bly gonna rip 'em off. But now, now brothaaa, I'm
    accessible! (ARIANO *laughs.*) Serious man, that's what
    this chick on the train told me yesterday. Ooooooh, Arrie!
    Una rubia down, boy. She almost be lookin' as good as
    Crystal, 'cept she ain't got no belly. (*He laughs.*) Blue eyes
    and fine. She said she never went out with a Spanish guy
    before ...
DOÑA HERNÁNDEZ: (*Interrupting.*) Puerto Rican!
SOLDIER: Yo, like that's what she meant!
ARIANO: Soldier!
SOLDIER: Nah, nah, wait up! Lookit what she tol' me. See, this is
    why I know my new look is on the money. She said that
    the reason she never dated any Spanish dudes before is
    because we all be lookin' like thugs an' shit, that I, listen
    to this, I could pass for Italian. Hah? Hah? (SOLDIER
    is thoroughly convinced this is the story and that he is the
    biggest macho out there. He whoops it up accordingly.)
    Well?

ARIANO: You collect any money for me today? (*There is a short silence.*)

SOLDIER: Your shit's weak, you know that, right?

ARIANO: Your brain is weak. (ARIANO *retrieves all the slips from the envelope.*) What's this?

SOLDIER: Some truck killed Rivera's dog up the block. Everybody's playin' the plate number.

ARIANO: 393, 393, 393. ¡Carajo! If that number hits, me jodí! (DOÑA HERNÁNDEZ *reaches into her bra, takes out a few dollars and hands them to* ARIANO.)

DOÑA HERNÁNDEZ: Here. For me.

ARIANO: 393?

DOÑA HERNÁNDEZ: I loved that dog just as much as anybody.

ARIANO: Andale pa'l infierno. Chelsea wants to break their banquero, it seems.

SOLDIER: Yo. I gotta book. You gonna give me the money or what? (ARIANO *pulls out a fifty and hands it to him.*) Crystal said at least a hundred, bee ... (ARIANO *bolts up and grabs* SOLDIER *by the neck, pushing him into a corner.*) Don't be touchin' me, homeboy!

ARIANO: I oughta break your little faggot ass!

SOLDIER: I don't want no lecture.

ARIANO: If you had half a brain I'd consider wasting the energy.

SOLDIER: Let me straighten you out, papito. I get paid to do pickups and drops, not to bring messages from your corteja!

ARIANO: If you like my money in your pockets, then you do whatever the fuck I tell you to do, homeboy! (SOLDIER *tries to play it off with a shrug and a weak laugh.*) And the next time I hear you call Crystal my mistress, for that matter, any time I hear my business coming out of your mouth ... you're a good employee, Soldier. I'd hate to lose you. (ARIANO *pulls out a wad of cash.*) Give me the fifty I gave you, G.Q.! (SOLDIER *complies.*) Here's a hundred. That's for you. Maybe you cool yourself down a bit. This one's for Crystal. That's what she asked for, right? (SOLDIER *nods.*) See you tomorrow.

SOLDIER: Can I get my box? (ARIANO *motions to it and* SOLDIER *retrieves it. He exits.*) Later. (*No sooner does* SOLDIER *exit than* DOÑA HERNÁNDEZ *swoops down.*)

DOÑA HERNÁNDEZ: What are you doing with that garbage? You can't get anyone better to work for you?

ARIANO: He knows the streets.

DOÑA HERNÁNDEZ: He knows a lot of other things too, I see.

ARIANO: He won't talk ...

DOÑA HERNÁNDEZ: M'ijo! Information is power. He'll talk when he thinks it can get him some of it. ¿Qué te pasa? Don't you think about these things?

ARIANO: Crystal has gotten close to him. She sends him for stuff. It's easier on me.

DOÑA HERNÁNDEZ: His kind is what gives us a bad name. They're stupid! They don't know what to do with themselves. You think he'd be smart enough to want to follow in your footsteps, but no! They want to be bums! Títeres de la calle. That's why Juancho and me never had any. Que Dios me perdone, but it's the truth. I would have killed them myself first before I let the street take them from me.

ARIANO: Believe me, he's more bark than bite. He's not gonna say anything.

DOÑA HERNÁNDEZ: I'll talk to Crystal. She probably doesn't know a thing about him.

ARIANO: Don't talk to Crystal.

DOÑA HERNÁNDEZ: She listens to me. Unlike some people.

ARIANO: Don't, really.

DOÑA HERNÁNDEZ: (*Suspicious.*) What? What is it? Tell me.

ARIANO: Nothing.

DOÑA HERNÁNDEZ: ¡Mentira! Don't lie to me Ariano.

ARIANO: (*Laughing.*) Nada. Nothing!

DOÑA HERNÁNDEZ: She don't like me, right? No le caigo bien ¿verdad?

ARIANO: (*Still laughing.*) Nothing like that.

DOÑA HERNÁNDEZ: No, si yo me lo imaginaba. People don't appreciate anything these days. You try to be nice ... Americana, al fin.

ARIANO: It's just the food. She doesn't like Puerto Rican food and she says you always bring her some and then make her eat it.

DOÑA HERNÁNDEZ: She has to eat! ¿Qué le pasa a la pendeja seca esa?

ARIANO: Calm down. It's no big deal.

DOÑA HERNÁNDEZ: That baby is half Puerto Rican. Tell her that! Remind her. He needs to eat food! ¡Arroz! ¡Habichuelas! Not that lettuce and carrots y mierda que se jartan esos gringos.

ARIANO: Once he's mine, you can give him all the rice and beans you can cook, okay, abuela? (ARIANO *gives her a big*

hug. After a pause.)
DOÑA HERNÁNDEZ: Ay, Ariano. A veces pienso ...
ARIANO: (*Interrupting.*) Please don't.
DOÑA HERNÁNDEZ: Es que ...
ARIANO: I need you to be strong for me, Doña. I'm walking on
    egg shells as it is.
DOÑA HERNÁNDEZ: Oyeme, oye. I know better than anyone
    how much Dolores loves you. More than I have known
    any woman to love any man.
ARIANO: I love her too. You think I don't love her?
DOÑA HERNÁNDEZ: Escúchame. Calma, calma. (*Pause.*) You
    want this child. He's everything you've ever wanted. But
    do you think Dolores is going to accept him into her
    home?
ARIANO: I've thought about that. Don't you think I've thought
    about that?
DOÑA HERNÁNDEZ: Ese nene va a salir blanquito. He's going
    to be white, no doubt. How do you think Dolores is going
    to respond. Ella es una trigueñita bastante fina, her fea-
    tures are white, pero still she is going to resent what she
    couldn't give you.
ARIANO: Which is why I have decided to leave. (*There is a stun-
    ning silence.*)
DOÑA HERNÁNDEZ: (*Quietly.*) What?
ARIANO: It's the best thing for us both. Start new lives. I've been
    looking at some property over in Connecticut. A lot of
    good opportunities over there.
DOÑA HERNÁNDEZ: I'll never see you. Or the baby.
ARIANO: I'll visit. You'll visit. Nothing will change.
DOÑA HERNÁNDEZ: It's not the same.
ARIANO: (*Interrupting.*) I can't put Dolores through that. (*Pause.*)
    And I can't back down from the kid either. It's too late.
    Maybe a couple of months ago ... but then a couple of
    months ago I was sure and now ... I don't know! All I do
    know is that just because I'm all screwed up doesn't mean
    my family has to suffer. She's better off and so is Serafín.
DOÑA HERNÁNDEZ: No, no, you're wrong. They need you.
    You need them. This wasn't supposed to happen.
ARIANO: Oh yeah? And what was? Can you tell me that? Now
    who's being stubborn?
DOÑA HERNÁNDEZ: But, you have so much to lose. Your busi-
    ness, all your property. You can't go. I saw Dolores the

other day. She was with Serafín. (*Lights up on* DO-
LORES *and* SERAFÍN. DOLORES *is preparing a meal
while* SERAFÍN *sits at the table doing homework.*) Oh,
Ariano, you should have seen how the whole block just
glowed as they walked past. ¡Esa mulata orgullosa con su
hijito al lao! Proud to be Mrs. Ariano Moreno. Proud to
have his son.

ARIANO: That's not fair, Doña. You're not helping things any.

DOÑA HERNÁNDEZ: It's not fair to us. We all love you here.
That baby can't mean that much, to give it all up!

ARIANO: Good night, Doña. And stop worrying please. It'll
all work out. Ten fe en Dios. Isn't that what you always tell me? Have faith? Well, I do. And I need to
have it too. Okay? (ARIANO *gives a very upset* DOÑA
HERNÁNDEZ *a big reassuring hug and kiss. Lights slowly
fade on them. Lights full up on* DOLORES *and* SERAFÍN.
*The apartment is in the process of being renovated. A step
ladder sits over in one corner with a few cans of white paint
on the rungs. A large tarpaulin, also white, covers furniture. A track light lies on the mantle. Also on the mantle
is a large portrait set in a guilded frame. It is wrapped
in clear plastic as is a small but expensive chandelier that
hangs over the dining table. Thousands are being spent on
this renovation.* DOLORES *wears a nurse's uniform while*
SERAFÍN *is in his school uniform shirt and pants. His
tie hangs loosely around his neck and his academy jacket
hangs on the back of his chair.* SERAFÍN *continues doing
his homework while* DOLORES *cooks.*)

SERAFÍN: (*Writing.*) I am a Puer-to Ri-can. From Puer-to-Rico.
We speak Span-ish and En-glish too.

DOLORES: (*Over his shoulder.*) Writing a report? (SERAFÍN *covers up his work.*)

SERAFÍN: Don't look! Don't look! I'm not finished yet.

DOLORES: (*Covering her eyes.*) Okay, okay! I didn't see a thing.

SERAFÍN: I'll show you when I'm finished. I drew a picture too.
(SERAFÍN *begins to write again.*) The food we eat is good.
(SERAFÍN *pauses and thinks.*) Because it tastes good.

DOLORES: You remember that the next time you decide you want
to skip dinner.

SERAFÍN: How do you spell tostones, Mommy?

DOLORES: Sound it out, canto-e-vago.

SERAFÍN: To, tow, tow.

DOLORES: "S." T-O-S.

SERAFÍN: Tos, tone, ton?

DOLORES: What else?

SERAFÍN: T-o-s-t-o-n-s! Tostones.

DOLORES: E-s, Popi. E-s. Good boy.

SERAFÍN: I like tostones and rice and beans! (*A young woman comes through the door and quietly sneaks up behind* SERAFÍN. *This is* CLARA, DOLORES's *best friend. She lives downstairs. As always, she is richly and fashionably dressed.*) I want to play the congas.

CLARA: So I can drive my Titi Clara crazy!! (CLARA *pounces on him with a tickle attack and a flurry of kisses. Then she puts down her bag and begins to beat on the table as if it were a conga drum.* SERAFÍN *joins in while* DOLORES *takes to doing an African dance.* CLARA *singing.*) ¡Africa! ¡Canta Africa! ¡Ay Changó! ¡Canta el guaguancó! ¡Epa! (*They enjoy this for a while until* CLARA *can no longer resist and grabs* SERAFÍN *to give him a big kiss.*) Tito Puente, eat your heart out! (DOLORES *gives* CLARA *a quick peck on the cheek and hurriedly returns to the stove.*)

DOLORES: ¿Cómo estás, mi'hija? How was your day?

CLARA: Pues, luchando, como siempre, ya tú sabes. But I tell you one thing. I'm gonna start dressing in battle fatigues from now on 'cause, baby, it is war out there. (*To* SERAFÍN.) ¿Verdad muñeco?

DOLORES: (DOLORES *burns herself.*) ¡Carajo!

CLARA: I hope you are not using any of your mother's colorful language in your report.

SERAFÍN: Mommy says that a dirty mouth keeps your thoughts clean.

DOLORES: (*To* CLARA.) ¡Coge! (*To* SERAFÍN.) Thank you. (*To* CLARA.) You think I'm defenseless?

CLARA: Actually, I don't think about you at all. Your wine, please!

DOLORES: (DOLORES *takes out a bottle of wine and searches for a crystal glass and hands them to* CLARA. *She then bows to her.*) Your majesty.

CLARA: You do that so well. But then, you've had so much practice, Mrs. Moreno.

DOLORES: Oh, we're sharp tonight.

CLARA: Razor, darling, razor! But! I've decided to spare you. My Serafín needs a mommy and, golly gee, you do it so well!

DOLORES: Ooooh! Not fair. You said you'd spare me.

CLARA: And you, if I recall, promised that you wouldn't curse in front of Serafín.

DOLORES: I never said that!

CLARA: Bullshit!

DOLORES: I rest my case.

CLARA: Fine! (*To* SERAFÍN.) If you want to be vulgar, Serafín, I guess you have your mother's approval.

DOLORES: Straighten out Titi's paranoia, son.

SERAFÍN: Titi! A dirty mouth keeps your thoughts clean.

CLARA: So I've heard.

SERAFÍN: But since I'm too young to have dirty thoughts, Mommy says that saying bad words doesn't serve a purpose!

DOLORES: Okay?

CLARA: Sure! Go ahead! Gang up on me. (SERAFÍN *laughs.*)

DOLORES: Oh, give me a break. We were "razor" only a few minutes ago. (*To* SERAFÍN.) Papito, go to your room and finish that so that Mommy can set the table and lick your Titi Clara's wounds. (*To* CLARA.) You missed your calling, querida. You should have been an actress.

CLARA: And compete with Rita and Chita? (CLARA *begins to tickle* SERAFÍN.) Oh, that rhymes, doesn't it? Rita, Chita, Rita, Chita. (SERAFÍN *collects his things and runs off. He comes back to kiss* CLARA.)

SERAFÍN: Mommy and I were just playing, Titi.

CLARA: Well, if you give me another kiss, I might believe you. (SERAFÍN *complies and* CLARA *squeezes him hard.*)

DOLORES: ¡Me lo mata, Dios mío! You're gonna kill him!

CLARA: ¡Ay, Mamá! ¡Si esto es lo más lindo que hay! How about the zoo tomorrow?

SERAFÍN: Yeah! Yeah!

CLARA: Okay! I'll pick you up at nine.

DOLORES: I'm glad some of us don't need any sleep.

CLARA: Ten. We'll make it ten. We wouldn't want to upset the drill sergeant now, would we?

SERAFÍN: I'll be ready. (SERAFÍN *gives her one last hug and exits.*)

CLARA: Ay, que Dios me lo bendiga. He has your heart.

DOLORES: And his father's good looks. Watch out, ladies!

CLARA: (*To herself.*) No, no Clara! Don't say it. Just take your glass and drink.

DOLORES: We are restrained tonight, aren't we? Vélame esto while I change. (DOLORES *runs into the room for a quick change.*)

CLARA: (*Sarcastically.*) And what are we making this evening?
    Muffins? Cookies? Apple Pie?
DOLORES: Drink, drink. The tongue's not numb enough yet.
CLARA: What are you on? Slow down, for Christ's sake!
DOLORES: Ariano'll be home soon.
CLARA: Ariano won't die if his food isn't ready. Relax. I tell you,
    I don't know how you do it. When I get home, I have to
    relax, sit down, watch T.V., read anything.
DOLORES: I'll just have to organize my time better, that's all.
CLARA: Pues m'ija, mira que sí. You'll have to do something
    'cause I get iron-poor blood just watching you.
DOLORES: You really shouldn't be so encouraging, Clara.
CLARA: Ariano can wait. (*To herself.*) Que te cocine a ti de ve'
    en cuando. Qué carajo. (DOLORES *comes out in a drop-
    dead little outfit, sure to please any eye.*)
DOLORES: Nobody'll have to wait now. Now I've got plenty of
    time. (CLARA *eyes* DOLORES *suspiciously, then, as if
    sensing something, swigs the wine straight from the bottle.*)
    Clara?
CLARA: We've played this game before. My odds are always im-
    proved if I'm stoned.
DOLORES: Don't you want to know why?
CLARA: Why what?
DOLORES: Why I'll have more time.
CLARA: Do I have to?
DOLORES: (*Interrupting.*) I quit my job today. Today was my last
    day.
CLARA: Weeeeeelll, guess you win, anyway. Maybe next time.
    (CLARA *gets up to leave.*)
DOLORES: Where are you going? Aren't you going to say some-
    thing? (CLARA *stands trying not to comment.*) Well?!
CLARA: ¡Pendeja!
DOLORES: Thanks a lot!
CLARA: What do you want me to say, for Christ's sake? You want
    my approval? You expect me to pat you on the back?
CLARA: (*Sarcastically.*) Okay, I'll just run and fetch a pair of
    floppy slippers and a bag of rollers I have downstairs. Oh
    wait, you probably want to go around barefoot. I'll eighty-
    six the slippers.
DOLORES: Is that necessary?
CLARA: Of course! If you're going to do drudge, then you might
    as well dress for the part!
DOLORES: Would you like to hear me out?

CLARA: You want to know something? I'm not surprised. Te lo
    juro that I expected this to happen sooner or later. And
    where does your husband fit into all of this? Now, tell me
    he hasn't anything to do with this?

DOLORES: I haven't told him yet.

CLARA: You mean to tell me that you made a decision without
    discussing it with the man of the house first? All by your
    little self? Well, at least that's some progress.

DOLORES: Clara, please.

CLARA: Your profession is important to you! How can you just
    quit!

DOLORES: I don't need to work!

CLARA: You want to play housewife? To whom? Serafin? God
    knows, your husband's never home.

DOLORES: Don't start with that again!

CLARA: You're depending on him for too much! He's only a small
    part, carajo!

DOLORES: There you are wrong! My family is everything to me.
    My husband! My son! You shouldn't talk about things
    you don't understand.

CLARA: Let me tell you something, Dolores. I'm not married,
    I have no children, by choice! I am as complete as any
    woman! I'm just not stupid.

DOLORES: I don't want to talk about it.

CLARA: Of course, not. You'd probably rather be in your room,
    knitting the bastard some underwear.

DOLORES: This discussion is ended!

CLARA: You're not making sense! If you want me to understand—
    and believe me, I'm going to need to understand very
    clearly—then you'd better explain.

DOLORES: Don't worry, Clara. I'm not going to take Serafín away
    from you, if that's your fear. You can still play mother.

CLARA: Oh yes! You are right, there. I do play the doting mother.

DOLORES: I'm sorry I said that.

CLARA: No, no, no! ¡Un segundito! Who was it that had me take
    care of Serafín for those first few months? You wanted to
    go back to work. Or so you said. You begged me to take
    care of him, you'd do anything, as long as he was out of
    Ariano's sight!

DOLORES: That was not the reason!

CLARA: I was the one who said that Serafín should be around him
    as much as possible. I was the one who kept warning you
    what would happen if you didn't get Ariano used to him.

DOLORES: All right, we have problems. I'm trying to work them out.

CLARA: By giving up everything?

DOLORES: I want it that way! (*There is a long pause.* CLARA *fills her glass.*) Yes. He can be a son-of-a-bitch sometimes. I know. I know.

CLARA: Dolores ...

DOLORES: Quiet! My turn! (DOLORES *lights a cigarette as is her custom when she gets nervous.*) Clara, I love you like a sister, or else I wouldn't be bothering with any of this, believe me.

CLARA: It's not about that.

DOLORES: Fine! Okay! It's not about that, you're right! But what makes you think, que yo soy una pendeja? That's what you called me, right? (CLARA *tries to interrupt again, but* DOLORES *steamrolls.*) No. No. I'm a jerk. You're right. Sometimes I am. As a matter of fact, I am a pendeja! I'm always trying to please everybody. Yeah, it's true! I'm the one who's always making the calls, finding out if everybody in the family is okay, if my brothers are all right, if someone needs money. If there's a fight, who's there always? That they call me la entrometida porque siempre tengo las narices metidas donde no pertenecen? Ah? Dolores, right? Sweet Dolores! Good Dolores! ¡Mira! Let me tell you something. I spent my childhood—10, 11, 12—taking care of people. You see my brothers ahora, Nestor y Mateo? Now they beat their chests, right? Big men! Successful with their business. Well, this one here remembers when they were out in the streets, hanging out like a bunch of fucking thugs, ready to get picked up by the first cop they crossed their eyes at! Now they call me pendeja, too. They say that Ariano is a comemierda. What am I doing with him, they say. My father! You see my father there, with that whore he's been living with for the last ten years! He can't stand my husband either. Why? Because he's jealous of him!

CLARA: My God, he's your father, Dolores ...

DOLORES: ¿Ese? ¡Ese lo que es es un hijo de la gran puta! Mira, Clara, if my family is together today it's because esta pendeja que tú ves aquí kept them together! Okay? My father was never home. After Mommy died, que en paz descanse, he left me in charge y se fue buscándosela por las calles, picking up any stray he could find. I cooked,

I cleaned, I ironed—got my ass kicked if he came home
encabronao o bellaco—and when he did manage to find
some slut que se lo hacía bien por allá, he'd bring her
home. Y yo era tan idiota—porque coño uno tiene que
ser bruta—that I would cook and clean for her too. No
hombre, no! Even when I finally left, seguían jodiéndome
la vida. They'd come over to bitch and complain about
Papi or ask for money, and Ariano never said no! Never!
Mira! ¡Ya estoy cansá! I'm tired. P'al carajo con todo el
mundo. I'm going to live by my rules, do what I want!
And this ... (DOLORES *goes around the room touching
things as she mentions them.*) this, this, this ... is what I
want. My home! My family! Everybody has something to
say about Ariano, always a comment. Que si "stuck up,"
que si dominante. Nobody stops to look ... see what he
has for me, nobody! All they can do is hablar mierda,
talk shit! Well, that's fine! 'Cause I don't force anyone
through that door and, please, don't think I'm directing
this at you, Clara. You are the only one, besides Ariano,
who respects me. You always have and I value that more
than you know. I don't want to lose you, but you have to
understand, I love my husband! We talk, have fun. He
has a mind! Sure we fight, but so do you and I. He got
me out of all that hysteria. It was with him that I got
to develop some sort of self esteem, some respect. You
know the wimp I was. He's never stopped me from doing
anything I've wanted, a lo contrario, he encourages any
and all my plans. He's the one who paid for me to finish
nursing school. I wanted dance classes, the same. That
he has moods? That sometimes these four walls suffocate
him? Me too. He was the first lover I had. The only
one. (*There is a pause.* CLARA *remains silent and finally
breaks into cynical laughter.*)

CLARA: Beeendiiito! Your mother's not dead, Dolores. Uh, uh.
She's locked up tightly inside you. And her mother's
locked tight inside her. And so on, and so on. (CLARA
lifts her glass in a toast.) Latina women! And their Latino
men. The ritual continues! Why, may I ask, are you cele-
brating in it? ¡Despierta boricua porque te lo quieren meter mongo! It's a penis, honey, not a goddamned scepter!
Aren't you tired of that, "Hey Mammi!" "Mira preciosa!"
rap? Honey, I had to clear all that away! In order for this
little number here to survive, I had to sweep up that crap

that stood in my way. I went through a period where I decided I was gonna have to play their game for a while. Hunt them down. Maybe take a few trophies. So I went to their lairs! Their salsa clubs! Sat there patiently until one of the horny mothafuckas came strolling over in one of those cute little polyester salsa suits. So macho! They made sure I heard they had balls, slam against the chair as they sat down, which was fine with me, 'cause that was the last they'd be seeing of those suckas! You see, after about five minutes, I'd plop them in my drink to cool my liquor! I tell you, the pleasure of watching these hombres as they watched their cojones melt in front of their stupid drunken faces can only be matched by the pleasure of having them pay for the act that ate their shit up! Another man! Another round! Every choice I see you make justifies every one I've made. You give up too much, querida!

DOLORES: I'm pregnant, Clara. That's why I quit.

CLARA: What?! Even after Serafín?

DOLORES: You got it.

CLARA: God, are you crazy? Don't you remember ...

DOLORES: (*Interrupting.*) I remember everything! (*There is a silence.*) Go ahead. I'm sorry.

CLARA: You're not gonna want to hear it.

DOLORES: I said, go ahead. Don't worry, I'll stop you if I have to.

CLARA: For eight months while you were pregnant, he went around the neighborhood showing everyone that picture of his mother he always has with him. "It will look just like her," he'd say. You never saw Daddy's picture, now did you? You think it fell out of his wallet? You think maybe he lost it by accident? (*She laughs.*) And then there are those who claim that there is no God.

DOLORES: Oh. So now Serafín was God's justice, is that what you're saying?

CLARA: Serafín, mi amor, was God's reminder to all good little Puerto Rican boys and girls of just how complicated we really are!

DOLORES: This is great! Me salvé yo ahora. Now I need your permission before I open my legs?

CLARA: Yes! Yes, if you expect me to help you raise this one too!

DOLORES: That's not fair, Clara, and you know it. Besides, I already told you that now my family has become my full

time obligation. I intend on making up for whatever mistakes I made in the past.

CLARA: Mistakes? M'ija, he's the only mistake ... (ARIANO *is
heard to come into the apartment. He stops when he sees*
CLARA. DOLORES *changes the tone to sweetness and
honey.*)

DOLORES: So. You'll be here at ten to pick up Serafín?

CLARA: Sure.

DOLORES: Why don't you make it nine? I'll make you both a
special breakfast. (CLARA *turns to leave.*)

ARIANO: I hope you're not leaving on my account?

CLARA: You've always provided for as good a reason why. (*To*
DOLORES.) Thanks for the invitation. I'll see you in the
morning.

ARIANO: Now is that nice? I'm trying to be sociable.

CLARA: Good. Keep trying. (*To* DOLORES.) Nos vemos mañana.
(CLARA *exits.*)

ARIANO: I try. You can't say I don't try. (ARIANO *embraces*
DOLORES *and kisses her sweetly. A split-second sadness
emerges in him but is quicky squelched.*)

DOLORES: Mmmmmmmm! You look hungry big boy.

ARIANO: Nice dress. (DOLORES *turns around slowly, seductively
as she models for her husband.*)

DOLORES: This old rag?

ARIANO: About my appetite.

DOLORES: Which one? (ARIANO *lets out a slow, gutteral laugh.
He pulls* DOLORES *forcefully to him.*)

ARIANO: Puuutita.

DOLORES: Moi? (ARIANO *kisses her again.*)

ARIANO: Fooood.

DOLORES: I'm ready.

ARIANO: (*Laughing.*) No, no, the kind that goes on the table.
(DOLORES *jumps on the table.*) ¡Coño! Mamita, please.
You're making this very hard ...

DOLORES: (*Interrupting.*) Oooooh! I hope so. (DOLORES *goes
to him once more.*)

ARIANO: (*Whiffing.*) I think I smell something burning. (DO-
LORES *lets out a small scream and races over to the stove.*
ARIANO *takes off his jacket and quickly sits.*)

DOLORES: No, papito. Nothing was burning, ooooh you sneak.

ARIANO: Works all the time. (DOLORES *runs over and tickles
him.* ARIANO *laughing.*) That's what you get for trying
to serve up the dessert before the main course.

DOLORES: Mi amor, as far as I'm concerned, I am the main course. (DOLORES *sits on his lap.*) But ... (DOLORES *gets up and goes back to the kitchen.*) Since you will need all that energy later on ...

ARIANO: Thaaaaank you!

DOLORES: Llámame al nene. He's in the room doing homework. (DOLORES *comes out and begins serving.*)

ARIANO: Honeeey. It's so much more romantic alone. He can eat later, no?

DOLORES: Well. He did stuff his face with doughnuts when he came home.

ARIANO: Chocolate?

DOLORES: Three.

ARIANO: Forget it. He won't be hungry for at least another ...

DOLORES: (*Interrupting.*)   Five minutes.   (ARIANO *laughs proudly. There is a short pause as they begin to eat.*)

ARIANO: (*Hesitantly.*) He have any, uh, problems at school?

DOLORES: Ay, cállate, no, ¡a Dios gracias! As a matter of fact, he came home in a good mood. Allí está en su cuartito drawing in his book.

ARIANO: Bastards!

DOLORES: He's a pioneer. The first Puerto Rican, whatta you expect? So he'll catch a few arrows now and then. We all do.

ARIANO: I know he blames me, I can feel it! He was happy where he was. I know he thinks it's all my fault.

DOLORES: (*Sternly.*) Hey! It's a good school. The best! He knows that, he loves you for that. And so do I. Although, you are spoiling him a little.

ARIANO: Spoiling him?

DOLORES: Well, actually you're spoiling us both.

ARIANO: So I bought a few things.

DOLORES: A few things? Honey, look at this place! They finished installing the marble in the bathroom today. I haven't seen so much of the stuff since we went to Rome, for Pete's sake.

ARIANO: What's wrong with marble?

DOLORES: It costs a fortune.

ARIANO: So?

DOLORES: Serafín doesn't really need an IBM home computer— with printer—while he's in the third grade.

ARIANO: I bet you all his other twerpy classmates have one.

DOLORES: And a VCR, and a 30-inch TV, new furniture.

ARIANO: Alright, alright, you've made your point. My answer is:
So what? Money we have, right?

DOLORES: That's not it, papito.

ARIANO: So then, what is it? I can't get things for my own family
now? That's a crime now too?

DOLORES: No, papito, no! I love everything you're doing, really.

ARIANO: Strange way of showing it.

DOLORES: I know, I'm sorry. Just being money-conscious, I
guess. (DOLORES *falls off into a silence.* ARIANO *con-*
templates her.)

ARIANO: Okay, what is it?

DOLORES: What's what?

ARIANO: There's something bothering you and I want to know
what it is. (DOLORES *breaks into a nervous laughter,*
gets up and goes over to him, putting her arms about the
back of his neck.)

DOLORES: Oooooh, my man! Knows his woman so well.

ARIANO: But he can't read her mind ... yet. (*There is a short*
silence as DOLORES *plays around with him, nibbling, etc.*
She is trying to get up the nerve to tell him about the job.)

DOLORES: I quit my job.

ARIANO: You what?!

DOLORES: Today was my last day.

ARIANO: You quit, Dolores? Just like that? Just up and gone?

DOLORES: No, no. I gave a months notice.

ARIANO: A month? You had this planned for a whole month and
you're telling me now?

DOLORES: Ooooh, you're mad. I knew you wouldn't understand.

ARIANO: Calm down and talk to me.

DOLORES: The timing was all wrong, renovating ahora, all that
money.

ARIANO: Dolores! Talk to me. Sit.

DOLORES: I want to stay home. I'm sick of the hospital. The
house is gonna look so nice, plus I figured we'd have more
time ...

ARIANO: You've given 5,000 reasons. Which is the real one?

DOLORES: Don't you think we could use some more time together?

ARIANO: Frankly, I think that things are fine the way they are. I
thought you did too.

DOLORES: I do. Things are fine.

ARIANO: And?

DOLORES: Nothing!

ARIANO: So?
DOLORES: Look, forget it. I guess I'm asking for too much. A
    new apartment and some more time with the man I love—
    Dolores, you glutton you.
ARIANO: No need for sarcasm.
DOLORES: I'll go in Monday and rescind my resignation. Simple.
ARIANO: I haven't asked you to do anything like that, we're still
    talking!
DOLORES: You're upset, it's obvious. But you're right. I should
    have consulted with you before I . . .
ARIANO: (*Interrupting.*) Look, it's your job! You have to pull the
    godamn shifts, so I'm not telling you that you need my
    permission or anything like that. You know I'm not like
    that!
DOLORES: Then what is it?
ARIANO: I just want to make sure that you're clear on your mo-
    tives. And your expectations. (*There is an uncomfort-
    able pause.*) Honey, I'm really tied up with my business
    right now. I'm giving up the numbers gig, negrita. I
    made enough money with it. I'm making some real es-
    tate deals, a few investments, I might even open up a few
    more stores.
DOLORES: How many laundries do you need, for Christ's sake.
ARIANO: I don't have time! Estoy tranquilo, it gives me piece of
    mind, knowing you have something to keep you occupied.
DOLORES: I have a son too. Have you forgotten that?
ARIANO: No, I haven't and he's in school all day. (*Pause.*)
    Nena, please. Let me keep on peddling my shit out there
    without having to worry that you're sitting here at home
    bored. (DOLORES *clears her plate and gets up to go to
    the kitchen.*) También, what if something ever happened
    to me? No more Ariano?
DOLORES: (*Jumping in.*) Alright! Alright! Before you start low-
    ering yourself into the ground, I surrender! I told you I'll
    go back!
ARIANO: Not surrender! I'm not making this decision for you.
DOLORES: Coulda fooled me.
ARIANO: Now it's my fault?
DOLORES: Look. I know you have every right to be mad. I should
    have consulted with you first. The way you do with me.
ARIANO: I don't always consult.
DOLORES: I'm talking about the important things. Papito, maybe
    you're right. Hey, you've always given me the best advice,

right? (DOLORES *tries to make peace and reaches for* ARIANO*'s hand. There is an awkward silence.*)

ARIANO: Wait. Wait, wait, wait. I've never stopped you from making any decisions before and that's not my intention now. You quit already, right? So stay home a while and see how you like it. (DOLORES *virtually jumps into his arms.*)

DOLORES: My man! I knew you'd say yes!

ARIANO: Oh no! You're the one making this decision, Dolores. Don't come blaming me later on.

DOLORES: I'll be the perfect housewife. Just call me Betty Crocker. (DOLORES *again embraces* ARIANO.) We're good for each other. You know that, don't you? (ARIANO *nods his head and kisses her hand.*) I need some cheap emotion. Tell me you love me.

ARIANO: I love you. Cheap enough? (DOLORES *pecks him on the nose and starts for the kitchen.*)

DOLORES: You could have thrown in a tip, stingy!

ARIANO: Ten minutes ago I was Nelson Rockefeller. Now I'm Scrooge. You can't win around here. (SERAFÍN *comes running out of his room carrying a drawing he has done and a cigar box of crayons.*)

SERAFÍN: I'm finished! I'm finished!

ARIANO: Serafín.

SERAFÍN: Hi, Papi! (SERAFÍN *kisses* ARIANO *and* ARIANO *pats his behind.*) Look, Mommy. I finished.

DOLORES: Ooooh! Let me see. Wow! That's excellent! Papi doesn't know it yet, but we have an artist in the family. It looks just like us.

SERAFÍN: I have to put the names still. See, that's yooouuu.

DOLORES: U-huh.

SERAFÍN: Thaaaaat's meeeee.

DOLORES: So handsome!

SERAFÍN: And that's Papi!

DOLORES: Magnifique! Look, honey.

ARIANO: I'm never gonna get to finish this.

DOLORES: Go show, Papi. Anda. (SERAFÍN *runs and makes a space for himself in* ARIANO*'s lap.*) I guess all that talent just runs in the blood.

SERAFÍN: Look, Papi. I made a picture for show-and-tell. Look, Papi! (SERAFÍN *pushes away* ARIANO*'s plate and places the picture in front of him.* ARIANO *is inattentive at first, trying to muster as much patience as possible. He slowly*

comes to notice the picture.) This is meee. This is Mom-
mmy. (ARIANO *suddenly grabs the picture.*)

ARIANO: What is this?!

SERAFÍN: It's for show-and-tell. I tooold you.

ARIANO: (*Blurting out.*) Can you please tell me what the hell this
is all about!

DOLORES: Ariano!

ARIANO: Who's this, Serafín? Who's this one in the middle? El
prieto ese? That black one in the middle? Is that supposed
to be me Serafín?

DOLORES: ¿Qué pasa?

ARIANO: Answer me! (SERAFÍN *tries to get down from* ARIA-
NO's *lap, but* ARIANO *holds him.* DOLORES *moves in
but is pushed away.*)

DOLORES: Stop! You're hurting him.

ARIANO: This is what you intend on bringing to school! Jesus
Christ, no wonder they're chasing you up and down the
halls.

DOLORES: Will you relax and let him go?

ARIANO: You stay out of this!

DOLORES: ¡Pues, no me lo toques! Don't hit him!

ARIANO: You encourage this garbage!

DOLORES: It's only a fucking picture!!! (ARIANO *slaps* DO-
LORES.)

SERAFÍN: Papi no! Papi! Don't hit Mommy! (SERAFÍN *starts
to cry.*)

ARIANO: I said be quiet! (ARIANO *drags* SERAFÍN *over to the
mirror.* DOLORES *puts her finger to her mouth, gestur-
ing for* SERAFÍN *to remain quiet.*) Look! Look in the
mirror. (SERAFÍN *turns his head away and looks at his
mother.* ARIANO *grabs him by the hair and forces him to
look.* DOLORES *runs to them.*) If you come any closer
I'll smack him. Serafín! I said look in the mirror!

DOLORES: ¡Ariano, por favor!

ARIANO: Leave me alone!

SERAFÍN: Okay, Papi! Okay! I'm looking.

ARIANO: And what do you see?

SERAFÍN: Just don't yell at Mommy.

ARIANO: What do you see! Is that a black face you see, Serafín?
Is it? Speak up, goddammit!

SERAFÍN: You, Papi. I see you and me.

ARIANO: And what color am I, Serafín?

DOLORES: Ariiiaaannno!

ARIANO: Puñeta, what color!!!! (ARIANO *pulls his hair.*)
SERAFÍN: Owwww, like me. Like me and mommy. (ARIANO
    flings SERAFÍN *around and they face each other.*)
ARIANO: No, Serafín! Not like you! Not like you!!!!
DOLORES: You son-of-a-bitch!
ARIANO: Where are your crayons? (SERAFÍN *points to them.*)
    Get them. (SERAFÍN *goes to the table and retrieves the
    crayons.* DOLORES *rushes to him and pulls him to her.*
    ARIANO *gets up and yanks him away. He sits him in a
    chair at the table.*) I said leave him alone!
DOLORES: What the hell's the matter with you, you crazy bas-
    tard. It's a picture for school, a fucking picture for school!
    (DOLORES *breaks down, but* ARIANO *is oblivious. Only*
    SERAFÍN *is concerned about his mother.*)
ARIANO: You're gonna have to learn the difference between your
    colors, kid. Now! Today! Believe me, everybody out
    there, especially in that freakin' school, knows the differ-
    ence in their colors. Nobody makes a mistake about that!
    (ARIANO *begins to explain this difference to his son. As
    he explains about each color, he will break the correspond-
    ing crayon to punctuate his point.*) You see these here?
    There! No more! No more black! No brown! That's
    the color of dirt and shit! No grey! No purple! Maroon!
    Suffering colors kid! Out! Pa'l carajo! You gettin' this?
    Bright colors, stupid! Bright!
SERAFÍN: Yes, Papi.
ARIANO: Nobody wants to see dark things, black things! Nobody
    likes the night time, Serafín. Don't you cry sometimes at
    night? Aren't you scared of the dark? Right? Right?
SERAFÍN: Sometimes.
ARIANO: Sometimes, yeah, because it's dark! It's ugly and scary
    and you get scared. Black scares people! Haven't you
    learned that yet? That's lesson number one in this U.S.
    of fucking A! I'm doing you a favor by telling you myself,
    so you don't have to come home crying anymore 'cause
    of those assholes in that school. (ARIANO *begins to cry.*)
SERAFÍN: Don't cry, Papi.
ARIANO: I'm doing you a favor. She don't understand! (ARIANO
    surrenders to his pain and pulls SERAFÍN *to him, burying
    his face into his child's neck.* DOLORES *tries to go to
    him. When she places her hand on his shoulder, he quickly
    snaps out of his lull. The rage is there again.*) Get away!
    (ARIANO *pulls* SERAFÍN *to the side and searches for the*

crayons. He finds them and dumps them on the floor. He takes the picture and turns it to the other side. He puts a crayon in SERAFÍN*'s hand.*) Start over.

DOLORES: No!

ARIANO: I said draw! (DOLORES *runs over and tries to grab* SERAFÍN. ARIANO *grabs her and holds her by the wrists.*)

DOLORES: ¡Déjalo ya, que ya es bastante! Leave him alone! (SERAFÍN *runs to them, thinking* ARIANO *is going to hurt his mother.*)

SERAFÍN: Papi, I'm doing it, look, Papi look.

ARIANO: He's gotta learn. Let him learn!

DOLORES: No me le des ... don't hit him, please! Please!

ARIANO: Ssssh! Ssssh! Relax. If he does what he's supposed to do, he won't get hit, go, stay out of it. I don't want to tell you again.

SERAFÍN: Mommy, don't cry.

ARIANO: There is nothing on this paper! I said do it over! (A-RIANO *does not have the patience. He takes over the job himself.*) These colors, Serafín! These! Orange! Yellow! Pink! White! (ARIANO *puts the white crayon up to his son's face.*) White! This is the most powerful crayon in the whole fucking box, you stupid son-of-a-bitch! (AR-IANO *lurches up and goes towards the portrait over the mantle and begins tearing off the plastic protective covering.*) Don't move! (*To* DOLORES.) And you shut up!

DOLORES: I haven't said anything!

ARIANO: My little artist! Color-shit-blind! (ARIANO *now takes the uncovered portrait and shoves it into* DOLORES' *hands so that* SERAFÍN *can see from it. He then goes back to* SERAFÍN.) You want something to show for school? How's this? (ARIANO *begins to draw.*) Here. Blue. For her eyes. Beautiful clear blue eyes. Like the sky from her island. See? Now pink. Isn't that pretty? You see how nice this color is? For her skin. Lightly, not too hard. See the contrast with her eyes? Gold! Her hair! Beautiful golden hair. Isn't that special? Aren't you proud of that? Wouldn't you like to show that instead? (ARIA-NO *looks at* SERAFÍN, *who is mute. He slams the table.*) This is what you show people! Have pride in your background, carajo! We're Puerto Rican! Not niggers! (A-RIANO *crumples up. He seems disoriented and confused. He takes the hallowed portrait away from* DOLORES, *who immediately runs to her son.* ARIANO *places the portrait*

back on its altar. He turns to leave.)
DOLORES: Where are you going? We have to talk!
ARIANO: (*Weakly.*) I ... I don't want to talk ... (ARIANO *exits.*
DOLORES *and* SERAFÍN *cling to each other.* DOLORES
inspects him for bruises.)
DOLORES: Papito? (SERAFÍN *does not answer.*) Serafín? Look
at Mommy. Look at me. Honey, are you okay? Huh? Are
you alright?
SERAFÍN: He hates me. Like the kids in school, he hates me.
DOLORES: No, no, papito, don't say that. That's not true. Serafín, I know what your father did was wrong; he knows that
too. Your daddy is in a lot of pain, papito. He doesn't
hate you. Really. He loves you. You know he does. All
those nice presents. Look, baby, we have to help Daddy.
We have to show him that we can help him, you know
like when someone is sick. You try and help them get
better, right? Riiiiight! Oh God! Everything is going to
be fine, papi! Just trust me. You trust Mommy don't
you? Huh? Mommy is going to make everything alright.
Okay? Okay? (DOLORES *rocks* SERAFÍN *and turns his
head away so as to not let him see her cry. Lights slow
up on* ARIANO *who kneels outside the door, slouched over
and moaning.*)
ARIANO: Ooooooh God! God help me please! Please! (*Lights
fade slowly on entire scene to blackout.*)

.... SCENE TWO ....

*In the darkness, "Desperado," a song performed by Linda Rond-
stad, is heard. Lights up slow on a small studio apartment; very New
York chic, in the minimalist mode. What catches the eye however is
a collection of frilly-laced dolls that are placed along the head board
of the bed. They are the traditional, Shirley Temple variations, i.e.,
white.* ARIANO *stands over by the wall, leaning against it. He
carries a paper bag. On the bed we see* CRYSTAL. *She is a human
version of the blue-eyed dolls that she collects. She is very beautiful
and very pregnant. She is knitting something while listening to the
radio. After a pause,* ARIANO *reaches over and shuts off the stereo,
ending the song.*

CRYSTAL: I don't see why you're getting yourself all upset. Ain't
the first time. (CRYSTAL *goes for the paper bag.*) God

that smells good.

ARIANO: (*Quietly.*) I hit them. I hit them both.

CRYSTAL: So you got a temper. You're Puerto Rican, right? Pas-
sion, switchblades, hysteria! Come on, we've all seen
"West Side Story." (ARIANO *gives her a contemptous
look.*) It's a joke! Jesus! Oh wow! Chinese! I know you
got me at least a dozen egg-rolls. (CRYSTAL *prepares to
enter gastronomic heaven.* ARIANO *picks up a strange
odor.*)

ARIANO: What's that shit I smell?

CRYSTAL: Incense, Lomein! Too much! Oh, I am going to pig
out!

ARIANO: What'a you, crazy? You know I don't go for any of that
shit. You're not supposed to be smoking. I have told you
over and over ...

CRYSTAL: (*Interrupting.*) And I don't listen! I don't listen! (A-
RIANO *swallows whatever he intended on blurting out.*)
Go ahead. Say something. You'll pop if you don't.

ARIANO: You're in your last month, Crys, it's almost over.

CRYSTAL: Did coke yesterday. Did a valium this morning.

ARIANO: You're trying to be funny, right?

CRYSTAL: You're paying for a kid. How I get through with it is
my business!

ARIANO: Yeah? Well I don't pay for damaged goods, remember
that!

CRYSTAL: You're such a fucking neurotic! Relax! Eat! (CRYS-
TAL *pulls* ARIANO *down on the bed with her.*) Come on.
Why don't you tell momma what happened. I love cheap
drama.

ARIANO: Nothing happened.

CRYSTAL: (*Unmoved.*) Okay. (CRYSTAL *continues to gorge her-
self and satisfy what appears to be an insatiable craving.*)
This is from the Cuban-Chinese over on 19th, right? (A-
RIANO *nods.*) I am still trying to fathom that concept.
But they sure as hell kick-ass in the kitchen. (*She laughs.*
ARIANO *contemplates her as she eats. He betrays a slight
disgust.*)

ARIANO: You're going to get sick if you don't swallow. Chew the
food and then swallow. That's the process.

CRYSTAL: Do you fucking mind! Jesus! The same goddam wind
always washes you up on my shore. Well, heave-ho, amigo,
'cause tide's out today. Go sail somewhere else. (ARIA-
NO *dives deeper into his funk.* CRYSTAL *would rather*

ignore him but decides to talk to him instead.) Look. You
wanna talk about it? I'll listen. Honest. (ARIANO *does
not respond.*) You wanna fool around? Come oooooon!
It'll make you feel better.

ARIANO: Can you please be serious, for once!

CRYSTAL: I'll let you be serious. I'll be seductive! (CRYSTAL
begins to massage ARIANO's *shoulders while kissing him
tenderly about the neck.* ARIANO *does not resist.*)

ARIANO: I'm such an ass-hole. What the hell's the matter with
me? (ARIANO *gets up.* CRYSTAL *tries to be patient.*)

CRYSTAL: Like you said, you're an ass-hole. (CRYSTAL *breaks
into laughter.* ARIANO *can't resist and joins her, somewhat reluctant.*) That's better. (CRYSTAL *motions to A-
RIANO so that he joins her on the bed. She kisses him
and indulges him as she would a little boy.* ARIANO
relaxes and surrenders.) It's almost over, babe. Not to
worry. A few more weeks and you'll have your kid, begin
your new life. (ARIANO *suddenly breaks down, burying
his head into* CRYSTAL's *shoulder. He is now a terrified
child.* CRYSTAL *has never seen this side of* ARIANO *and
is momentarily caught off guard.*)

ARIANO: (*Crying.*) I'm scared, Crys! I'm so fucking scared!
(CRYSTAL *cannot respond. She just holds him, hoping
it will be enough. After a pause.*)

CRYSTAL: Ssssssh. Hey, hey. Come on, now. Forget about all this
stuff here. You're going to Connecticut. Arrie?

ARIANO: Crys, I don't know what the hell I'm doing anymore. I
can't stay here, don't wanna go there. I'm too old for this
shit, you know?! I'm not a kid.

CRYSTAL: You love that house. It's what you've always wanted!
And so's this baby. Come on. You can't fall apart now.
You've come too far.

ARIANO: A three-bedroom house? Tell me, what the hell do I
need a three-bedroom house in Greenwich, Connecticut?
Can you tell me please?

CRYSTAL: Company?

ARIANO: I don't know how to raise a kid. Don't have any friends.

CRYSTAL: I'll write.

ARIANO: Come.

CRYSTAL: What? With you?

ARIANO: Why not? (*Again,* CRYSTAL *is caught off guard. She
catches herself considering the proposal for a moment but
snaps out of it. She knows better.*)

CRYSTAL: Naaaaah! I can only take you in spurts. (CRYSTAL, *enjoying what she thinks is a clever pun, laughs.* ARIANO *laughs as well, however, more at her than with her. There is a pause.*) Thanks for the invite, though. I'm flattered . . .

ARIANO: (*Interrupting.*) Hey, no sweat. Don't worry about it. (ARIANO *gets up. He is uncomfortable. He works at recomposing himself.*)

CRYSTAL: No. It's real sweet that you think of me that way . . .

ARIANO: (*Interrupting.*) I don't! We were joking around, it was a joke, right?

CRYSTAL: (*Softly.*) Yeah. Right.

ARIANO: I got a Mercedes too.

CRYSTAL: A Mercedes too, my, my.

ARIANO: Yep. I'll be okay.

CRYSTAL: Got a lot for those laundries, I see.

ARIANO: That's not my primary source of income. Who told you about the laundry? Soldier? (CRYSTAL *glares at him and takes a moment to answer.*)

CRYSTAL: Come on. No way you're gonna run things from Puerto Rico, right? Common sense told me. Not Soldier. By the way, I hope you haven't found the need to dip into my fee for any of these little goodies of yours. (ARIANO *looks at her smugly and pulls out his wallet. He produces a cashier's check and tosses it to her. It falls to the floor.*)

ARIANO: Cashier's check. (CRYSTAL *scoops it up off the floor.*)

CRYSTAL: You're walking around the streets of New York with $10,000 in your pocket?! Are you fucking looney-tunes?

ARIANO: Keeps me arrogant, what can I tell you?

CRYSTAL: (*Sweetly.*) You can tell me to keep it. It's only a few more days.

ARIANO: Ooooooh no! Hand it over. Half at conception and half at delivery. That was, if you recall, El Deal. (CRYSTAL *begrudingly returns the check.*)

CRYSTAL: (*To check.*) See you soon, honey. Got your deposit slip all filled out and everything.

ARIANO: Thrifty, thrifty.

CRYSTAL: That's right. That money is the start of my new life. California here I come! (ARIANO *sits staring into space. There is a long uncomfortable pause.* CRYSTAL *then begins to ramble with* ARIANO *interjecting frequently.*)

CRYSTAL: You know, Arrie. You ain't that bad. Don't be so hard on yourself. Really. I've seen worse.

ARIANO: Don't worry about it.

CRYSTAL: Believe me, I've come across some real shit bags, but you're fair, up front. You always come through. (ARIANO *gets up and walks away.*)

ARIANO: Fine. Drop it.

CRYSTAL: Look at this place. You didn't have to set me up like this. We agreed on a fair price. But no, you wanted to take care of me too.

ARIANO: Any food left?

CRYSTAL: You've just had some hard luck with women, that's all. It happens.

ARIANO: That's not true.

CRYSTAL: But one day you'll find the kind of girl you want, and she'll fall in love ...

ARIANO: That isn't the problem.

CRYSTAL: ... with you and I'll bet she'll be real blonde and real blue-eyed.

ARIANO: Will you please shut up! Shut up! (CRYSTAL *is startled into a minute pause but quickly lashes back.*)

CRYSTAL: Don't tell me to shut up, who the hell are you? Here I am trying to make you feel good, you're telling me to shut up in my house?!

ARIANO: You don't know me! You only know what I want you to know about me! My wife knows me! Dolores! Not you! (CRYSTAL *walks slowly to the door.*)

ARIANO: You really think you're something, don't you?

CRYSTAL: Compared to you? Uh huh. Yep. (CRYSTAL *holds the door open for him to leave.*)

ARIANO: You're real funny.

CRYSTAL: No. I'm real tired. Good night. (*There is a short pause. A repentant* ARIANO *reaches for her hand.*)

ARIANO: I'm sorry, Crys. You're a friend. Of course, you know me. (CRYSTAL, *still miffed, backs away to her bed and flops onto it.* ARIANO *closes the door, leaving it slightly ajar.*)

CRYSTAL: No shit, Sherlock ... (ARIANO, *childlike again, snuggles his head into her lap.*)

ARIANO: Friends? (CRYSTAL *bursts into laughter and caps it off with a blood-curdling scream.*) Sssssssssh! Hey! Quiet.

CRYSTAL: You're insane!

ARIANO: See. You do know me pretty good. (*They both laugh.*) And for your information, I had plenty of blondes after my tight, Puerto Rican buns.

CRYSTAL: Oh yeah? Well, we have been known to slum occasion-
　　　　ally.

ARIANO: You are so evil tonight! Evil, evil, evil!

CRYSTAL: You bring out the best in me, what can I say? (*They
　　　　settle down.* CRYSTAL *runs her fingers through his hair
　　　　and stares down at him.*)

ARIANO: That's not true. There was only one.

CRYSTAL: One what?

ARIANO: One blonde.

CRYSTAL: Oh yeah?

ARIANO: Yep.

CRYSTAL: Serious? I mean, love-love? Or lust-love?

ARIANO: Love-love. We were going to be married.

CRYSTAL: Married?! Well why the fuck didn't you then? Jesus
　　　　Christ! Do you know the grief—-not to mention all the
　　　　cash—-you could have saved yourself?

ARIANO: I wanted to! She wanted to! But marrying Puerto Ricans
　　　　was not the family tradition. Irish.

CRYSTAL: Oooops!

ARIANO: When Jeannie's father found out, God! I still see his
　　　　face whenever I close my eyes. (ARIANO, *trying to re-
　　　　create the moment, bellows in the voice of Jeannie's father.*)
　　　　"I'm allergic to spics!" (CRYSTAL *blurts out a laugh but
　　　　swallows it upon seeing* ARIANO's *stern look.*)

CRYSTAL: Sorry.

ARIANO: It is sorry. It's very sorry. Lookit how sick the bastard
　　　　was that he could say to me that we couldn't be together,
　　　　Jeannie and I, but because should his daughter give him
　　　　any Puerto Rican grandkids, he wouldn't be able to hold
　　　　them and enjoy them like he could normal kids. The rea-
　　　　son being, he said, that he'd be too busy sneezing and
　　　　slobbering all over them. So he warned me. He said,
　　　　that if by chance his daughter ever did produce Rican
　　　　grandkids, he'd have to wipe my 18 year-old ass off the
　　　　street. (CRYSTAL *kisses his cheek and lays him in her
　　　　lap.*) Trouble was, Jeannie was already pregnant.

CRYSTAL: That past is the past. Forget about it.

ARIANO: That sucka had a heart of ice. He didn't care who his
　　　　daughter fucked, he said, but when it came to living with
　　　　the evidence, well, that was a different story. That man
　　　　gave me $2,000 to stay away and forget about the whole
　　　　thing. He paid me because, according to him, he under-
　　　　stood my trying' to better myself by marrying white.

CRYSTAL: Well, that was sorta decent of him ...
ARIANO: (*Interrupting.*) $2,000?!! For somebody that I loved?
    For my baby? (*He laughs.*) So now, now when somebody
    asks, "Whatever happend to that polite, shy, little boy?
    Ariano? Whatever became of him?" I'll just turn around
    and tell them that that boy died! Looooong ago! Yes!
    That naive little shmuck is no more! Struck down on the
    welcome-mat of that all-American home and $2,000 paid
    for his funeral! Two thousand reasons that told me in
    green! Why love is not pure! Love is not sacred! And
    love, for damn sure, is not fucking blind!
CRYSTAL: Easy, it's history.
ARIANO: I stood there. Like an idiot! Waiting for Jeannie to say
    something to her old man. "Just like that?"
CRYSTAL: What? (ARIANO *now addresses* CRYSTAL *as if she
    were Jeannie as he relives the moment.*)
ARIANO: Defend me! Defend what we have. (ARIANO *abruptly
    grabs* CRYSTAL *and kisses her desperately. He stops and
    slowly releases her. They are both embarrassed.*) Dolores
    made me forget. I fell apart and Dolores put me back
    together. Jeannie was supposed to be the prize. If I be-
    haved, studied, didn't hang out, I'd pass and get the prize.
    But Dolores was the prize.
CRYSTAL: You're gettin' yourself all upset, stop.
ARIANO: She helped me start the business—the laundry. "Go
    back to college," she said, I went. Always optimistic, al-
    ways undefeatable! No problems too big! None! She has a
    solution. Always! She loves me. I love her. I do, Crystal.
    I love her ... (*The door crashes wide open as* SOLDIER*'s
    powerful slam with his fist startles them both.*)
SOLDIER: (*Sing-song.*) Doors open! Muy peligroso in New York
    City!
CRYSTAL: (*Recovering.*) Jesus Christ. (ARIANO *is furious and
    lurches at* SOLDIER, *grabbing him by his lapels.*)
ARIANO: You little shit bag!
SOLDIER: Hey! Hey!
CRYSTAL: Arrie, Arrie! Stop! Stop, I was expecting him.
SOLDIER: Step-off, bee. You heard the lady. (ARIANO *reluctantly
    sets him loose.* SOLDIER *brushes himself off.* ARIANO
    turns away, still trying to come down from the scare.)
ARIANO: Don't you knock first?
SOLDIER: I did knock. Guess I don't know my own strength,
    that's all. (SOLDIER *flexes for all concerned.*)

ARIANO: He's delivering the money now?
CRYSTAL: No. He brought it already. You mean the hundred
    bucks?
ARIANO: Yes, I mean the hundred bucks! You did ask for it,
    didn't you? Or is this jive-ass con-man beatin' my meat?
    (CRYSTAL *stands between them trying to calm* ARIANO.)
SOLDIER: Let him come. I'm tired of his shit, anyway.
CRYSTAL: Quiet, Soldier! Arrie, I sent him to the drug store
    for some pills. I wasn't feeling too good. (ARIANO *says
    nothing and stares down at* SOLDIER, *who looks away at
    first and then, irritated, hits back.*)
SOLDIER: You heard the lady. What you lookin' at me for?
ARIANO: You're pushing it! (SOLDIER *breaks past* CRYSTAL
    and goes up into ARIANO's *face.*)
SOLDIER: Naw, man, you're pushin' it! She just finished tellin'
    you that she sent me out ta get her something. Ain't that
    what you just finished tellin' me this fuckin' aftanoon? To
    help the bitch out? (ARIANO *turns to* CRYSTAL. SOL-
    DIER *takes the opportunity to hide a silver foil packet. He
    waves it behind* ARIANO's *back so that* CRYSTAL *sees
    where he puts it. He hides it.*)
CRYSTAL: You're blowin' this all outta proportion, Arrie.
ARIANO: If you screw this up, Crystal! If anything happens to
    this kid ... (ARIANO *abruptly grabs* CRYSTAL's *arms
    and raises her sleeves looking for track marks.*)
CRYSTAL: What the hell are you talking about?! Are you nuts?!
    Put the brain in park kiddo and give us all a break, why
    don't ya?!
ARIANO: You're a walking pharmacy for Christ sake!
CRYSTAL: I don't know what you're talking about.
SOLDIER: A little suga' neva' hurt anybody, Arrie. Come on now,
    lighten up ...
CRYSTAL: (*Interrupting.*) Soldier, will you please get outta here?!
ARIANO: Your pills, Crystal. What about your pills?
SOLDIER: Sorry, Crys, store ran out. (SOLDIER *laughs.* ARIA-
    NO *lunges at him, grabbing him again.*)
ARIANO: And so's my patience! So you better take a hike, boy!
    Your services are no longer required! (*With the speed of
    light,* SOLDIER *flicks open a switchblade, bringing it up
    to* ARIANO's *face.* ARIANO *does not even blink.*)
SOLDIER: Don't fuck with me like this, Arrie! You better step off!
    (ARIANO *smiles and raises his chin so that it rests upon
    the tip of the blade.*)

ARIANO: Do it! You'd be doing me a great favor. (*There is a long, tense moment as* SOLDIER *holds the blade in place, but does not follow through. He lowers it slowly.*) I didn't think so. (SOLDIER *breaks away and steps back.*)

SOLDIER: The crime—or the slime—ain't worth my time. You dig? (ARIANO *starts to laugh.*)

ARIANO: Look at me. What am I doing here? What the fuck am I doing here? On my right, a tramp. On my left, a convict. What the fuck is this place? I got a home ... a family ...

SOLDIER: (*Interrupting.*) Cut the high and mighty shit, 'cause you ain't no better than us, mothafucka. You eat rice and beans just like I do, and that bitch over there is bought and paid for, so don't even try it!

ARIANO: I'd be quiet if I were you and leave while you still could.

SOLDIER: I'm bookin', don't worry. But remember, no matter how much you wanna be, you ain't! You hear me, Ariano? (SOLDIER *by this time is outside the door.* ARIANO *slams it shut in his face.* SOLDIER *yells from outside.*) You ain't! ¡Maricón! (ARIANO *prepares to leave. He seems maniacal, his gestures, nervous.*)

CRYSTAL: You have no right!

ARIANO: You just did me a big favor!

CYSTAL: Oh really?

ARIANO: Yes, really!

CRYSTAL: You're totally wrong. You know that.

ARIANO: Right, wrong, I don't care! You can do whatever the hell you want, honey, 'cause you just lost yourself a good customer.

CRYSTAL: Slow down! This is not about hagglin'! We made our deal.

ARIANO: For a baby! A healthy baby!

CRYSTAL: I told you I'm not taking anything!

ARIANO: Come on.

CRYSTAL: All right, all right! A little grass. That's it! So what? You ain't backin' outta this, José! No way!

ARIANO: I wanna thank you. I wanna thank you 'cause suddenly I'm as clear as a bell. You and that orangoutan showed me that I belong at home. With my wife. My kid. Oh, and if I ever see your face ...

CRYSTAL: Oh, you'll see my face, all right! 'Cause this face is gonna be up in your face, if you try and pull what you're talking about! (ARIANO *tries to exit. She blocks him.*)

I don't want this baby, Ariano, you do! And I ain't Dolores or Doña Aida, so don't think you can railroad my
ass the way you do theirs! I know too much, baby! You
seem to forget that I was looking over your shoulder every step of the way while you drew up those blueprints to
casa cuchifrito up in Connecticut land. And I warn you
that I will be up there like (*She snaps her fingers.*) this
to detonate the bomb that'll bring the shit down around
your ears! So I expect to see you—daddy—the day Pan-
cho Villa Jr. here decides he wants to do his little hat
dance, with I remind you, the rest of my money!

ARIANO: If it's healthy and if it's normal, then we'll talk about it,
Crystal. We'll talk about it! (ARIANO *bolts out the door.*)

CRYSTAL: No talk! Ten thousand more! Just like we agreed!
Or I swear to God ...! (*She slams the door. She is livid.
She immediately goes to the place where* SOLDIER *hid the
packet, retrieves it, goes to her bed and begins preparations
to smoke it.*) You don't know who you're fucking with,
mister. You really don't know. (*End of Act One.*)

ACT TWO

.... SCENE ONE ....

The next morning. ARIANO's *apartment. At rise,* CLARA
and DOLORES *sit across from one another in silence. Both are in
night gowns. They both drink coffee.* DOLORES *smokes and is lost
in thought.* CLARA *is very concerned. There is a long silence.*

CLARA: Te ves cansada. You look bad. (*There is no response.*)
You told him about the baby? (DOLORES *shakes her
head "no."*) No te apures. He'll be back. He's just letting
off steam.

DOLORES: It was bad, Clara.

CLARA: Heck, it was an argument; of course, it was bad. Be real,
please.

DOLORES: You have to do something for me.

CLARA: Seguro, m'ija. Anything.

DOLORES: I want you to take Serafín for a while.

CLARA: ¿Que qué? What did you say?

DOLORES: Ay, Clara, he hit him last night! He was crazy. I never saw him that bad. He hit me too!

CLARA: Then throw him the fuck out! Call the police!

DOLORES: Clara! Sssssh! You'll wake up Serafín!

CLARA: Serafín! Where is he? I want to see him!

DOLORES: ¡Cálmate! He's all right. I swear he is. He finally fell asleep a few hours ago. I was up with him all night.

CLARA: ¡Bueno, m'ija! Llegamos al colmo. ¿Tú no crees? This is it! !¡¿Y tú no te abochornas, carajo?!! You're not embarrassed?

DOLORES: Embarrassed? For what? What did I do?

CLARA: It's what you're not doing? Dammit, Dolores, doesn't this convince you? Don't you finally see what I've been talking about all these years?

DOLORES: He needs help!

CLARA: What he needs is for somebody his size to come and kick his ass, but good!

DOLORES: That's gonna solve a lot, right?

CLARA: And you're even willing to give up your son for him?

DOLORES: I am not giving him up! How can you even think that! It's only temporary. He'll be right downstairs with you. I need time. I can help Ariano, I know I can. I just want to make sure that Serafín never has to go through something like that again.

CLARA: He needs more time than you can give him. And you're pregnant again. God, Dolores, have you gone crazy?

DOLORES: But that's just the point! This baby will solve everything! Oh, Clara, I know you may not understand, but trust me! You're all I've got right now.

CLARA: I'm sorry. I can't! I can't just sit on the sidelines, mute, and watch you give that man another child! That you would even consider such a thing is beyond my comprehension.

DOLORES: This will be different.

CLARA: What are you going to do, carajo?! Pour bleach on your coffee?

DOLORES: Maybe I already have! (*There is a long silence. The two women stare at each other until* CLARA *can no longer look.*) There's something I should probably tell you.

CLARA: Stop!

DOLORES: Please. Listen.

CLARA: I don't want to know anything. ¡Cállate!

DOLORES: Let me explain.

CLARA: ¡Por favor! I can't! Don't you understand? I can't take this thing to another level. I couldn't deal with it.

DOLORES: Then will you at least help me? Please, Clara!

CLARA: I love you, Dolores. More than anything. So I hope you understand where I'm coming from. I can't, no puedo dejar that you jeopardize yourself or Serafín. If you don't throw that bastard out, or leave him yourself, then I'll take Serafín, all right. But I swear, te lo juro por los huesos de mi madre! I will do everything in my power to keep him from you!

DOLORES: ¡Tú estás loca, muchacha!

CLARA: No. I'm not crazy! I'll go to court. I'll have him arrested. (*There is a sudden knock on the door, which renders both* CLARA *and* DOLORES *mute.*)

DOÑA HERNÁNDEZ: Dolores, soy yo. Es Doña Hernández.

DOLORES: Shit! (DOLORES *hesitates, trying to compose herself.* CLARA *walks to the table and sits.* DOLORES *to* CLARA.) Please. Okay? (CLARA *does not respond and turns away.* DOLORES *opens the door and* DOÑA HERNÁNDEZ *comes in.*)

DOÑA HERNÁNDEZ: ¿Cómo estás m'ija? Perdona la molestia, ay, si Clará esta aquí también! Hi, Clara!

CLARA: How are you, Doña? How are you feeling? The last time I saw you, you had a cold.

DOÑA HERNÁNDEZ: Baah! No more cold! That night, I took un palito, a nice shot of Don Q, sent my husband to sleep on the couch and poof! ¡P'al carajo se fue el catarro! Straight to hell! (*She laughs.*)

DOLORES: ¿Quieres café, Doña? Some coffee?

DOÑA HERNÁNDEZ: ¡Ay sí! If it's not any trouble. I'm not bothering? (DOÑA HERNÁNDEZ *makes a courteous attempt to get up.*)

DOLORES: No! No! Please. Siéntate, sit. Please.

DOÑA HERNÁNDEZ: Okay. Make mine with milk, then. Light. No sugar. (*To* CLARA.) Diabetes.

CLARA: Really?

DOLORES: And you, Clara? Coffee?

CLARA: A little more. Black, this time.

DOÑA HERNÁNDEZ: You look very good, Clara. Did you ever make it to that hairdresser I told you about? I told him you would make an appointment.

CLARA: I went, Doña, but I really didn't feel the urgency to have my hair hot pressed, which is all he seemed to want to do.

DOÑA HERNÁNDEZ: Y ¿por qué no? Estiraíto. Un estilito así como la Farrah Fawcett. You would look nice.

CLARA: I don't think so.

DOÑA HERNÁNDEZ: Well. I try, no? (*She laughs. To* DO-LORES.) ¿Y tú, linda? How are you?

DOLORES: Good Doña. I'm okay, a Dios gracias.

DOÑA HERNÁNDEZ: ¿Y Serafinsito?

DOLORES: Durmiendo. I let him sleep late Saturdays.

DOÑA HERNÁNDEZ: Qué bien. That's nice. (*There is an awkward silence as* DOLORES *serves the coffee.* DOÑA HERNÁNDEZ *surveys the apartment.*)

DOLORES: Anything wrong, Doña?

DOÑA HERNÁNDEZ: Oh no, no. A little sad. I was so worried! I wanted to make sure that I got a chance to see you before you left.

DOLORES: What? (DOLORES *then follows* DOÑA HERNÁNDEZ*'s stares around the apartment. She now understands and laughs softly.*) No, Doña. We're renovating and redecorating.

CLARA: (*Dryly.*) That's right, Doña. You couldn't get her outta here with a crowbar.

DOÑA HERNÁNDEZ: Really? You're not moving, then?

DOLORES: You heard Clara. I'm very content here. Why would I have to move?

CLARA: Excuse me. I've got this sudden urge to go to the bathroom. (CLARA *gets up to go, but stops dead in her tracks as* DOÑA HERNÁNDEZ *continues.*)

DOÑA HERNÁNDEZ: Perdón, entonces. I guess that since Ariano sold the laundries, pues everybody's jumping to conclusions.

CLARA: What? What did you say?

DOLORES: (*Interrupting.*) Clara, excuse me. (*To* HERNÁNDEZ.) What was that, Doña? Where did you hear that?

DOÑA HERNÁNDEZ: You mean you didn't know about it? The streets are buzzing.

CLARA: (*Sarcastically.*) Oh, of course Dolores knew. Ariano tells her everything, doesn't he, querida?

DOLORES: Okay. Doña. What's this all about? What are you really here for?

DOÑA HERNÁNDEZ: Era para decir adiós, to say goodbye. I thought you'd be leaving. Why else would Ariano sell his business.

DOLORES: He did not sell anything! It's gossip! Bochinche!

DOÑA HERNÁNDEZ: Oh noooo! He has sold them. Mr. Vélez,
tú sabes, el bodeguero from next door. He bought them
all.

CLARA: Coge, bruta. ¡Sigue oliéndole el fondillo al pendejo ese!

DOÑA HERNÁNDEZ: So, you didn't know! I'm glad I came.

DOLORES: Oh, I'm sure of that.

DOÑA HERNÁNDEZ: ¡Defiende lo tuyo, hija! There are those
who want to take it from you.

DOLORES: Will you please speak your mind!

CLARA: ¡Dolores! ¡Más respeto!

DOÑA HERNÁNDEZ: No, déjala. She has every right to be upset. I don't blame her. Mira, Dolores. You know me
for many years. You know I don't like to get involved in
other people's affairs. ¡Entrometida no soy! But you and
Ariano, ¡imagínate oye! ¡Son familia! Like family.

DOLORES: What, may I ask, does this have to do with the laundry?

DOÑA HERNÁNDEZ: Every marriage goes through its difficult
times, querida.

DOLORES: (*To* CLARA.) Are you sure you've told enough people.
Didn't leave out anybody, did you?

CLARA: What, are you crazy or something? You don't know me
better than that ... (DOLORES *and* CLARA *begin to argue, but* DOÑA HERNÁNDEZ *jumps in.*)

DOÑA HERNÁNDEZ: ¡Hijas, hijas! ¡No! ¡Por favor! ¡Dolores!
Please! Don't get excited! Everything will be fine, but
you can't go crazy. Listen, escúchame, you have to understand. Your husband, he is a very good-looking man!
He's also very successful. Women look at him, play up
to him. Of course, el siendo macho al fin, being a typical
man, if they put it in front of him, se lo estrellan en la
cara, naturally ...

DOLORES: That's enough!

CLARA: Hear her out!

DOLORES: I said shut up! Both of you! How dare you! Come
into my house, sit at my table ... Doña Hernández, please
leave!

CLARA: Dolores!

DOLORES: You too! Out! I don't need any of this shit!

DOÑA HERNÁNDEZ: She is nothing! You don't have to worry!
Una americana, hinchá, seca, fea, ugly! (DOLORES *opens*

the door for them.) Well. At least now you know. You can fight! Ariano can't leave. You must make things work, you must stay here.

DOLORES: Goodbye! (*Blockout.*)

.... SCENE TWO ....

Lights up outside of CLARA's *apartment, a few hours later.*
CLARA *appears as* ARIANO *arrives. He is very tired.*

CLARA: We have to talk.
ARIANO: Not now, Clara. (ARIANO *proceeds towards his apartment.*)
CLARA: Sí, Ariano, ahora.
ARIANO: No. Not now. (ARIANO *continues on his way.*)
CLARA: You don't want to go in there. She knows.
ARIANO: What are you talking about?
CLARA: About the blonde. (ARIANO *stops dead in his tracks; however, he says nothing.*) Can we talk? (ARIANO *does not respond. He merely looks her straight in the face.*) You're a fighter, Ariano. And, putting anything else I may feel about you aside, it's the one thing I admired about you. I've seen you struggle for many, many years, piling up success after success and it made me feel good. It made me feel good, carajo, because you were one of my own kind! Un puertorriqueño.
ARIANO: Please make your point.
CLARA: I couldn't understand why, with all God had given you, you were still so unhappy. Then, Serafín was born.
ARIANO: That's as far as you go, lady.
CLARA: I know what you're going through!
ARIANO: Really? So you know all about Ariano, is this what you're saying to me? You got me all figured out, is that it?
CLARA: Laying up with Barbie is not gonna make you Ken! (A-RIANO *makes a move to depart but* CLARA *holds on to his sleeve.*) I'm not making fun of you, Ariano. I am the last one who can point a finger, 'cause I've had to dance with those demons same as you. I was a blonde for years, remember? An acid-rock gringo on each arm and a bottle of Miss Clairol in my knap-sack. That was Clara. And thank God they weren't pushing blue contacts back

then, 'cause I'm sure I would have found a way to have
the mothafuckas glued in! You see, Ariano, I didn't like
looking in that mirror any more than you did, because all
I'd see was this, this Puerto Rican, rice and beans face,
staring right back at me. And that, mi amor, has never
been in fashion!

ARIANO: Is that why you still let out such a sigh of relief any-
time someone tells you, "Gee, but you don't look Puerto
Rican."

CLARA: Unlike yourself, I don't give a flying fuck about what
people think or say. Some of us grow up!

ARIANO: I'm glad that you've been able to "transcend" all that,
Clara. I'm sure the world is glad as well.

CLARA: Have you "transcended," querido? I don't think so.

ARIANO: You just don't know when to stop, do you?

CLARA: Last night you hit them! What about the next time? What
about the next time?

ARIANO: Whatever happens, in my house, with my family, is my
business!

CLARA: That lady and that child are the only family I got! So you
see, Mister, it is my business.

ARIANO: You're way out of line on this one. Where do you come
off telling me how to run my life?

CLARA: I'm not that presumptous! I don't have any answers for
you! You have to work things out the way we all did.
What I'm suggesting is that you go away for a while. See
what it is you really want. You need to go away, Ariano!

ARIANO: You've wanted that for a long time.

CLARA: No more than you have! Don't you see? No more than
you.

ARIANO: I'll handle things the way I've always handled them—
my way.

CLARA: Leave, Ariano. Leave, or the next time I'll call the police.
I'll have you arrested. (*Lights down.*)

.... SCENE THREE ....

Lights up on ARIANO's *apartment a few moments later.* DO-
LORES *stands at one end of the table facing away from* ARIANO,
who stands at the opposite end. There is silence.

DOLORES: ¿Dónde tú estabas? Where were you?

ARIANO: I want to apologize for last night. To you and Serafín.

DOLORES: I said, where were you last night?!

ARIANO: Walking. Around. Hit a few bars. Who cares? Where's Serafín?

DOLORES: He's sleeping in your room, so be quiet! He was up all night crying.

ARIANO: Jesus! I want to see him. I want to tell him I'm sorry.

DOLORES: You can do that later. We have things to discuss.

ARIANO: Look, I was wrong. I admit it. I'm an asshole, what can I say?

DOLORES: Well that's very gallant. Any other concession while we're being so humble? (ARIANO *says nothing.*) I just got a visit from *El Diario* a few minutes ago.

ARIANO: Excuse me?

DOLORES: Doña Hernández dropped by. She didn't come to talk about the weather, either. (ARIANO *says nothing and just shakes his head from side to side.*)

DOLORES: Are you going to say something?

ARIANO: (*Quietly.*) I guess that explains everything.

DOLORES: What?

ARIANO: Nothing.

DOLORES: You know, Ariano, she seemed very concerened about us. Particularly about the state of our marriage. Normally I wouldn't trust her for the time of day, but she put on too good a show to dismiss her completely. (ARIANO *will remain silent as long as he can.*) She said you sold all the laundromats. (ARIANO *gives off a nervous laughter. He sits.*) Then, she's right?

ARIANO: It was supposed to be a secret. I wanted to surprise you.

DOLORES: What kind of friggin' surprise is that?!

ARIANO: Calm down, all right! Jeez, easy. What did we talk about last night? That you quit your job, right? So! After last night, I got to thinking about this togetherness thing. Maybe you were right. Maybe it was time to switch gears. Vélez has been after me for months for the stores. He offered a good price, so last night I dropped by and we did it. They're his now.

DOLORES: Just like that, huh? He had a few thousand in his hip-pocket and said, "here ya go!" What did he do write out a receipt on a shopping bag?

ARIANO: What are you talking about?

DOLORES: Hernández said he paid you cash, up front.

ARIANO: No, no. No money changed hands. We made a verbal
　　　　agreement, that's all. We'll sign the papers later on this
　　　　week. You know Doña Ida. You know she exaggerates.

DOLORES: She does, huh? Was that blonde she said she saw you
　　　　with a figment of her imagination too?

ARIANO: (*Exploding.*) What do I have all around me, dammit,
　　　　spies?!! Nobody has anything better to do than keep track
　　　　of my fucking life?

DOLORES: Was she or was she not hallucinating? Answer me!

ARIANO: She's talking about Soldier's girlfriend! She comes to the
　　　　store because she knows she can always reach him there.
　　　　Doña Ida is bochinchando, like always! God, Dolores,
　　　　you know how she feels about me. She gets jealous if
　　　　she thinks she's not the center of my attention twenty-five
　　　　hours-a-day! You'd think she was my wife!

DOLORES: But she's not. I am. And you're right. I am aware of
　　　　how much Doña Ida loves you. She loves you so much,
　　　　as a matter of fact, that something must have scared her
　　　　real bad, for her to come over here and do what she did.
　　　　Maybe she panicked? Maybe she thought that she would
　　　　never see you again. Is that it, you think, Ariano? Do you
　　　　suppose that she had some reason to believe that you're
　　　　going away?

ARIANO: Is that what you want to believe?

DOLORES: I don't know what to believe. (ARIANO *bows his head
　　　　and is silent.*) So you're saying that the talk about the girl
　　　　is a lie.

ARIANO: She exists, but Doña Ida is getting her wires crossed.
　　　　She's Soldier's girl. I swear.

DOLORES: And why didn't you tell me about the laundry?

ARIANO: I wanted it to be a surprise. Negrita, look. I'm sorry
　　　　about last night. And if you can forgive me ... Honey.
　　　　Let's go away. Leave all this shit behind. We can go to
　　　　Puerto Rico. Serafín won't have to take more crap in that
　　　　school, we can live peacefully, with our own kind.

DOLORES: You want to leave?

ARIANO: Uhuh! Away from everybody! We can leave tomorrow,
　　　　start fresh. (ARIANO *takes her hands.*) If you give me
　　　　another chance, you won't regret it! I'll change! I swear!
　　　　It's this place. It's, it's evil! It takes control. I love you,
　　　　Dolores. I love you and Serafín! But sometimes, my mind
　　　　... my mind thinks about so many things, I don't know
　　　　what happens. I change, I act crazy.

DOLORES: What things? Talk to me. E' que you never talk to me.

ARIANO: It doesn't matter now. If you tell me you want to be with me, if you say to go, then we'll go! And everything will change. I'll make you happier than you've ever been, I swear.

DOLORES: Ariano, I don't know. You make so many promises. (DOLORES *breaks down and cries.* ARIANO *embraces her.*)

ARIANO: Please don't, nena. Negrita, por favor. Not over me. (ARIANO *showers her with kisses and tries to console her.*) You're more than good for putting up with my shit and I know that. You are the best, Dolores! I swear on my mother's grave that nobody could ever satisfy me like you. Nobody! Mamita, I'll tell you the truth. I came in here this morning ready to pack up and leave.

DOLORES: (*Startled.*) What?!

ARIANO: If that's what you wanted. Hey, only if that's what you would have wanted.

DOLORES: Is that what you want?

ARIANO: No. I want to stay here with you and Serafín. I want to be a family again. (*They embrace.*)

DOLORES: I want another baby. Tell me you want one too. (A-RIANO *embraces her.*)

ARIANO: Anything! Anything. Vente. We'll start now. We'll make 100 babies.

DOLORES: I'm already pregnant. (ARIANO *is stunned. A loud knock comes from the door.*)

ARIANO: We're having a baby? (DOLORES *nods. Another anxious knock on the door.*)

DOLORES: I was afraid to tell you before. (ARIANO *sweeps her into his arms. He is elated. The knocking grows louder.*)

ARIANO: Afraid?! No, no! Never be afraid ever. It's perfect! Perfect!

SOLDIER: (*Outside.*) Arrie! Open up!

ARIANO: Goddammit!

DOLORES: It sounds like Soldier, honey.

ARIANO: I fired him yesterday. (ARIANO *flings open the door.* SOLDIER *comes in respectful and nervous.*)

ARIANO: This better be important.

SOLDIER: Yo, Arrie. It's uhhh Chris. He's bad, man. I went over to his pad and like he was stretched out on the floor.

DOLORES: Who?

ARIANO: A guy I do business with, m'ija. (*To* SOLDIER.) Just
    call the cops. I can't do anything.

SOLDIER: The cops are already there. And an ambulance too.
    It didn't look to me like he was gonna make it, you now
    what I'm saying?

DOLORES: M'ijo, vete a ver. (ARIANO *hesitates, then gets his
    jacket.*)

ARIANO: I'll be right back, babe. This won't take long. Then we
    celebrate! (*He pecks her on the cheek and starts to exit
    with* SOLDIER.)

SOLDIER: Yo, Arrie, I'm sorry about yesterday, you know.

ARIANO: We'll talk about it later, Soldier.

SOLDIER: That's good. (*They exit.* DOLORES *smiles and goes
    into a long, tension-relieving stretch. She is elated.*)

DOLORES: ¡Gracias te doy, Señor! Thank you! That's all I wanted.
    My family. My family! (*Fade to black.*)

.... SCENE FOUR ....

*The stage is in darkness. We hear music. The salsa version of
the song, "New York State of Mind," as interpreted by the group,
Charanga '76. Lights up slow reveal* ARIANO's *livingroom, fully
redecorated. The stereo plays the tune.* CLARA *is at the table with*
SERAFÍN. *He is again coloring and* CLARA *helps him. They are
enjoying themselves. We will hear* DOLORES *and* ARIANO *in the
bedroom as they joke and kid around. They are getting dressed to
go out. The time is one week later.*

SERAFÍN: Titi, you draw lousy!

CLARA: Well, excuse me, Picasso!

SERAFÍN: That's okay. I'll teach you.

CLARA: Now, that part I like. (CLARA *gives him a hug and goes
    for some wine.* DOLORES *calls from the room.*)

DOLORES: We'll be out in a minute, m'ija.

CLARA: (*Shouting.*) Take your time.

DOLORES: There's wine in the cabinet.

CLARA: Good idea. I'll go get some.

SERAFÍN: Give me some.

CLARA: Ay. Míralo a él. This is for grown-ups, mister. (SERAFÍN
    stands up on the chair.) Well, I guess you are at that. A
    sip. (CLARA *lets* SERAFÍN *sip and then pulls away the
    glass.*)

SERAFÍN: Mmmmmmm!

CLARA: Like that, huh? Well, if you're old enough to sip, you're old enough to take out your Titi and dance. Vente. (SE-RAFIN *jumps off the chair and begins to salsa with* CLARA. *They enjoy themselves immensely.* CLARA *is so taken with* SERAFÍN *that she cannot help but laugh.*)

SERAFÍN: You should have been with us on the trip, Titi. It was fun.

CLARA: You like the woods, huh?

SERAFÍN: Yeah! Papi took me fishing! We got up real early. Mommy was still sleeping. We went in the lake.

CLARA: You caught anything?

SERAFÍN: I got a big fish. Like Jaws!

CLARA: Like Jaws?

SERAFÍN: Papi only caught a little one. (SERAFÍN *starts to laugh.*)

CLARA: I guess you're the champ, then.

SERAFÍN: Yep! That's what papi told me too. He gave me a big kiss when I got it. A biiig kiss, Titi! (CLARA *bends down to him.* SERAFÍN *stops dancing as well.*)

CLARA: You like that, huh, papito?

SERAFÍN: Yes, Titi. I liked it a lot. (CLARA *and* SERAFÍN *embrace each other.*)

CLARA: Good, m'ijo, good. I'm glad you like it a lot. That's all Titi wants to hear. That you're happy. That makes me happy too. (DOLORES *comes gliding out on a cloud. She is radiant in a splendid black gown. She carries some jewelry and her clutch and some makeup.*)

DOLORES: We made reservations everywhere! Dinner! Theatre! Salsa!

CLARA: You're a knock-out! (CLARA *primps the dress.*) I'm getting good, carajo.

DOLORES: This design is fabulous! And bullshit, you've always been good!

SERAFÍN: You look nice, Mommy.

DOLORES: Thank you, papito! (DOLORES *throws him a kiss.*) ¡Deja que tú veas a Ariano! We almost decided to do our own little merengue in there.

CLARA: A week in the woods with the chipmunks and squirrels did all this.

DOLORES: You've got to do it. Very hot! Very romantic!

CLARA: With my luck the only thing that would brush up against me would be poison ivy. Y de meter—m'ija quizás a splinter—¡quizás!

DOLORES: You don't mind, do you? Babysitting on such short notice?

CLARA: Please! (DOLORES *continues to put on the finishing touches.*) I know it's been a week. We haven't really had any time to talk. I just got that note that said you guys went upstate. Are we going to make believe that the other day never happened?

DOLORES: Can we?

CLARA: What do you think?

DOLORES: Mira. I think, that there were a lot of things that I've wanted to say to you for a long time, and that I shouldn't have waited for an argument to say them. A lot of things came out the wrong way. M'ija I know you feel that I should be more like you. And for a while there I used to think so too. I felt that somehow I was inferior, less evolved, 'cause I could never handle things the way you did. I would constantly ask, "What would Clara do in a case like this?" Or, "How would Clara do it?" Querida, until finally I realized that I am not you! And that your answers are not my answers. I listen to you, Clara. And I always will because I trust you and, more important, I love you. I know you feel good about yourself, but I feel good about myself too! My decisions are just as valid as yours and I don't feel I should have to be made to apologize for them. Especially to you. (DOLORES *and* CLARA *embrace while a quiet moment passes between them.*)

CLARA: I am wonderful. Am I not?

DOLORES: Which doesn't mean that I can't give you a humbling little kick in the culito every now and then.

CLARA: Likewise, I'm sure. (*There is a short silence.*) He knows?

DOLORES: Yep.

CLARA: You still want me to take Serafín for a while?

DOLORES: No. But I do want you to love him as much as you always have.

CLARA: The easiest thing you've asked me all evening. (CLARA *goes to* SERAFÍN *and kisses him.*)

DOLORES: Mira, uhhh, how can I put this?

CLARA: Gently. Whatever it is.

DOLORES: Ariano wants to call a truce.

CLARA: A truce.

DOLORES: He's committed, he says, to winning your affections. Friends? Maybe?

CLARA: (*Laughing.*) Maybe. (ARIANO *comes into the room dressed in an elegant black tuxedo. He is nervous in dealing with* CLARA *at first, but warms up to it.*)
ARIANO: Ready! (ARIANO *goes to* CLARA *and kisses her on the cheek.*) Hello.
CLARA: You look nice.
ARIANO: Thank you. (SERAFÍN *comes running over to* ARIANO, *who swoops him into the air.*) Hey champ! (ARIANO *kisses him.*) Un besito a papi. (SERAFÍN *kisses him.*) Ready, nena?
CLARA: Well. Let me get going. Come on, Serafín.
ARIANO: I'll drop him off before we leave, Clara.
CLARA: Okay. (CLARA *begins to exit. She stops and turns to* ARIANO.) I'm sorry about your friend. (ARIANO *looks a bit tense and there is an awkward silence.*)
ARIANO: Thanks.
CLARA: Be careful driving.
DOLORES: Excuse me? The Morenos—drive? We rented a limo, darling?
CLARA: And the babysitter gets minimum wage, I love it! (CLARA *exits.*) Have fun. (ARIANO *sneaks up behind* DOLORES *and gives her a warm embrace.*)
ARIANO: Whoa there, foxy lady. Can I have this dance? (SERAFÍN *races over and clings to them both.*)
SERAFÍN: Me too, me too! (*They move about a bit, enjoying a nice moment.*)
ARIANO: So. You guys liked the country?
SERAFÍN: Yeaaaahh!
DOLORES: That's good enough to win my vote.
ARIANO: Good. Because I bought us a house in the country.
DOLORES: ¿Que qué? You didn't!
ARIANO: (*To* SERAFÍN.) We got us a beautiful house in Connecticut, champ! And it's just like the place up on the lake. Trees, grass ...
SERAFÍN: Yeaaaaahh!
ARIANO: We're gonna live there! And we'll always go to the lake and we'll play baseball and football. You like that?
SERAFÍN: With you and Mommy?
ARIANO: With me and Mommy and ... you want a baby brother?
DOLORES: Sister!
ARIANO: Sister.
SERAFÍN: I could play with her?
ARIANO: I got a new car too. A Mercedes!

DOLORES: But how?

SERAFÍN: Can I drive?

ARIANO: In about fifteen years or so, sure!

DOLORES: Ariano, when? How?

ARIANO: I got everything under control, baby. Let your man take
    care of you!

DOLORES: No argument from me. (*They kiss.*)

ARIANO: Lets get your stuff, big guy. Your mommy and daddy
    have got a date. (ARIANO *leads* SERAFÍN *to the room.*
    DOLORES *continues to primp. There is sudden pounding*
    on the door that draws their attention.)

CRYSTAL: (*O.S.*) Ariano!

DOLORES: Who the hell is that? (DOLORES *goes to open the*
    door.)

ARIANO: Don't!

CRYSTAL: (*O.S.*) Ariano! Open this fucking door! I know you're
    in there!

DOLORES: Excuse me ... (DOLORES *goes to the door but* ARI-
    ANO *blocks her way.*)

ARIANO: Go in the next room, honey. This has to do with Soldier,
    there might be problems.

DOLORES: Oh, there's gonna be a problem, all right. If you don't
    get out of my way, there's gonna be lots of problems! (*The*
    banging is incessant.)

CRYSTAL: (*O.S.*) Ariano!

ARIANO: Get the hell outta here! (DOLORES *gets past* ARIANO
    and opens the door. A very tired and disheveled CRYSTAL
    faces her.)

DOLORES: Who the hell do you think you are, banging on my
    door like that?

CRYSTAL: I want Ariano!

DOLORES: I'm his wife!

CRYSTAL: Yeah, well you didn't look like the friggin' maid!
    (CRYSTAL *pushes past* DOLORES *and goes after* ARIA-
    NO.)

ARIANO: You have two seconds to get the fuck outta here!

DOLORES: I said, what do you want?!

ARIANO: Honey, let me handle this, please. (ARIANO *grabs*
    CRYSTAL *and tries to eject her.* CRYSTAL *breaks free*
    and goes deeper into the apartment.)

CRYSTAL: Get offa me, you son-of-a-bitch! (SERAFÍN *enters the*
    room unnoticed and crouches in a corner.)

DOLORES: Stop it!

ARIANO: Honey, let me handle this. I'll just throw her out.

DOLORES: Quiet! Now, either you let her talk, or I leave.

ARIANO: It's lies, baby! All lies! She's a junkie, she's trying to squeeze me for cash! She's garbage!

CRYSTAL: Now I'm trash, right? I was good enough before but now I'm garbage! (ARIANO *again makes an attempt to get* CRYSTAL *but* DOLORES *pushes him with all her might away from her.*)

DOLORES: I want to hear what she has to say. I want to hear! So either you let us talk here, or I'll take her somewhere else where we won't be disturbed. (ARIANO *stands his ground.*)

ARIANO: I can't believe you're letting her get away with this.

DOLORES: (*To* CRYSTAL.) All right! You've got five minutes.

CRYSTAL: It'll be less than that ... Maria! My time is precious too. Your husband owes me money! Ten thousand! (*To* ARIANO.) We had a deal!

ARIANO: You liar! We had nothing, you junkie mothafucka! Nothing!

CRYSTAL: I fell! It was an accident! It could have happened to anybody!

ARIANO: Get outta here, Crystal!

CRYSTAL: Look, I'm sorry about the baby, I really am. But that ain't the point now. I did my eight months and I want my compensation! Pay me! (*There is a silence.* ARIANO *is trying to see how this is affecting* DOLORES. *Without taking her eyes off of* CRYSTAL, DOLORES *speaks.*)

DOLORES: Is this the woman you told me about, Ariano? (ARIANO *is dumbfounded by the remark, as is* CRYSTAL. A-RIANO *plays along.*) Listen, miss. You'll get your money. My husband told me all about you, so don't get pushy in my house. Come back tomorrow and I'll give you the money myself.

CRYSTAL: Nope. Now! He's got it.

DOLORES: That's not pocket change.

CRYSTAL: In his wallet. He's got a check. (DOLORES *looks over to* ARIANO. *She goes to him and places her hand in his jacket.* ARIANO *tries to stop her but* DOLORES *will not have it. She pushes his hand away and removes his wallet and searches for the check. She finds it, pulls it out, gazes at it. She does not, however, lose her composure.*)

DOLORES: (*To* ARIANO.) Is this what you were going to buy our home with?

CRYSTAL: Hell. That's old news, toots. He's had that house so long already that property values have probably doubled by now, ain't that right, pumpkin? Did you tell her about the Mercedes too? (ARIANO *begins to charge again but* DOLORES *holds firmly onto his jacket sleeve.*)

DOLORES: Don't you dare!

ARIANO: Dolores, don't ...

DOLORES: Please. I don't want to hear anything. (DOLORES *folds the check and delivers it back hand. As* CRYSTAL *approaches it,* DOLORES *lets it drop to the floor.* CRYSTAL *remains still for a moment. She looks at* ARIANO *and then bends to retrieve the check. She quietly puts it away. There is a pause.*)

CRYSTAL: (*Quietly to* ARIANO.) Just like that?

DOLORES: You got what you came for, so get out! Or do you want him as well?

CRYSTAL: Oh nooooo! That's your basket-case, sweetheart. It seems that I've suddenly developed an allergy! (CRYSTAL *turns to exit, then stops, suddenly remembering something. She turns to* ARIANO.) Oooops! Almost forgot. Let it not be said that good ole' Crystal is without compassion. (CRYSTAL *reaches into her shopping bag and produces a doll. One from her collection. It is unclothed. She holds it by the leg, and thrusts it at* ARIANO.) I hope you don't mind. I named her Conchita! That's Puerto Rican ain't it? (DOLORES *can no longer contain it and breaks down.* ARIANO *takes the opportunity and lunges at* CRYSTAL, *grabbing her by the lapels. He flings the doll across the room. The doll lands in the proximity of* SERAFÍN, *who is over in a corner.*) Yeah! Go ahead! Hit me! I'd love to haul your ass into court! I'd sue you for everything you had, bastard! Everything! (ARIANO *hesitates at first and then drags her over to the door, opens it wide, and then pushes her out.* CRYSTAL *stands in the doorway.*) You're filthy, Ariano. You're nothing but a piece of shit! (ARIANO *stands in the doorway as* CRYSTAL *leaves. He does not turn towards* DOLORES.)

ARIANO: (*After a pause.*) It wasn't about love or anything like that. (DOLORES *is motionless, trying to contain the storm within her.* ARIANO *goes to her.*) I didn't love her!

DOLORES: ¡Dilo a tu madre, canto 'e cabrón! Serafín!

ARIANO: Let me talk to you ...

DOLORES: Serafín! (SERAFÍN *gets up from where he is crouched.*

DOLORES *is stunned that he was present.* ARIANO
touches her.)
ARIANO: M'ija. (DOLORES *attacks him.*)
DOLORES: You bastard! I hate you! Son-of-a-bitch! (*As* ARIANO
grapples with her, SERAFÍN *comes between them.*)
SERAFÍN: Mommy! Papi! No! Stoooop!
ARIANO: Papito, don't worry. Nothing's going to happen. (DO-
LORES *frees her hand and slaps him again and quickly
backs away.* ARIANO *takes the slap and merely bows his
head.* SERAFÍN *clings to* ARIANO. *He cries.*)
SERAFÍN: Mommy, noooo, pleaaaaase! (ARIANO *bends and hugs*
SERAFÍN. *He breaks down and cries.*)
ARIANO: Papito, I'm sorry! ¡Serafín! ¡Serafín, perdóname, hijo!
Forgive me, please! Please!
DOLORES: ¿Ahora? Ahora is too late, m'ijito! (DOLORES *pulls*
SERAFÍN *away from* ARIANO, *who does not move. He
remains kneeling on the floor.*)
DOLORES: (*To* SERAFÍN.) Pack a few things, Papi—no toys, no
junk! Just a few pants, some underwear, put them in the
knapsack from the camping trip.
SERAFÍN: (*Scared.*) No, Mommy, no!
ARIANO: Dolores, por favor.
DOLORES: Do as Mommy says!
SERAFÍN: I wanna stay!
DOLORES: Move! (DOLORES *pushes* SERAFÍN *to his room. She
turns and begins plucking off her jewelry and throwing it.*)
ARIANO: Dolores. I love you. ¡Te quiero! ¡M'ija, please!
DOLORES: You don't love me, Ariano.
ARIANO: I do! I do! I swear.
DOLORES: Naaaaah! Impossible! You don't even love yourself.
How can you say you love me?!
ARIANO: I've changed. Give me another chance.
DOLORES: Did she remind you of Jeannie? Was that it? (ARIA-
NO *tries to hold her.*)
ARIANO: No, that wasn't it at all.
DOLORES: She must have been good, eh? Better than me? I hear
white girls are freaky in bed. Was she freaky? Is that it?!
ARIANO: Dammit, don't do this! I told you, I swear! She meant
nothing to me. It was business.
DOLORES: Business?! Business, Ariano?! (DOLORES *lets out a
nervous laughter.*) ¡Te la comiste ahí! I wasn't expecting
that one! (ARIANO *touches her.*)
ARIANO: Negrita, don't!

DOLORES: (*Backing away.*) ¡Ahí llegaste! ¡Negrita! That's right!
¡Yo soy negrita!

ARIANO: I didn't mean it like that ...

DOLORES: Didn't you? I think you did. I think every time you've
said it that's exactly what you meant! ¡¡¡Negrita!!! (DO-
LORES *now takes his hand and makes him pass it over
her skin.*) She's white, and I'm the negrita!!

ARIANO: No!

DOLORES: Say it!

ARIANO: Stop it!

DOLORES: Negritaaa!

ARIANO: Negrita.

DOLORES: Again.

ARIANO: Negrita.

DOLORES: Louder godammit!

ARIANO: ¡Negrita! Negrita, negrita, negrita ... stop!! (DOLORES
takes his face firmly in her hand.)

DOLORES: That word, canto 'e idiota, means love. Love! All my
life the same thing. And from my own people! Que si
who's from Spain, who's not from Spain. Good hair, bad
hair, white features, black features, que si uno es indio, no
indio ... por eso, that's why, estamos tan jodío, puñeta!
¡Eso es por que nosotros los puertorriqueños seguimos
comiendo tanta mierda!

ARIANO: ¡No, m'ija! Don't say that. It's not true. That's not how
I think!

DOLORES: ¡Tú lo que eres es un acomplejao!

ARIANO: M'ija, no. The only complex I have maybe is that I
have always wanted the best for my family. Everything
had to be the best! But in order to do that, you have
to be a certain way—think a certain way. I didn't make
the rules, honey, I'm only playing by them. Don't you
understand?

DOLORES: I am a woman of color, your son and you, believe it
or not, are colored también! Same as that island you're
always crying over! Colored people who live in a world
full of color. Don't you understand?

ARIANO: (*Pleading.*) ¡No, carajo, no! Baby, look at us. Look at
all we have. We're not like the rest of the Puerto Ricans
here, Mommy. We've made it. We made it because I had
to make a choice. Here you have to make a choice. If you
say you're a nigger, then they'll treat you like a nigger!

DOLORES: Don't you think I know? Do you really think that
you were the only one? I'm darker than you are and my
family still tried to tell me que yo era una blanquita! That
we were white! But I have eyes, carajo! You have eyes!
That seed of self hatred has been with me ever since the
day I was born Puerto Rican! And every time an aunt
would pinch my nose to make it pointier, every time my
grandmother would try to weave silk out of wool, combing
my hair, yanking at it! Every time some white asshole
decided he was gonna piss on me, decided he was gonna
water that seed, I knew, I knew that if I let it, it would
grow! It would grow and rip right through me the way it's
ripped through you! So I grabbed that shit by its roots
and tore it out! And I bled and I hurt, but I'm still here!
And I'll be damned if I'm gonna let you come along and
plant another one. Noooo waaaaay! (ARIANO *goes to
her, holding her by the shoulders, pleading with her.*).
ARIANO: That's the past. I'm gonna be different. We have to
think about our future now. Our baby, honey, our baby!
(DOLORES *breaks into a nervous laughter.*) Stop!
DOLORES: Our baby, Ariano? (DOLORES *holds his face in one
hand, looking straight into his eyes.*) It's not yours, querido, ... (ARIANO *grabs her by her wrists and holds onto
them tightly, putting* DOLORES *at a distance from him.*)
You wanted white ... so I got white! (ARIANO *releases
her hands and turns away from her.*) The label on the
specimen was very clear ... blonde. Blue eyes.
ARIANO: Shut up! Be quiet!
DOLORES: It was a simple procedure. You would have never
known. Because I loved you, Ariano. I loved you so
much. (ARIANO *goes to* SERAFÍN *and tries to take him.*)
ARIANO: Serafín. Come on. We'll go for a walk. Mommy needs
to be alone right now. (DOLORES *snatches* SERAFÍN
away from him.) He shouldn't be hearing this. He can't
hear this shit, Dolores!
DOLORES: This is exactly what he has to hear! ¡Para que aprenda!
So he learns! ¡Todo el mundo se la pasa con la lengua
metía en el culo, pues ya estoy cansá! I'm tired! (DO-
LORES *brings* SERAFÍN *over to the same imaginary mirror of Act One. She stands behind him as they look out
over the audience.*) Vente, Papi. Because the last time
someone put you in front of this mirror, they lied to you!
They said that what was staring back at you was no good.

ARIANO: Don't tell him that, Dolores, please.
DOLORES: See?! Do you see there, mi amor? No! You're not
    black. And you're not white! You're not red or yellow or
    any one color! You are all of these! That is the beauty of
    what a Puerto Rican is, and don't you let anybody ever
    tell you any different! You tell them, mira, look at me,
    Papito ... (DOLORES *stands tall and erect with her chin
    up.*) You tell them, yo soy el nuevo puertorriqueño! I'm
    the new breed! And I love myself! I respect mysel! And
    if you believe it, then they'll believe it! Y el que no pueda
    apreciar eso, whoever doesn't like it, que se vaya pa la
    mierda! Straight to hell! (*There is a silence now. ARIANO
    stands his ground, paralyzed in humiliation and shame.
    He is in tears but dares not utter a word. SERAFÍN picks
    up the doll, which DOLORES quickly snatches out of his
    hand. She places it in ARIANO's hands.*)
DOLORES: (*Quietly.*) That's your father's.
ARIANO: (ARIANO *takes the doll. SERAFÍN hugs his father's legs
    fiercely. When ARIANO tries to reciprocate, DOLORES
    pulls SERAFÍN away and exits. ARIANO stands alone
    now. He looks around the apartment without taking a
    step. He is totally distraught. He begins to breathe deeply,
    almost heaving. He finally lets out a long bellow.*) Do-
    loreeeeeeees! (*Quietly.*) Serafín. (*He lunges over to the
    table. He pulls out the chair where SERAFÍN sat in the
    crayon scene. He places the doll on the table. He begins
    to speak to the chair as if SERAFÍN were there.*) Serafín,
    Serafín, don't hate me. Don't hate me, papi! Listen to
    your mother. Don't be like me. Listen to her! Listen
    ... (ARIANO *suddenly stops crying for a moment, as if
    that last word had hit home. He looks up from the chair,
    pensive. He slides the chair away and slowly notices the
    mirror.*) You have eyes, carajo! I have eyes. (*He looks
    slowly into the mirror.*) Not white, not black, not red or
    yellow. All of these. (*Eyes closed.*) I am the new Puerto
    Rican. (*Silence. He opens his eyes. He looks at him-
    self. The words come out easier this time.*) I am the New
    Puerto Rican! (ARIANO *is now strong and determined.*)
    And whoever doesn't like it ... can go to hell! (ARIANO
    *stands there in front of the mirror, gaining strength by the
    moment, as lights fade to black.*)

Family Scenes

by

Ivette M. Ramírez

Characters:

SOPHIA, twenty years old, rebellious and hot-tempered. She lives with her mother and sister.

PAULA, twenty-three years old, mostly even-tempered, very conservative. She's Sophia's sister.

MARGARITA, forty years old, she is an older version of Paula. She is Paula's and Sophia's mother.

BENNY, twenty-seven years old, has lived a fast life with women, dresses in flashy clothes and doesn't take life seriously. He's Paula's boyfriend.

EDUARDO, fifty years old, it's obvious that he's lived a hard life and that it's taken its toll on him. He's Sophia's father.

SAMUEL, fifty-five years old, he's an easy going man, who takes life as it comes but is tenacious in his relationships. He's Margarita's lover.

JIMMY, twenty-one years old, he's a casual guy, who hasn't had a conventional lifestyle and is looking for something permanent in his life.

.... SCENE ONE ....

The set is a small three-room apartment located in a poor, but well-kept neighborhood in the Bronx. The three rooms are set on a low platform. The center of the apartment is the kitchen with a bedroom on stage left with a doorway leading to the bathroom and the living room barely visible behind the kitchen. Stage right is the door to the apartment and the stoop of the brownstone building. The front of the stage represents the street, with a fire hydrant and lamppost. The apartment is furnished with mostly old furniture which is kept in good condition.

PAULA, dressed casually but fashionably, is in the bedroom admiring a wedding dress which hangs on a closet door. A light flickers from the living room television as MARGARITA watches it. SOPHIA comes up the steps of the brownstone to the door, fumbles for the house keys in her bag, drops it, tries the door and, finding it open, goes in.

SOPHIA: Mami, I'm home.

MARGARITA: (*From the living room.*) It's time you got home. Your food's on the counter. Eat it before it gets cold. I wish you would call when you're going to be late.

SOPHIA: (*Looking at the plate of food.*) I had to work late. (*To herself.*) Nag, nag, nag. (SOPHIA *places her handbag on the kitchen counter, picks up the plate and places it on the table. She goes to the refrigerator and pours herself a glass of milk; she then sits down at the kitchen table to eat.*)

PAULA: (*From the bedroom.*) Was that the door? (PAULA *comes out of the bedroom with a bride's magazine in her hand.*) Oh, it's you.

SOPHIA: (*Seeing the magazine.*) How come you're still looking at those? Didn't you tell Mami you were wearing her dress?

PAULA: I know, but it doesn't hurt to look. Besides, there's other things in here.

SOPHIA: You shouldn't have told her you were wearing her dress. You're going to hurt her feelings if you don't wear it.

PAULA: (*Reluctantly.*) I wouldn't do that. There's stuff in here about how to wear your hair ...

SOPHIA: Anything in there about when not to get married?

PAULA: Shut up, okay. I know you don't like Benny, but I'm the one who's marrying him, not you.

SOPHIA: (*Mocking her.*) Oh, well, ain't that precious. (*Pause.*) Sorry, I didn't mean it.

PAULA: He's not such a bad person, if you just give him a chance.

SOPHIA: I'm not saying nothing. I'm minding my own business.

PAULA: I really wish you would. He's coming over in a little while, so you better behave yourself.

SOPHIA: I'll be a good little girl, just like I always am.

PAULA: Please don't mess this up for me.

SOPHIA: What?

PAULA: (*Begins to go back into the bedroom.*) I want my wedding to be special.

SOPHIA: (*To herself.*) Well, maybe you should change the bridegroom.

PAULA: What did you say?

SOPHIA: Nothing.

PAULA: Can't you see how important this is to me?

SOPHIA: Yeah, sure.

PAULA: He's really a nice person. He has problems, but he loves me.

SOPHIA: You know, I'm sick of hearing about this. I'm sick of him hanging around here.

PAULA: He's my boyfriend and he can come whenever he wants.

SOPHIA: Big deal. I personally wouldn't go telling that to people I knew. (MARGARITA *enters carrying a plate and glass to the sink. She's in a housedress with a flower print, her hair is pinned up. She has the tired look about her but becomes animated when speaking to her daughters.*) Mami, tell her she can't have Benny over here every night.

PAULA: What do you care, you're never around, anyway.

MARGARITA: Will you stop fighting?

SOPHIA: Sure, go ahead take her side.

MARGARITA: (*Being patient.*) I'm not taking sides.

SOPHIA: Then tell her Benny can't come over every night.

MARGARITA: Do your dishes ... and mine.

SOPHIA: Mom, I just got home?

PAULA: You're so damn lazy.

SOPHIA: (*To* PAULA.) You know you're really stupid. (PAULA *reaches over to hit* SOPHIA *and* MARGARITA *steps between them.*)

PAULA: Sure, defend her, that's why she's such a spoiled ... (MARGARITA *grabs* PAULA *by the face.*)

MARGARITA: I thought you said you had a date with Benny?

PAULA: Yeah, yeah. (PAULA *reluctantly exits to the bedroom. MARGARITA turns to her youngest daughter; she slaps her gently on the head.*)

SOPHIA: Hey, what's that for?

MARGARITA: Haven't I told you a million times to leave your sister alone about Benny?

SOPHIA: But, Mom, he's just so ...

MARGARITA: He loves your sister and wants to marry her, so leave it alone.

SOPHIA: If you knew how people talk about him ... (MARGARITA *slaps her on the head again, this time a little harder.*) Ma, you're giving me a headache.

MARGARITA: I don't want to hear gossip, is that clear?

SOPHIA: Mom, why do you want her to marry Benny?

MARGARITA: I don't want anything. She's a good girl, she works hard and she should marry and settle down and have a family.

SOPHIA: Ugh, gross. (PAULA *comes out of the bedroom, looking at her watch.*)

MARGARITA: What time is Benny picking you up?

PAULA: Twenty minutes ago.

MARGARITA: Maybe he had to work late.

PAULA: I talked to him at home.

SOPHIA: (*Smiling.*) Maybe he's not coming.

PAULA: Why do you say that?

SOPHIA: (*Wide grin.*) Maybe he found something better along the way, maybe Dolores across the street got to him before he made it here.

MARGARITA: I warned you. (MARGARITA *reaches over and slaps* SOPHIA *on the head.*)

SOPHIA: Jesus, it's a miracle I'm not retarded.

MARGARITA: Sophia, don't you have something to do so you won't be in the same room as your sister?

SOPHIA: I'm eating, where would you like me to go, the toilet?

PAULA: That's a good place for you. (BENNY *comes strutting up the steps. When he gets to the door he stops a moment to smooth his hair before ringing the doorbell.* MARGARITA *raises her head up as if praying for peace.*) I'll get it. Hopefully it's Benny so I can get the hell out of here.

SOPHIA: You owe me one, I won't forget it. (PAULA *opens the door and* BENNY *enters.*)

PAULA: (*Kisses him lightly and clutches his arm.*) I told Mom we're going out for a while.

MARGARITA: Don't be too late, we all have to work tomorrow.

BENNY: Hello, Doña Margarita, how are you doing?

MARGARITA: (*Forcing a smile.*) Just fine, Benny; how are you?

BENNY: (*Rubs SOPHIA's head as if she's a kid.*) Hi, Sophie.

SOPHIA: (*Pushes his hand away.*) Don't do that.

BENNY: What's with you?

SOPHIA: Nothing, just keep your hands off me. (SOPHIA *picks up her dish and takes it to the sink.*) Mami, do I have to do the dishes?

MARGARITA: Yes, and you better do them now, 'cause one of your friends will call you and you'll be out the door and forget to do them.

PAULA: Mom, did I get a letter from Dad today?

MARGARITA: No, we didn't get any mail today.

PAULA: I need to know if he's going to be here for the wedding to give me away.

BENNY: What's the hurry, we still have six months.

SOPHIA: (*Without looking up from the sink.*) The condemned man speaks.

BENNY: (*To* SOPHIA.) Have I done something to you?

SOPHIA: You're breathing ain't you?

PAULA: (*To* SOPHIA.) If you don't stop it ...

SOPHIA: What did I do?

MARGARITA: (*Exits to the living room.*) Paula, Benny, why don't you go, so I can get some peace around here?

PAULA: (*Going into the bedroom.*) I have to get my purse.

BENNY: (*To* SOPHIA.) Really, sweetie, couldn't you even try to like me a little?

SOPHIA: What for? (PAULA *comes out of the bedroom.*)

PAULA: I'm ready. (BENNY and PAULA *exit the apartment and stop by the stoop.*

SOPHIA: (*Wipes her hands and takes a letter out of her bag. The letter is still sealed, she looks it over and then tears it into pieces. The phone rings and she goes into the bedroom to answer it. While in there she picks up a picture of her father on the dresser, looks at it for a moment, then opens a drawer and throws it in. She answers the phone as the lights go down on the apartment.*) Hello ... yeah, hi Jimmy ...

.... SCENE TWO ....

The light goes up on PAULA *and* BENNY *kissing in the hallway.* PAULA *is struggling a bit.*

PAULA: Benny? (BENNY *ignores* PAULA *and continues to caress her and presses harder up against her.*) Benny, please. (PAULA *pushes him away.* BENNY *leans up against the door and sulks.*) Don't be mad.

BENNY: I ain't mad.

PAULA: You could've fooled me. What's wrong?

BENNY: Honey, it's the same old story. I'm a man not a kid, or a machine you can turn on and off. I've got hormones.

PAULA: You better keep them under control.

BENNY: (*Taking her hand and kissing it.*) When are you going to stop being such a proper lady?

PAULA: When I have the wedding ring on my finger and it's official.

BENNY: No one waits anymore.

PAULA: Oh, really? Well, things aren't so simple anymore.

BENNY: (*Kissing her hand.*) There's no one but you, honey. I'll use protection, you don't have to worry.

PAULA: You want me to be like all those other girls you've gone out with before?

BENNY: (*Kissing her neck.*) Well, maybe just a little.

PAULA: (*Pushes him away by the face.*) Which one would you like me to be like, Denise, Sandy, Karen?

BENNY: Jesus, you're going to kill a guy for trying. You know they don't mean anything to me. You're the one I'm going to marry.

PAULA: Benny, sometimes ...

BENNY: (*Kissing her very gently.*) Why don't you trust me, uh? Don't I do everything you tell me?

PAULA: (*Enjoying* BENNY*'s caresses.*) I trust you ...

BENNY: (*Kissing and caressing her.*) I'm not just any guy, I love you, I really do.

PAULA: We could move up the wedding date.

BENNY: (*His hand pulling up her skirt.*) We'll have the best and biggest wedding and our apartment will have the best furniture and we'll live in the best building.

PAULA: (*Coming to her senses.*) How much have you saved this week?

BENNY: (*Dropping his hand.*) Well, you see babe ...

PAULA: (*Pulling away.*) Didn't you put anything away?

BENNY: Honey, I'm a little short this week. I had to give my mother some money.

PAULA: Your mother?

BENNY: Yes, my mother, swear to God, honest. Ask her.

PAULA: You know your mother would say you could fly like Superman if you asked her to.

BENNY: No, she wouldn't. Well, anyway, I was wondering if you could lend me a few bucks until payday.

PAULA: Honestly, we'll never have enough money for the wedding in November.

BENNY: (*Kissing her gently.*) Oh, babe, it will be all right, trust me. Don't I have a deposit on our rings at the jewelers, didn't I let you pick them out? Besides, who else could settle me down like you have, uh? You know a few bucks this week won't make that much difference. I'll put more away next week. I promise. (PAULA *looks doubtful, takes money from her purse and hands it over to* BENNY.) That's my precious babe. Thanks, honey, honest I'll pay you back on Wednesday, promise. (BENNY *holds up his hand and* PAULA *takes it and they walk off stage. The light on the stoop fades.*)

.... SCENE THREE ....

The lights go up on the bedroom where SOPHIA *is still on the* phone.

SOPHIA: I just don't want to go out with all those people, why can't it be just us two? Oh, Jimmy, they're so boring, all the girls talk about is their clothes and hair. (MARGARITA *goes into the kitchen as the lights in the kitchen go up. She stands by the wall phone in the kitchen.*)

MARGARITA: (*Yelling in* SOPHIA*'s direction.*) I need the phone.

SOPHIA: Jimmy, I got to get off, Mom's yelling. I'll meet you there later. Sure, sure, I have to get off. (SOPHIA *gets off the phone and goes into the kitchen.* MARGARITA *picks up the phone and dials.*)

MARGARITA: Hello ... yes, I'm leaving now ... okay. (*She hangs up the phone.*)

SOPHIA: Where are you going?

MARGARITA: Bingo.

SOPHIA: Like I needed to ask. Don't you get tired of that?

MARGARITA: Do you get tired of dancing?

SOPHIA: That's different.

MARGARITA: Kids always think that.

SOPHIA: Ma, I'm not a kid. Is Samuel going to be there?

MARGARITA: (*Ignoring the question.*) Where are you going?

SOPHIA: Just out, no place special.

MARGARITA: With who?

SOPHIA: With Jimmy.

MARGARITA: Why doesn't he pick you up here? You ashamed of something?

SOPHIA: No, Ma, of course not. It's just easier to meet at the ... uhh, bowling alley.

MARGARITA: What kind of boy is this Jimmy?

SOPHIA: Ma, he's just a friend, I ain't marrying the guy.

MARGARITA: Why can't you be more like your sister, huh? Find yourself a nice steady boy?

SOPHIA: Well, I think she should be more like me and maybe she wouldn't even think of marrying someone like Benny. Me, I'm never getting married.

MARGARITA: Don't say that. What's wrong with Benny? He works, is with her all the time, and is going to marry her.

SOPHIA: What about all the women he was involved with, huh? They still come around I hear. And that job, God, he only has it because his uncle owns the store.

MARGARITA: I don't want you talking that way about Benny to people.

SOPHIA: Why Mom? Why is it so important that she get married to Benny? Or is it that you don't care who she marries as long as she gets married?

MARGARITA: Don't you talk to me like that. I've only wanted what's best for you and Paula, always, nothing else have I thought of. Maybe I just know a little more than you since I've been through so much.

SOPHIA: All right, Mom, truce, I don't want to get into your troubles with Dad, okay.

MARGARITA: I used to be real smart, just like you.

SOPHIA: (*Kissing her mother.*) Mom, you go out with Samuel and have a good time, okay.

MARGARITA: I'm going to bingo.

SOPHIA: Yeah, I know, and so is Samuel, I know he goes same as you. So have a good time, okay.

MARGARITA: You watch that new boy.

SOPHIA: Mami, don't start. Jimmy's a nice guy.

MARGARITA: No such thing as a nice guy.

SOPHIA: Mom, stop living in the dark ages, don't be paranoid.

MARGARITA: You listen to me, no boy respects a girl who is easy. Paula is very smart that way.

SOPHIA: Yeah, sure, Mom, I thought we called a truce.

MARGARITA: (MARGARITA *smiles, pinches her daughter's cheek.*) Yeah, be careful, okay. You're the one I worry about.

SOPHIA: Don't worry about me. (MARGARITA *leaves and the light on the stage fades.*)

.... SCENE FOUR ....

The stage is dark except for a light on the bedroom and a very dim light coming from the living room. SOPHIA is watching television while in bed. PAULA comes up the stairs to the brownstone, then quietly into the apartment and tiptoes into the bedroom.

PAULA: What are you doing up?

SOPHIA: Mommie was piss furious when she went to bed.

PAULA: It isn't that late.

SOPHIA: Tell that to her. You have a good time?

PAULA: (*Getting undressed.*) Shut up and leave me alone.

SOPHIA: What I do? Just 'cause I wasn't Miss Sweet with that jerk.

PAULA: Don't call him a jerk.

SOPHIA: I can't help it if he's a low life.

PAULA: What's with you?

SOPHIA: He's just using you and you know it.

PAULA: You don't know what you're talking about. Benny loves me.

SOPHIA: Sure, he does.

PAULA: What's with you, anyway. Benny and I have been going out for over six months, why are you acting so obnoxious now?

SOPHIA: You know that wedding of yours is going to upset everyone.

PAULA: What are you talking about?

SOPHIA: You asked Dad to come to the wedding. Do you really think Mom wants to see him after all these years? Do you? Why do you have to have him at the wedding?

PAULA: None of this is any of your business, so stay out of it.

SOPHIA: Why do you want to hurt Mom that way?

PAULA: I'm not hurting Mom, or anything, I just want my wedding to be proper. He is my father and he should give me away.

SOPHIA: How come you act so ancient. He's nothing to us, when we needed him where was he? When we were on welfare?

PAULA: You don't know anything. That was a long time ago. You don't know what happened between them, we had nothing to do with it.

SOPHIA: Well, where has he been all these years? He's in Chicago living this wonderful, carefree life, no responsibility. He never sent us a dime.

PAULA: That's not true.

SOPHIA: Oh, excuse me, a few miserable dollars every few years, maybe a gift at Christmas. I'm sorry I can't forgive him for what he did.

PAULA: Who's asking you to do anything. It's my wedding and this is what I want, a proper wedding. Now, if that bothers you, tough.

SOPHIA: It's going to be tough on you 'cause he doesn't give a shit about us or this wedding. He ain't going to come.

PAULA: You mean he doesn't care about me. He's always loved you best.

SOPHIA: You're wrong, he doesn't care about either of us or Mom.

PAULA: (*Finding the picture in the drawer.*) Sure, that's why the first person he asks me for is you when I call him. Why do you hate him so much? (PAULA *places the picture back on the dresser and gets into bed.*)

SOPHIA: I just don't like fairy tales. I don't believe in them.

PAULA: Sure, you don't have to. If you were getting married, Dad would be here like a shot. But I made sure he'd answer my letter this time.

SOPHIA: What you do?

PAULA: I told him you were looking forward towards the wedding and wanted to see him again.

SOPHIA: How could you do that?

PAULA: I'm sure I'll get a letter from him soon.

SOPHIA: I don't want to hear it anymore, he ain't anything to me. (SOPHIA *buries her head in her pillow.*)

PAULA: (*Turning off the light.*) You're such a bitch.

SOPHIA: Yeah, but a smart bitch. (*The light in the living room goes off leaving the stage dark.*)

.... SCENE FIVE ....

As the lights go up SOPHIA *and* PAULA *are in the middle of their ritual of preparing for work.* MARGARITA *is still in her robe, drinking coffee at the kitchen table.* SAMUEL *is standing by the stoop trying not to be noticed; he is smoking.*

MARGARITA: (*Yelling towards the bedroom.*) Eight o'clock! (PAULA *comes out first. She kisses* MARGARITA.)

PAULA: (*Drinking from* MARGARITA's *cup.*) How come you're not ready, the factory burn down?

MARGARITA: Don't you know coffee is bad for you? (*Pause.*) I have some errands to run, I took a vacation day.

PAULA: I'm sorry I was late last night, I promise it won't happen again.

MARGARITA: Where did I hear that one before?

PAULA: Mom ... (SOPHIA *comes out of the bedroom; she walks slowly, putting her hair up in a ponytail. She stretches and then gives her Mom a big hug and kiss.*)

SOPHIA: Morning, Mamita. (SOPHIA *pours herself a cup of coffee.* SOPHIA *and* PAULA *exchange harsh looks.*)

PAULA: I have to get to work. I'll be home early, Benny and I are going to his uncle's for dinner. (PAULA *exits and passes* SAMUEL; *he turns his back and she doesn't notice him as she walks off the stage.*)

MARGARITA: What is this thing between you two?

SOPHIA: What?

MARGARITA: Stop being so innocent.

SOPHIA: Ma, how come you're not dressed for work?

MARGARITA: I took the day off, I've things to do.

SOPHIA: Yeah, like what?

MARGARITA: Don't change the subject.

SOPHIA: Don't worry about it, Mami.

MARGARITA: You and your sister shouldn't fight so much. It seems like lately all you do is fight.

SOPHIA: I can't help it, she picks on me.

MARGARITA: Sophia ...

SOPHIA: Okay, okay, but you know Benny is all wrong for her. And wanting that man at the wedding ...

MARGARITA: You mean your father? (*Pause.*) How can you be so sure that Benny is wrong for Paula? Paula wants to get married, that's what all women want.

SOPHIA: All women, Mami?

MARGARITA: Well, if they're smart.

SOPHIA: Well, where did marriage get you? (SOPHIA *regrets the words as soon as they're out of her mouth.*) Mom, I'm sorry.

MARGARITA: We were talking about Paula. Benny's not a bad person, he loves Paula. (SOPHIA *kisses her mother.*)

SOPHIA: I got to go, enjoy your day off. (SOPHIA *passes SA-MUEL on the stoop as she exits; she stops and turns around.*) Hi, Sam. (*She doesn't wait for him to respond and exits off the stage.*)

SAMUEL: Shit. (SAMUEL *goes up the stairs to the apartment and seeing the door open, he walks in.*) Hello. (MARGARITA *doesn't even look up.*) What's wrong?

MARGARITA: Nothing. (SAMUEL *kisses her and she doesn't respond.*)

SAMUEL: Now, what?

MARGARITA: I'm tired.

SAMUEL: (*Playful.*) Well, we could lie down for a while before we go shopping.

MARGARITA: I'm not in the mood.

SAMUEL: For lying down or shopping?

MARGARITA: Pick one.

SAMUEL: What's wrong, you're the one who asked me to take a day off to go look at bedroom sets for Paula's wedding gift.

MARGARITA: Something's happening between Paula and Sophia, and I can't quite figure it out. They're fighting all the time.

SAMUEL: Sister's always fight.

MARGARITA: No, they weren't like that. Since Paula said she's marrying Benny and told us that she's asking Eduardo to walk her down the aisle, Sophia has been impossible.

SAMUEL: Maybe she's jealous. Besides, it's only one day. Once Paula is married, everything will settle down.

MARGARITA: Yeah, well, I heard Sophia and Paula fighting last night. Sophia doesn't want anything to do with her father. She's really upset that Paula wrote to him.

SAMUEL: It's all going to work out, you'll see.

MARGARITA: I'm so worried that he'll come. I really hope he doesn't.

SAMUEL: Why?

MARGARITA: What if he tells them that we were never married and that Paula's not his daughter?

SAMUEL: You should have told them a long time ago.

MARGARITA: Oh, sure, let me tell them that I hardly knew Paula's father and that Eduardo never married me because he never thought me good enough.

SAMUEL: What happened to you could have happened to anyone.

MARGARITA: Yeah, I trusted him. I'll never trust another man . . .

SAMUEL: You can trust me.

MARGARITA: Yeah, the man who's been getting a divorce for the last three years.

SAMUEL: That's not fair, you know my wife's got me by the short hairs because of the business. I can't afford to lose everything I've worked for all my life. You're being unfair. I'm trying to get that divorce and I've wanted to bring our relationship into the open since the beginning.

MARGARITA: I know you have. I'm sorry, but I can't let you meet my daughters until you're divorced and that's final.

SAMUEL: Your mantel of respectability, uh . . .

MARGARITA: Oh, please, Sam, I'm really worried about this. You don't know Eduardo. He's kept his mouth shut all these years because it's been convenient. As long as I didn't hassle him for child support. What if he gets drunk and decides to confess all, where does that leave me?

SAMUEL: Maybe you should tell them before the wedding, then.

MARGARITA: I can't, I have to find a way to keep him away from here. Maybe I can get Paula to change her mind. (SAMUEL *pours himself some coffee.*)

SAMUEL: I think you should tell them the truth. (*Pause.*) You know that Sophia is a smart girl. I think she knows about us.

MARGARITA: Yeah, she goes around hinting about us, but I don't think she really knows anything.

SAMUEL: I saw her outside and she said hello and she had this smart-ass smile.

MARGARITA: That's all I need.

SAMUEL: She's a smart girl, I don't think she disapproves.

MARGARITA: Of course she doesn't disapprove because it stamps
the seal of approval on her running around with all different kinds of boys.

SAMUEL: I think you underestimate your daughter.

MARGARITA: I better go get dressed, if we're going to get out
of here. (MARGARITA *goes into the living room and*
SAMUEL *follows her. Their shadowed figures can be seen
from the kitchen.* SAMUEL *puts his arms around her.*)
What are you doing?

SAMUEL: Shh, I'm concentrating.

MARGARITA: Sam, we have to get to the store.

SAMUEL: I love you.

MARGARITA: (*After a pause.*) I guess we have time. (*The lights
on the stage fade.*)

.... SCENE SIX ....

It is late in the evening. The apartment is semi-dark. SOPHIA
and JIMMY *go up the steps to the brownstone and then up to the
door of the apartment.* SOPHIA *opens the door.*

JIMMY: You sure this is okay?

SOPHIA: Are you kidding, Mom is playing bingo and Paula is out
with Benny. They won't be home for hours. (SOPHIA
leads JIMMY *into the bedroom. She puts on the radio
and starts dancing.* JIMMY *throws himself on the bed
and watches her for a few moments and then pulls her on
top of him.*)

JIMMY: (*Kissing her neck.*) You're something else.

SOPHIA: (*Pulling at his shirt.*) Who me?

JIMMY: (*Grabbing her hands.*) Wait a minute, I want to ask you
something.

SOPHIA: What?

JIMMY: We've been hanging out for a about a month, maybe we
should sort of make it steady?

SOPHIA: You mean just you and me?

JIMMY: Yeah.

SOPHIA: Why? I like things they way they are, why do we have
to change them.

JIMMY: I thought we had something real going here.

SOPHIA: We do, but there's no reason to label it.

JIMMY: You sound like my mother. She doesn't believe in commitment either. I can't count the number of guys she's brought over to the house this year.

SOPHIA: I'm not your mother, okay. (*Pause.*) Where's you dad?

JIMMY: They're divorced, he's got a new family. I really envy him. His wife, she's real pretty and they got a little girl.

SOPHIA: What about you?

JIMMY: What do you mean?

SOPHIA: How do you fit into this new family? You get along with his wife?

JIMMY: I guess she's nice, but they don't really have time for me.

SOPHIA: Well, I'm glad my father lives in Chicago. He's divorced from his wife. If they were here I know I'd hate it.

JIMMY: Is that why you don't like the idea of commitment?

SOPHIA: Is your mother's lack of morals why you want to commit? (JIMMY *looks hurt.*)

SOPHIA: I'm sorry, but I hate to be analyzed. I'm just the way I am, okay.

JIMMY: Okay. I love you the way you are, I just want, uh, more . . .

SOPHIA: (*Pulling at his shirt again.*) More? (JIMMY *kisses her and turns over so that he's on top of her. The light fades in the bedroom and goes up in the kitchen and in front of the house.* PAULA *and* BENNY *come up the steps. They have been arguing and stop by the stoop.*)

PAULA: You're a pig, there's no justifying what you did at your uncle's.

BENNY: What did I do so wrong? Okay, so I looked at the girl, so what?

PAULA: Benny, what you did wasn't looking, you were . . . well if you were a dog you'd have been drooling . . . come to think of it, you were . . .

BENNY: She's just a kid, the neighbor's daughter.

PAULA: Sure, Benny, I can still see the sweat. Oh, go take a cold shower. (PAULA *goes up to the door and stops short.*) Why's the kitchen light on?

BENNY: How the hell should I know.

PAULA: Shhh.

BENNY: You asked me.

PAULA: No one is supposed to be home.

BENNY: It's probably your mom.

PAULA: No, I don't think so.

BENNY: (*Pushes* PAULA *behind him.*) Let me go, it's probably
　　　Sophia. (*He walks towards the bedroom and* PAULA *follows him slowly.*) I hardly think a thief would listen to
　　　music. (*Yelling.*) Hope you're decent in there, I'm coming through. (BENNY *enters the bedroom. Backing out of
　　　the room.*) Oops!

PAULA: What is it?

BENNY: Don't go in there, I don't think your sensitivity could
　　　handle it.

PAULA: (*Enters the bedroom.*) Damn it, Sophia. (SOPHIA *is
　　　putting on her blouse and* JIMMY *is fumbling with his
　　　pants.* PAULA *follows* BENNY *back into the kitchen.*)

BENNY: Guess your sis hasn't got your problem about sex.

PAULA: Shut up, just shut up. (JIMMY *and* SOPHIA *enter the
　　　kitchen.*)

SOPHIA: What are you doing home so early?

PAULA: How could you do this in our bedroom?

SOPHIA: Oh, what are you making such a big deal for?

PAULA: This is our home, not a cheap motel.

SOPHIA: Oh, give me a break with your holy virgin act, like you
　　　never ... (SOPHIA *regrets the words as soon as they're
　　　spoken.*)

JIMMY: I think I better go.

SOPHIA: I, uh, no, don't go, Jimmy.

PAULA: I want him out of here right now.

SOPHIA: Excuse me, but who died and left you in charge?

PAULA: What about Mami?

SOPHIA: Mami's too busy doing her own thing.

BENNY: (*To* JIMMY.) Doesn't this all sound very interesting.
　　　Guess things are going real good for you, uh?

JIMMY: Who are you?

BENNY: I'm her boyfriend, the one who doesn't ...

JIMMY: Hey, I think I better go.

PAULA: Good idea, I think you both should go home.

BENNY: Me? Oh, no, I think this is getting interesting.

JIMMY: (*To* SOPHIA.) Look, I'll meet you at the bowling alley.

BENNY: Hey, Sophia, why don't you go with him, I want to talk
　　　to Paula about her little act.

SOPHIA: I think slugs should just crawl and not talk.

PAULA: (*To* SOPHIA.) How could you do this?

SOPHIA: I'm not you.

PAULA: (*Grabbing* SOPHIA *by the shoulders.*) You're stupid, stupid. How many guys have you brought here? (SOPHIA *breaks loose from* PAULA *and* BENNY *steps in between.*)
BENNY: Hey, stop that.
SOPHIA: Your problem is that you can't face reality. You think you have a trophy between your legs, that a guy has to jump through hoops just right in order to win the prize.
JIMMY: Look, I'm going ...
SOPHIA: I'm not asking for any promises and what I do is because I enjoy it. You want to be married fine, but don't put your lousy morals on me. (PAULA *slaps* SOPHIA.)
PAULA: You're a slut and it's going to kill Mom the day she finds out.
SOPHIA: You think because you're marrying Benny that's going to make you respectable.
PAULA: Get out of here, get out! (SOPHIA *takes* JIMMY*'s arm.*)
SOPHIA: We're leaving. But, if you tell Mami about this, remember I have a few things I can tell too.
PAULA: How could you be so unfeeling? How could you not care about hurting her?
SOPHIA: Oh, spare me. What do you think, uh, that Mom is a saint? What do you think's been going on with her and Sam all these years? You're so stupid. Or maybe you don't see what you don't want to. Every time Mom tells you she's going to bingo, you believe her. Bingo is that sleazy motel on the highway.
PAULA: I don't believe you. You're making that up.
JIMMY: Sophia, come on, let's get out of here.
BENNY: Yeah, he's right, you'd better go, you've gone too far.
SOPHIA: I haven't gone far enough.
BENNY: (*Holding on to* PAULA.) Hey, I said that's it, now leave her alone.
SOPHIA: Yeah, sure, her knight in shining armor. What a joke. (SOPHIA *and* JIMMY *walk out of the apartment and stop by the stoop.* BENNY *holds* PAULA.)
BENNY: You going to be okay?
PAULA: Yeah. You better go home.
BENNY: I think we'd better talk.
PAULA: My mother's not involved with Samuel.
BENNY: Paula, I don't care about that. Have you been putting me on all these months? Have you been with someone else?
PAULA: What's the matter, afraid you're going to get damaged goods?

BENNY: I just want to know if you've been making a jerk out of
me all this time.

PAULA: Why should it matter to someone like you? There's not
anyone around here you haven't been with. Don't you
know that I know, even Dolores across the street?

BENNY: I never realized what a low opinion you had of me. Why
do you stay with me?

PAULA: (*Touching his face lightly.*) I don't know.

BENNY: Jesus, you don't know? (*Pause.*) I thought you loved me?

PAULA: Love? I do love you. I guess I just don't believe you really
love me.

BENNY: I know I messed around in the past, but I'd be a jerk to
mess things up with you.

PAULA: Why?

BENNY: 'Cause I love you. (*Lights go down as* BENNY *takes*
PAULA *gently in his arms and kisses her. The lights come
up on* SOPHIA *and* JIMMY *standing by the front of the
house.*)

SOPHIA: Come on, lets go to the bowling alley.

JIMMY: No. You were really vicious in there.

SOPHIA: I hate all their lies. I know I shouldn't have said those
things to her.

JIMMY: You tore her apart.

SOPHIA: Sure, make me feel better.

JIMMY: That's all I'm here for, isn't it?

SOPHIA: Jimmy, please don't start. She goes around with this air
about her, like she's so much better than everyone else.
Like she's special or something. Oh, God, I hope I didn't
screw things up with Benny. Mom's going to kill me.

JIMMY: You want to go to my place? Mom's not home.

SOPHIA: Yeah, I may need a place to hide out. (JIMMY *takes*
SOPHIA *by the hand and the lights fade.*)

.... SCENE SEVEN ....

It's the next morning and MARGARITA *is cleaning up the
kitchen.* PAULA *and* SOPHIA *are snuggled in their beds.* EDUAR-
DO *stops by the front of the building, checks a piece of paper and
then looks up at the building. He goes to the front door and knocks.*

MARGARITA: Yeah, who is it?

EDUARDO: I am looking for Margarita Hernandez. (MARGA-
RITA *opens the door slowly.*) I thought it was you. Your
voice hasn't changed. (*He waits for* MARGARITA *to say
something; she says nothing.*) Aren't you going to ask me
in?

MARGARITA: (*Reluctantly stepping aside.*) What are you doing
here?

EDUARDO: That's all you can say after all these years?

MARGARITA: Oh, well, excuse me. How are you? Family in
Chicago okay?

EDUARDO: I got divorced, remember?

MARGARITA: Oh, yes, took you to the cleaners, I heard.

EDUARDO: Well, I guess I should have known this wasn't going
to be easy. Look, Paula wrote me, said she was getting
married and thought it would be nice if I walked her down
the aisle.

MARGARITA: The wedding is in November, six months away.

EDUARDO: Well, I've decided to move back to New York.

MARGARITA: Why, for God's sake?

EDUARDO: This is my home. Why are you acting like this? Can't
we let the past be? I just want to share in a little of the
happiness, with the wedding and all.

MARGARITA: Paula doesn't need your help for the wedding, she's
saved her money for it.

EDUARDO: You've become mean spirited. (*Pause.*) What about
Sophia, my daughter?

MARGARITA: Please, Eduardo, stay away from Sophia, you know
how she is.

EDUARDO: I don't have to be careful around my own daughter.

MARGARITA: You have two daughters, you owe me that much.

EDUARDO: I'm not going to say anything to them, I just want to
see them.

MARGARITA: Well, they're sleeping now and I'm not going to
wake them.

EDUARDO: Don't make this hard for me. I'm moving back and
I want to be part of their lives.

MARGARITA: What if they don't want to be part of your life.
Sophia doesn't want to have anything to do with you.

EDUARDO: Maybe if you talked to her, tried to make her understand that I had no choice but to leave for Chicago.

MARGARITA: How can I make her understand something I never
understood myself?

EDUARDO: I had a job in Chicago.

MARGARITA: You had a woman in Chicago.

EDUARDO: What did you expect me to do when you refused to go with me?

MARGARITA: You refused to marry me. Why do you want to drag up the past?

EDUARDO: Nothing has to change. Won't you help me to get my daughters back into my life? If you don't help me, how do you explain why I won't walk Paula down the aisle when I'm living in the same city?

MARGARITA: In other words, if I don't get Sophia to change her mind about you, you'll tell them everything.

EDUARDO: I just think that Paula will ask questions and I'll have to answer them.

MARGARITA: I can't promise anything. She's not as gullible as Paula. She sees things for what they are.

EDUARDO: Maybe you've made her that way.

MARGARITA: Look, come back at around eight o'clock, after dinner, and you can talk to both of them. You convince Sophia about your good intentions. I won't interfere.

EDUARDO: Thank you, Rita. Remember how I always called you Rita?

MARGARITA: Sure, Eduardo, I'll see you at eight. (MARGARITA *backs away and* EDUARDO *exits. Then* PAULA *and* SOPHIA *begin to stir.* SOPHIA *gets out of bed, disappears into the bathroom for a moment, then goes into the kitchen.* MARGARITA *has been sitting at the kitchen table.*)

SOPHIA: Did I hear you talking with someone?

MARGARITA: Yes, your father was here.

SOPHIA: He was?

MARGARITA: Yes, he was.

SOPHIA: What did he want?

MARGARITA: To see you ... and Paula.

SOPHIA: What for, I don't want to see him.

MARGARITA: Sophia, please, you're going to have to be sensible about this, he is your father and Paula is getting married.

SOPHIA: Well, I hope she still is.

MARGARITA: What do you mean? What's happened?

SOPHIA: Oh, Paula and I got into a fight last night and I said some things I shouldn't have.

MARGARITA: What did you say?

SOPHIA: Oh, Mami, nothing, really.

MARGARITA: Did you start in on Benny again. Oh, my God, Sophia, what am I going to do about you? Can't you learn to keep your mouth shut?

SOPHIA: Well, she started it.

MARGARITA: I'm going to have peace of mind in this house, do you understand me, if it's the last thing I do. Now, you make up your mind what you want, because I want you to make peace with your sister and Benny. I don't want any more bickering. And, as for your father, you're going to be civil to him, do you understand me. And, if Benny and Paula have broken up and it's your fault, I'm going to take my shoe to you, do you understand? (SOPHIA *has been listening very solemnly. Then she leans over and kisses her mother.*)

SOPHIA: You sound just like you did when we were little girls and you threatened us with our lives if we didn't listen.

MARGARITA: I mean it, Sophia. Your father is coming back at eight tonight.

SOPHIA: (*Taking some coffee.*) Okay, Mom, I'll be good, I promise. I at least owe Paula that much after last night. I also stole the letter Dad sent her. I guess it didn't do any good.

MARGARITA: You what?

SOPHIA: Oh, Mami, don't get a fit, he came anyway. But, I have a date with Jimmy and I'm not canceling it, so his visit better be short. What's he doing in New York?

MARGARITA: He's moved back.

SOPHIA: I hope he doesn't expect to make us one big happy family.

MARGARITA: Sophia, you promised.

SOPHIA: Oh, I'll be good, I will, but I'm not going to go overboard. I'm sure Paula can be excited enough for the both of us. (*The lights fade.*)

.... SCENE EIGHT ....

The lights go up in the kitchen. SOPHIA *is in the bedroom.* MARGARITA *and* PAULA *are in the kitchen.*

PAULA: Mom, you sure I look all right? I haven't seen Daddy in such a long time.

MARGARITA: Honey you look great. I'm sure he's not going to care about your dress.

PAULA: I know. (SOPHIA *comes out of the bedroom dressed in jeans and a sweatshirt.*) Is that what you're wearing?

SOPHIA: Jimmy and I are going to a movie later.

PAULA: What about Daddy?

SOPHIA: I'll be here, but I'm not staying all night. You're the one who has to talk to him about the wedding. You do have the wedding still, don't you?

PAULA: (*Looking at her mother.*) Yeah, of course. I called Benny, he'll be over in a little while.

MARGARITA: Is Benny going to be here on time?

PAULA: Yeah, of course, he is. Is Jimmy meeting you here?

SOPHIA: Yeah.

PAULA: Do you think that's a good idea, I mean with Daddy coming over and everything?

SOPHIA: What's that got to do with anything?

MARGARITA: Is that the new boy that you're seeing?

SOPHIA: Yes, and he's very nice.

MARGARITA: They're all very nice.

SOPHIA: No, Mom, he really is very nice and I really like him.

PAULA: He should like you.

MARGARITA: What?

SOPHIA: (*To* PAULA.) Don't start with me.

MARGARITA: I warned you Sophia. (*The doorbell rings.* SOPHIA *goes to answer it, but* PAULA *rushes in front of her to the door.*)

PAULA: No, let me. (PAULA *smoothes out her dress and then opens the door. It's* BENNY.)

PAULA: Oh, it's you.

BENNY: You're going to have to stop being so excited about seeing me, honey. (*He kisses her on the cheek.*) You're okay?

PAULA: Yeah, I'm fine now. You look very nice.

BENNY: As per your instructions on the phone. Doña Margarita excited about seeing the old man?

PAULA: Benny!

MARGARITA: Water under the bridge.

BENNY: Doña Margarita, isn't Saturday night a bingo night for you?

MARGARITA: Yes, I'm going later, why?

SOPHIA: Benny, I'll kill you.

BENNY: Hey, Sophia, you talking to me these days?

SOPHIA: Cool your shit, or I'll put you out of commission.

BENNY: Still crazy about me, I see. (PAULA *is very quiet and* SOPHIA *notices this.*)

SOPHIA: Aren't you going to say anything, what's wrong with you?

PAULA: Nothing. (*The doorbell rings again and this time* MAR-GARITA, *stepping in front of* PAULA, *answers the door.* EDUARDO *is carrying a couple of packages.*)

EDUARDO: Rita, you look very nice.

MARGARITA: Don't call me that. Well, here they are just as you wanted. (PAULA *goes over to* EDUARDO *and gives him a hug and kiss.* SOPHIA *barely lets* EDUARDO *kiss and hug her.*)

EDUARDO: Well, I'm glad to see both my beautiful girls again. I've brought you both a little something. (*He hands them each a package.* SOPHIA *looks at it without opening it, but* PAULA *tears off the wrapping.* BENNY *is standing around a bit uncomfortable.*)

MARGARITA: I'm sorry, Eduardo, this is Benny, Paula's fiance.

EDUARDO: (*Shaking hands with* BENNY.) Good to meet you. Sophia, aren't you going to open your gift? (PAULA *takes out a beautiful shawl from her package.*)

PAULA: (*Kissing him.*) Oh, Daddy, it's beautiful. Thank you. (SOPHIA *opens her package and takes out a beautiful China doll.*)

SOPHIA: It's a really nice doll, thanks. (*The doorbell rings and* SOPHIA *goes to open it. It's* JIMMY.)

JIMMY: Hi. (SOPHIA *gives him a warm kiss and hug.* EDUAR-DO *notices this.*)

EDUARDO: Who is that?

SOPHIA: He's a friend, Daddy, we're going to the movies.

EDUARDO: What about my visit?

SOPHIA: You came to talk to Paula about her wedding, we can talk another day.

EDUARDO: Aren't you a bit young to be going around like this?

SOPHIA: Around like what? I'm going on a date.

MARGARITA: Eduardo, the girl has a date, I think it would be a good idea if you let her go.

EDUARDO: I haven't seen her in over five years and she's going on a date.

SOPHIA: My life is supposed to stop because you're here?

MARGARITA: You promised, Sophia.

JIMMY: Have I come in on another family thing?

SOPHIA: No, because we're leaving.

BENNY: Yeah, Don Eduardo, we have a lot to tell you about the wedding.

EDUARDO: I want Sophia to stay.

JIMMY: Maybe we could make it another night, uh, Sophia?

EDUARDO: That's a good idea.

SOPHIA: Why? (MARGARITA *steps back to watch the exchange.*)

EDUARDO: Don't you want to sit and talk to me?

SOPHIA: About what? I don't need to talk to you, Paula's the one
    with the wedding.

PAULA: Don't you want to talk to me, Daddy?

EDUARDO: Of course, I do, but I also want Sophia here.

SOPHIA: Well, I don't want to be here, okay.

PAULA: You always do this, it's always her you want to see, always
    her, never me.

EDUARDO: What are you talking about?

SOPHIA: Yeah, what's this thing you have that you always want
    me around when you know I can't stand you?

BENNY: Didn't you do enough damage last night? (*At this* MAR-
    GARITA *steps back in.*)

MARGARITA: What are you talking about?

BENNY: Nothing, nothing.

SOPHIA: I'm leaving, come on, Jimmy.

MARGARITA: No one is leaving until I find out what happened
    last night.

JIMMY: I think I better go.

MARGARITA: Leave if you want, but Sophia is staying until I
    get some answers. Now, you tell me what happened last
    night.

BENNY: It wasn't a big deal.

JIMMY: I don't want to get involved in this family thing.

SOPHIA: My knight in shining armor. Maybe Mom is right: no
    man can be trusted.

EDUARDO: Is that what you've taught them?

JIMMY: Sophia, what do you want me to do?

PAULA: Is it true, Mom, are you seeing Samuel?

MARGARITA: What?

PAULA: Are you sleeping with Samuel?

EDUARDO: Well, I see you haven't changed any.

SOPHIA: Don't you talk to my mother like that.

EDUARDO: Excuse me, young lady, but she was my wife first.

PAULA: Oh, who the hell are you kidding ... (SOPHIA *grabs*
    PAULA *by the arm.* MARGARITA *puts her hands to her*
    mouth.)

SOPHIA: No, Paula, don't.

PAULA: Why not? You think you're the only one who's tired of
    all the secrets, of all the lies.

MARGARITA: How long have you known?

SOPHIA: Mami, we know everything. We've always known.

EDUARDO: How do you know?

PAULA: Why is it that adults think that kids are deaf? That because you're little you can't hear or understand when someone is shouting in the other room. We both knew, we always knew, the walls of that dingy apartment were very thin. I guess I knew about Samuel too, but I didn't want to admit it.

SOPHIA: Where did you get the wedding dress? We always wondered.

MARGARITA: At a thrift shop. I saw it hanging in the window. It made me feel like I really had worn it. I can't figure out why I was so adamant that you wear it. (JIMMY *and* BENNY *have backed away from the women and stand as outsiders.* EDUARDO *stands hopelessly next to them as they talk.*)

PAULA: I wanted to live up to your image of goodness, even when I knew it was a lie. But, I didn't I ... Who was my father?

MARGARITA: Oh, honey ... he was a boy from school. He was young, too young to be a father. (*Pause.*) Of course, it didn't matter that I was too young too. His family shipped him to Puerto Rico, then I met Eduardo.

EDUARDO: I took you in.

MARGARITA: Yeah, you took me in. Promised me marriage and I got nothing.

EDUARDO: It wasn't like that.

PAULA: Really? Well, why did you go to Chicago without us?

EDUARDO: I asked her to come.

MARGARITA: What, to be your mistress? I knew about that woman you were marrying, that she was waiting for you with her respectable family and a business for you to run.

EDUARDO: I wouldn't have married her if you had come with me.

MARGARITA: Well, isn't that a revelation, considering she had the church all booked and the dressed picked out.

SOPHIA: Dad, go back to Chicago, that's where you belong.

EDUARDO: I have nothing there.

SOPHIA: You don't have anything here. (EDUARDO *looks at* MARGARITA *and then* PAULA.)

MARGARITA: Please, Eduardo, don't expect compassion from me. All these years I never stopped you from seeing them. I wanted my daughters to have something to look up to, so

that they wouldn't be ashamed, ashamed of me. I always
thought the truth would ruin them.

SOPHIA: Oh, Mom, you can't hide that kind of truth forever. The
lies hurt more than the truth.

MARGARITA: I love you girls more than my life. I didn't want
you to be ashamed of me.

PAULA: You were ashamed of us.

MARGARITA: No, not ashamed, just worried that I provided a
bad example.

EDUARDO: (*To* PAULA.) I'd still be proud to walk you down the
aisle.

PAULA: No, I think it's time to face reality, don't you think so,
Benny?

BENNY: Yeah, I think we did that last night.

PAULA: I think we should postpone the wedding.

BENNY: You can't be serious?

PAULA: Only a postponement.

BENNY: (*To* SOPHIA.) This is all your fault. You've always hated
my guts.

SOPHIA: I just think she's marrying you for the wrong reason.

BENNY: Because she feels she can't do any better?

SOPHIA: Maybe.

PAULA: Benny and I talked last night, I told him everything.

SOPHIA: You told him about the joke in high school.

PAULA: Yeah.

SOPHIA: And?

MARGARITA: What is this about?

PAULA: It was this boy I dated, you remember him, very clean cut
and polite. He got me pregnant and Sophia helped me get
an abortion.

MARGARITA: You couldn't have!

SOPHIA: Why did you tell her?

PAULA: I thought you wanted the truth. (*To her mother.*) Oh, I
sure did have an abortion. I wasn't going to make your
mistake. I wasn't going to have a kid without being married. So, I had an abortion. How do you like that, Mami?
I'm very respectable, just like you. I'm respectable on the
outside, but on the inside ...

MARGARITA: Don't say that.

PAULA: I'm all right. It doesn't mean I don't love you.

SOPHIA: You didn't have to tell her.

PAULA: No, I didn't. But, I'm glad I did, I'm tired of carrying
this load all alone.

SOPHIA: You aren't alone, I'm here.

PAULA: Why don't we get out of here, I think I need some air.

EDUARDO: You can't go like this.

PAULA: Go back to Chicago, Eduardo, it's where you belong.

MARGARITA: Paula?

PAULA: Don't worry, Mami, we'll be home eventually. (*The two couples walk out the door and leave* EDUARDO *and* MARGARITA *staring at each other.*)

EDUARDO: They can't mean this.

MARGARITA: I really did the best I could, didn't I?

EDUARDO: I can make it up to them.

MARGARITA: I don't think we can.

EDUARDO: There must be something I can do.

MARGARITA: I won't stand in your way. But, I can't help you either. I have enough of my own damage to repair. (E-DUARDO *goes to the door, takes one look back before leaving. He walks out to the front of the stage going past* SAMUEL *who is waiting for* MARGARITA *by the stoop.* MARGARITA *lays her head on the kitchen table and cries out.* EDUARDO *stands underneath the lamppost smoking, the light lingers a bit on him before the stage goes dark.*)